Lecture Notes in Computer Science   13540

More information about this series at https://www.springer.com/bookseries/558

Shandong Wu · Behrouz Shabestari ·
Lei Xing (Eds.)

Applications of Medical Artificial Intelligence

First International Workshop, AMAI 2022
Held in Conjunction with MICCAI 2022
Singapore, September 18, 2022
Proceedings

Editors
Shandong Wu
University of Pittsburgh
Pittsburgh, PA, USA

Behrouz Shabestari
National Institute of Biomedical Imaging
and Bioengineering
Bethesda, MD, USA

Lei Xing
Stanford University
Stanford, CA, USA

ISSN 0302-9743   ISSN 1611-3349 (electronic)
Lecture Notes in Computer Science
ISBN 978-3-031-17720-0   ISBN 978-3-031-17721-7 (eBook)
https://doi.org/10.1007/978-3-031-17721-7

This Springer imprint is published by the registered company Springer Nature Switzerland AG
The registered company address is: Gewerbestrasse 11, 6330 Cham, Switzerland

Preface

The First Workshop on Applications of Medical Artificial Intelligence (AMAI 2022) was held as a hybrid event in Singapore on September 18, 2022, in conjunction with the 25th International Conference on Medical Image Computing and Computer Assisted Intervention (MICCAI 2022).

Along with the quick evolvement of artificial intelligence (AI), deep/machine learning, and big data in healthcare, medical AI research goes beyond methodological/algorithm development. Many new research questions are emerging in the practical and applied aspects of medical AI, such as translational study, clinical evaluation, real-world use cases of AI systems, etc. The AMAI 2022 workshop created a forum to bring together researchers, clinicians, domain experts, AI practitioners, industry representatives, and students to investigate and discuss various challenges and opportunities related to applications of medical AI.

The aims of the AMAI workshop are to introduce emerging medical AI research topics and novel application methodologies, showcase the evaluation, translation, use case, and success of AI in healthcare, develop multi-disciplinary collaborations and academic-industry partnerships, and provide educational, networking, and career opportunities for attendees including clinicians, scientists, trainees, and students.

In the inaugural edition of this workshop, two submission tracks were included: full papers and abstracts (one page). The idea for the abstract track was to attract participation from researchers and clinicians primarily in the medical communities. AMAI 2022 received a strong response in submissions, including 26 full papers and 29 abstracts. All submissions went through double-blind review by the Program Committee and ad hoc reviewers, and each submission was reviewed by at least two qualified experts in the field. Finally, 17 full papers were accepted: 16 are included in this Springer LNCS volume and one was invited to be published in the partnering journal of *Radiology: Artificial Intelligence*. The 14 accepted abstracts were made publicly accessible on the workshop's website.

The organizers are grateful for the hard work of the Program Committee members and the ad hoc reviewers in undertaking their quality and timely reviews of the submissions. We thank all the authors for submitting their work to this new workshop. The collective efforts of all participants made this workshop successful.

September 2022

Shandong Wu
Behrouz Shabestari
Lei Xing
Niketa Chotai

Organization

Program Committee Chairs and Workshop Organizers

Shandong Wu	University of Pittsburgh, USA
Behrouz Shabestari	National Institute of Biomedical Imaging and Bioengineering, USA
Lei Xing	Stanford University, USA
Niketa Chotai	RadLink Imaging Centre and National University of Singapore, Singapore

Program Committee

Dooman Arefan	University of Pittsburgh, USA
Bettina Baessler	University Hospital Wuerzburg, Germany
Douglas Hartman	University of Pittsburgh Medical Center, USA
Yu Jing Jan Heng	Harvard Medical School, Beth Israel Deaconess Medical Center, USA
Mireia Crispin Ortuzar	University of Cambridge and Cancer Research, UK
Chang Min Park	Seoul National University Hospital, South Korea
Adam Perer	Carnegie Mellon University, USA
Nicholas Petrick	U.S. Food and Drug Administration, USA
Zhiyong (Sean) Xie	Pfizer Inc., USA
Yudong Zhang	The First Affiliated Hospital, Nanjing Medical University, China

Contents

Increasing the Accessibility of Peripheral Artery Disease Screening with Deep Learning

Adrit Rao[1(✉)] and Oliver Aalami[2]

[1] Palo Alto High School, Palo Alto, CA, USA
adrit.rao@gmail.com
[2] Stanford University, Stanford, CA, USA
aalami@stanford.edu

Abstract. Peripheral arterial disease (PAD) is estimated to affect 200 million people worldwide and is one of the leading causes of limb loss. The early diagnosis and treatment of PAD is crucial in preventing adverse clinical outcomes. However, the current point-of-care diagnostic evaluation for PAD, the ankle-brachial index (ABI), has significant limitations making it underutilized. The goal of this study is to develop a deep learning-enabled system which can predict clinically relevant ABI ranges directly from circulatory sounds of an artery derived from a hand-held doppler. Our IRB-approved clinical study focuses on ubiquitous, efficient, and secure collection of data for training of our system as well as a pipeline for continuous validation across multiple sites. We approach the collection of data and deployment of our AI through a mobile application which provides a simplistic and intuitive platform to be used by vascular technologists and clinicians. Our work can contribute a unique point-of-view into the deployment of AI for niche medical applications and the usage of a mobile application to streamline AI clinical studies.

Keywords: Peripheral arterial disease · Deep learning · Audio

1 Problem

Peripheral arterial disease (PAD) is a common form of arterial occlusive disease which involves the blockage of arteries supplying the lower extremities due to a build up of plaque or atherosclerosis [3–5,11]. PAD affects an estimated 200 million worldwide and is one of the leading causes of limb loss or amputation leading to life-long disability in patients [14]. The early diagnosis of PAD at the point-of-care is crucial in enabling timely treatment and preventing the progression of disease into irreversible stages. Currently, standard of care point-of-care diagnostic evaluation for PAD is the ankle-brachial index (ABI) [15]. The ABI is a value derived through measurement of bilateral brachial and tibial pressures with blood pressure cuffs using a hand-held continuous wave doppler to assess

S. Wu et al. (Eds.): AMAI 2022, LNCS 13540, pp. 1–7, 2022.
https://doi.org/10.1007/978-3-031-17721-7_1

arterial flow. However, the current methodology used in ABI evaluations has various limitations which make it clinically underutilized. The ABI measurement is time consuming and technically challenging for non-trained individuals. Also the traditional approach using a blood pressure cuff is unable to accurately derive ABIs in those with calcified non-compressible tibial vessels typically found in patients with diabetes or end-stage renal disease [6,8,9]. These limitations have led to limited point-of care use of the traditional exam. Without a definitive point-of-care PAD screening methodology, patients are referred to formal vascular laboratories which can significantly delay treatment. The goal of this study is to improve the screening of PAD by improving ABI evaluations using deep learning. This short paper presents an overview of our on-going two-fold clinical study focused on collection of ABI data to train our deep learning system and the validation of our system at the point-of-care. We also describe the technology used and the design of our deep learning system.

2   Related Work

Deep learning-based sound classification algorithms have not yet been leveraged for ABI predictions from continuous wave hand-held doppler sounds as demonstrated in our study. However, the capability of classifying sounds through deep learning has been leveraged previously in the medical context. For example, deep learning algorithms have been applied to the classification of heart auscultation sounds to classify murmurs in the cardiovascular field [1]. Similar algorithms have also been applied to the classification of breath and respiratory sounds to help diagnose COVID-19 [2]. Deep learning-based sound classification in the medical domain can have a major impact due to its ubiquity.

3   Data Collection Study

The goal of this study is to develop a deep learning-enabled system which can predict clinically relevant ABI ranges directly from circulatory sounds of an artery derived from a hand-held doppler. The continuous wave hand-held doppler is a widely used clinical tool used for evaluating arterial flow and is used during ABI examinations. If ABI values can be directly derived from sounds of a doppler, pressure-based measurements can be eliminated alleviating the current limitations while also increasing efficiency of evaluation and increasing objectivity in diagnosis. The first part of our clinical study focuses on collecting continuous wave doppler sounds paired to their corresponding ABIs at multiple vascular laboratories. Data is collected in a formal vascular lab by registered vascular technologists (RVT) in this Institutional Review Board (IRB) approved study with informed consent in patients scheduled for formal ABI examinations at Stanford University. An iOS smartphone (iPhone, Apple) data collection app was developed to capture 4-s doppler audio recordings during examinations.

Recordings were labeled with ground truth ABI values, non-compressibility status (which included falsely elevated ABIs), waveform phasicity (triphasic, biphasic, monophasic), laterality (left or right), and artery name (dorsalis pedis or posterior tibial). Formal ABI examinations were performed using the Parks Flo-Lab 2100 doppler machine (Parks Medical Electronics, Aloha, OR) and ABI output from the machine was used as a reliable ground-truth for data labeling. Non-compressible arteries (including falsely elevated ABIs) were defined as, 1) visible waveforms with ankle cuff pressure >220 mmHg, or 2) ankle cuff pressures 40 mmHg greater than highest arm cuff pressure. Patient demographics were not collected, however, all patients were standard referrals for formal ABI measurement to an Intersocietal Accreditation Commission (IAC) accredited vascular lab. Upon collection of the dataset, sound files were manually screened for quality and labeling was confirmed by a trained vascular physician (O.A). The dataset was split into subsets with the <0.5, 0.5–0.7, 0.7–0.9, and >0.9 cutoffs. An ABI less than 0.5 can be clinically interpreted as severe arterial insufficiency, 0.5–0.7 as moderate arterial disease, 0.7–0.9 some arterial disease, and greater than 0.9 as normal (open to further clinical interpretation). A total of 268 recordings were collected in 67 patients used for model training and validation excluding those with non-compressible tibial vessels.

4   System Development

Upon collection of the ABI dataset, the 4-s recordings are split into 1-s audio clips. Each clip contains an audible single waveform phase. Performing this conversion not only allows for a more detailed representation of each waveform phase but also increases the dataset size significantly. The files are processed by performing a stereophonic to monophonic conversion allowing for spectrogram plotting. The goal of spectrogram plotting is to enable distinct visual features between the ABI ranges based on the intensity and frequency of circulation. This technique is similar to spectral doppler ultrasound waveforms plotted by doppler machines such as the Parks Flo-Lab 2100 used in our study. Spectrogram images of the doppler recordings were generated through a Short-Time Fast Fourier Transform (STFT) filter through window-wise separation and conversion to time frequency domain. Data augmentation such as rotations, random zoom, and sheer were additionally added to the images in order to increase dataset size and potential features learned during deep learning. Additionally, spectrograms were passed through a Butterworth high pass filter to perform cleaning and reduction of noisy visual features introduced from surrounding machinery in the clinical setting. Figure 1A shows a sample of visual spectrograms generated for each ABI range in our dataset. As shown, greater ABI ranges (0.7–0.9 and >0.9) have an increased length and definition in amplitude corresponding to a higher phasicity while lower ABI ranges (0.5–0.7 and <0.5) have less amplitude definition in line with a lower phasicity. By converting the doppler sounds into visual representations, a popular format for deep learning classifiers, we enable the use of a standard image classifier to create an end-to-end predictive system. Spectrograms are finally converted to be 32 × 32 pixels. For classification of the visually differentiated spectrograms, we employ the convolutional neural network (CNN) algorithm [10]. The CNN is popularly leveraged for various image classification problems, for example in the medical domain where it is used to detect disease across various imaging modalities (CT, CXR, MRI, and more) [7]. We construct a 9-layer architecture which consists of the main components of a CNN to fit our smaller sized dataset (shown in Fig. 1Bx). Our CNN architecture consists of convolution operations for feature extraction, pooling for computational size reduction, and finally dense and flatten layers for branching predictions into a final ABI range. The algorithm is trained across 30 epochs with the sparse categorical cross entropy loss function and adam optimizer (LR 0.001), with 80% of the dataset used for training and 20% for validation. Implementation was carried out with Tensorflow and Keras in a high-ram environment with the NVIDIA P-100 GPU in the Python programming language in Google's CoLab IDE.

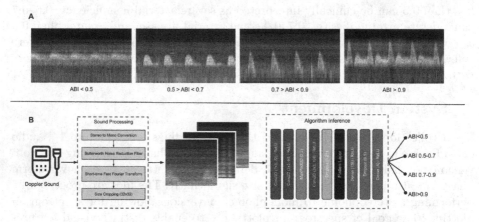

Fig. 1. (A): Visual spectrograms for each ABI range differentiated through amplitude peak length and definition, (B): Deep learning model architecture (consists of signal sound processing and convolutional neural network algorithm inference).

5   Validation Study

Our deep learning system went through an in-depth statistical validation receiving a cumulative testing accuracy of 98.85%. The system averaged a multi-class precision of 0.911, recall of 0.909, F1-score of 0.9065, and AUROC of 0.991. Metrics are shown per class in Table 1.

As the main focus of this paper is on the clinical aspect of our study, further standard validation methods are not documented here. To perform clinical validation of our system at the point-of-care setting, another iPhone application was developed to house our deep learning system. The CoreML framework from Apple is used to compress and integrate our model into the app in an on-device format without reliance on internet connectivity to perform computation. Both iOS apps in our study are deployed on the TestFlight ecosystem

Table 1. Precision, recall, F1-score, and AUROC scores per ABI range.

Class	Precision	Recall	F1-score	AUROC
<0.5	0.866	0.987	0.923	1.00
0.5–0.7	0.942	0.912	0.926	0.981
0.7–0.9	0.849	0.928	0.887	0.998
>0.9	0.988	0.809	0.890	0.986

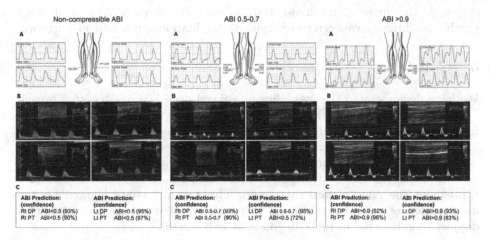

Fig. 2. First patient: 75 year old female with diabetes mellitus who has had bilateral toe amputations, Second patient: 92 year old male presents with bilateral lower extremity claudication symptoms with walking approximately one block, resolved with five minutes of rest. Approximate four year history of symptoms and worse in the past twelve months. Risk Factors include: hypertension and hyperlipidemia, Third patient: patient presents for screening exam and does not report claudication symptoms.

allowing for simplistic beta deployment in various sites. For usage of the validation app, the clinician simply taps a button which triggers a 12-s recording from the microphone. The model performs inference on each 1-s clip and the most frequent prediction is outputted. Due to deployment of the app on a Cloud beta platform, when any changes are made to the model, a new version is simply redeployed. Patient data was not collected during the data collection part of our study but is collected in validation of our model to keep track of weak points in inference and to track patterns. The deployment of a mobile app allows for efficient testing which can be done during examinations. In Fig. 2, we present 3 specific patient testing examples from our on-going clinical validation. The first patient on the left had non-compressible tibial vessels, the middle patient had a moderate ABI in the range of 0.5–0.7, and the patient on the right had a normal ABI >0.9. Panel (a) shows continuous doppler waveforms bilaterally, non-compressible arteries (ankle cuff pressures >230 mmHg). Panel (b) shows spectral doppler ultrasound waveforms of the same vessels. Panel (c) lists the

ABI predictions of the continuous wave doppler audio sounds using our models. In the first patient with non-compressible vessels, the results of an ABI<0.5 are concordant with the Monophasic phasicity of the patient. In the second patient with an ABI 0.5–0.7, the model made a single misprediction of <0.5 for the left posterior tibial artery. In the third patient with an ABI>0.9, the model made all correct predictions. Our deep learning system has shown the preliminary ability to derive ABI ranges from sounds of a continous wave hand-held doppler, even in non-compressible tibial vessels. Our clinical study is on-going and in very early stages. At the current point in our study, around 40 different PAD patients with varying conditions have been tested using the validation app across all 4 arteries.

6   Conclusion

We have demonstrated the feasibility of a novel deep learning-based approach for accurate prediction of ABI ranges through analysis of arterial sounds derived from hand-held dopplers. Significant validation work outside of the vascular lab in the "wild" at our center as well as other centers with a greater variety of continuous wave doppler probes is required. Once validated, this model could provide a low cost, objective, point-of-care solution to assess limb perfusion throughout the point-of-care continuum. This two-fold study allowed for the development of other works related to prediction of waveform phasicity from doppler sounds to aid in PAD diagnosis as well [12,13].

Prospect of Application: This study presented the development of a deep learning-enabled system which can predict clinically relevant ABI ranges directly from circulatory sounds of an artery derived from a hand-held doppler. Our work presents the rapid development of sound-based deep learning for clinical problems through our app-based two-fold study with a custom algorithm.

References

1. Amiriparian, S., Schmitt, M., Cummins, N., Qian, K., Dong, F., Schuller, B.: Deep unsupervised representation learning for abnormal heart sound classification. In: 2018 40th Annual International Conference of the IEEE Engineering in Medicine and Biology Society (EMBC), pp. 4776–4779. IEEE (2018)
2. Coppock, H., Gaskell, A., Tzirakis, P., Baird, A., Jones, L., Schuller, B.: End-to-end convolutional neural network enables COVID-19 detection from breath and cough audio: a pilot study. BMJ Innov. **7**(2) (2021)
3. Criqui, M.H.: Peripheral arterial disease-epidemiological aspects. Vasc. Med. **6**(1_suppl), 3–7 (2001)
4. Criqui, M.H., et al.: Mortality over a period of 10 years in patients with peripheral arterial disease. N. Engl. J. Med. **326**(6), 381–386 (1992)
5. Hirsch, A.T., et al.: Peripheral arterial disease detection, awareness, and treatment in primary care. JAMA **286**(11), 1317–1324 (2001)
6. Hyun, S., Forbang, N.I., Allison, M.A., Denenberg, J.O., Criqui, M.H., Ix, J.H.: Ankle-brachial index, toe-brachial index, and cardiovascular mortality in persons with and without diabetes mellitus. J. Vasc. Surg. **60**(2), 390–395 (2014)

7. Litjens, G., et al.: A survey on deep learning in medical image analysis. Med. Image Anal. **42**, 60–88 (2017)
8. Mohler III, E.R., et al.: Utility and barriers to performance of the ankle brachial index in primary care practice. Vasc. Med. **9**(4), 253–260 (2004)
9. Mourad, J.J., et al.: Screening of unrecognized peripheral arterial disease (PAD) using ankle-brachial index in high cardiovascular risk patients free from symptomatic PAD. J. Vasc. Surg. **50**(3), 572–580 (2009)
10. O'Shea, K., Nash, R.: An introduction to convolutional neural networks. arXiv preprint arXiv:1511.08458 (2015)
11. Ouriel, K.: Peripheral arterial disease. Lancet **358**(9289), 1257–1264 (2001)
12. Rao, A., Battenfield, K., Aalami, O.: Waveform phasicity prediction from arterial sounds through spectrogram analysis using convolutional neural networks for limb perfusion assessment. In: 2021 IEEE International Midwest Symposium on Circuits and Systems (MWSCAS), pp. 462–466. IEEE (2021)
13. Rao, A., Chaudhari, A., Aalami, O.: Development of the Next generation hand-held doppler with waveform phasicity predictive capabilities using deep learning. In: Oyarzun Laura, C., et al. (eds.) DCL/PPML/LL-COVID19/CLIP -2021. LNCS, vol. 12969, pp. 56–67. Springer, Cham (2021). https://doi.org/10.1007/978-3-030-90874-4_6
14. Shu, J., Santulli, G.: Update on peripheral artery disease: epidemiology and evidence-based facts. Atherosclerosis **275**, 379–381 (2018)
15. Winsor, T.: Influence of arterial disease on the systolic blood pressure gradients of the extremity. Am. J. Med. Sci. **220**, 117–126 (1950)

Deep Learning Meets Computational Fluid Dynamics to Assess CAD in CCTA

Filip Malawski[1,2], Jarosław Gośliński[1], Mikołaj Stryja[1],
Katarzyna Jesionek[1], Marcin Kostur[1,3], Karol Miszalski-Jamka[1],
and Jakub Nalepa[1,4(✉)]

[1] Graylight Imaging, Gliwice, Poland
{fmalawski,jgoslinski,mstryja,mkostur,kjamka}@graylight-imaging.com,
jnalepa@ieee.org
[2] Institute of Computer Science, AGH University of Science and Technology,
Krakow, Poland
[3] Faculty of Science and Technology, University of Silesia, Katowice, Poland
[4] Department of Algorithmics and Software, Silesian University of Technology,
Gliwice, Poland

Abstract. Early diagnosis and effective monitoring of the coronary artery disease are critical in ensuring its effective treatment. Although there are established invasive examinations to assess this condition, the current research focus is put on non-invasive procedures. Here, the coronary computed tomography angiography is the first-choice modality, but its manual analysis is cost-inefficient, lacks reproducibility, and suffers from significant inter- and intra-rater disagreement. We tackle those issues and introduce an end-to-end deep learning-powered pipeline for automated analysis of such imagery which additionally exploits computational fluid dynamics to capture the functional vessel characteristics. Our experiments, performed over clinically acquired scans, revealed that the suggested segmentation approaches not only outperform state-of-the-art nnU-Nets, but also lead to the blood-flow parameters which are in strong agreement with those elaborated for the ground-truth delineations.

Keywords: Coronary arteries · Segmentation · U-Net · CCTA · Blood flow simulation · Coronary artery disease

1 Introduction

Cardiovascular diseases (CVDs) is a class of disorders that affect the heart or blood vessels, and are one of the most common causes of death in both developing and developed countries [11]. They are often associated with a build-up of fatty deposits inside the arteries which leads to an increased risk of blood

This work was supported by the National Centre for Research and Development (POIR.01.01.01-00-0664/16). JN was supported by the Silesian University of Technology funds through the grant for maintaining and developing research potential.

clots. Coronary artery disease (CAD) is one of such conditions, accounting for approx. 7 million deaths yearly—its early diagnosis plays a pivotal role in effective treatment [1]. There are several exams which are clinically used to assess CAD. They span across both invasive and non-invasive procedures, with the latter exploiting medical imaging to quantify anatomical and physiological measures prognostic for the patient's risk. Here, the coronary computed tomography angiography (CCTA) is the first-choice image modality. Unfortunately, manual analysis of such data may lead to inconsistent results and high inter- and intra-rater disagreement, strongly dependent on the experience of a reader [6,13].

Once a scan is acquired, it is visually investigated to detect coronary artery stenosis. However, to understand its functional significance, the patients undergo the invasive angiography to extract the fractional flow reserve (FFR) [22]. Unfortunately, due to low specificity of CCTA, there is a significant number of such invasive and costly procedures performed unnecessarily [12]. To tackle it, the automated quantification of the functional significance of stenosis in CCTA has been researched [27]. We distinguish the algorithms to (i) simulate the blood flow to obtain the functional characteristics of the stenosis (or the arterial plaques), and to (ii) analyze the left ventricle myocardium. The simulation techniques mainly focus on estimating FFR [9,19], whereas the others do not benefit from the computational fluid dynamics [5,25], but require clinical validation [27].

Inaccurate segmentation of the coronary vessels can deteriorate the quality of extracted biomarkers [20]. Their manual delineation is cost-inefficient, and it is affected by inter- and intra-rater variability. Therefore, automating this process can not only accelerate the diagnosis, but is also key in ensuring its reproducibility, which is of utmost importance in clinical settings. Although there are classic algorithms to segment coronary vessels [14], the current trend focuses on the deep learning segmentation approaches [17]. Such techniques often exploit multi-scale analysis offered by the fully-convolutional architectures [3], also deployed in a cascaded fashion [4,15]. To benefit from the shape characteristics of the coronary vessels, we can utilize their (manually- or automatically-extracted) centerlines [23,26]. Such "straightened" view of the scan is routinely used by radiologists for reporting the stenosis degree, and may be exploited to improve the segmentation [18]—we follow this research pathway. To the best of our knowledge, the impact of the segmentation quality on the simulation results has not been quantitatively investigated so far. We address this research gap as well.

In this paper, we introduce an end-to-end and reproducible pipeline to extract the quantitative biomarkers from CTTA, in which the deep learning algorithm is used for segmenting coronary vessels. They are later fed to the computational fluid dynamics (CFD) engine for blood flow simulations (Sect. 2). Our multifaceted experiments performed over the clinical CTTA data revealed that the suggested segmentation techniques not only outperform the state-of-the-art nnU-Nets [8], but also improve the quality of the blood flow pressure parameters extracted using the Lattice Boltzmann Method (Sect. 3). To our knowledge, such quantitative analysis which can shed more light on the impact of the segmentation quality on the CFD simulations has not been performed so far.

2   Automated Assessment of CAD in CCTA

We utilize a deep learning approach for segmenting coronary vessels which are fed to the blood flow simulation engine which exploits the Lattice Boltzmann Method (Sect. 2.4). The U-Net-powered segmentation algorithm (Sect. 2.3), which operates on the upsampled CTTA data, benefits from the straightened representation of the vessels (Sect. 2.1) to better capture their local (contextual) characteristics. Also, the proposed mesh-based ground-truth representation allows us to maintain sub-pixel peculiarities of the vessels (Sect. 2.2).

2.1   Straightened Representation of the Coronary Vessels

Once a centerline (CL) of the vessel of interest is extracted[1], it is smoothed and interpolated using the $\mathcal{B}$-spline interpolation [2]. Afterwards, we determine the tangent vector for each point $\mathcal{P}_{CL}^i$, positioned on CL, where $i = 0, 1, \ldots, |\mathcal{P}_{CL}|$, and $|\mathcal{P}_{CL}|$ denotes the number of sampled points along CL (Fig. 1a). It becomes the normal vector of a plane for each $\mathcal{P}_{CL}^i$, and the original CTTA data is sampled (using Gaussian interpolation) during the segmentation process to generate a 2D image in this plane (Fig. 1b). Such stacked 2D images created along CL constitute the straightened vessel's representation. Capturing the positions of the sampled CL points enables us to conveniently reverse this transformation.

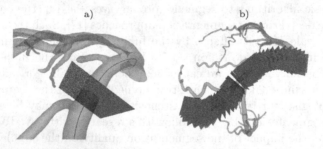

Fig. 1. Creating the straightened vessel's representation using the points (in dark blue) sampled along CL: a) a single 2D image for a selected $\mathcal{P}_{CL}^i$, together with b) a subset of all 2D images which constitutes the straightened representation. (Color figure online)

---

[1] Extraction of the CLs can be manual or automated. In the former case, we emphasize that this process is much faster than delineating the entire vessel tree, hence it is still a valid approach in the clinical settings. Our preliminary experiments showed that the avg. time required to manually delineate the left and right coronary arteries was 14 h, whereas segmenting their CLs only would reduce this time by 75%.

2.2   Representing Ground-Truth Segmentation as a 3D Mesh

To train a data-driven segmentation model in a supervised way, the ground-truth (GT) segmentation, commonly prepared by a human reader in a manual or semi-automated process, is utilized. In medical image analysis tasks, GT delineations are often generated as per-voxel binary masks, where each voxel is annotated with one or more class labels. In our approach, we exploit a 3D mesh representation of the GT, as it can allow us to capture sub-pixel peculiarities of the vessels in a much easier way, especially using dedicated software tools [24]. Such 3D meshes can be voxelized (therefore, they may be transformed into the per-voxel masks), hence they may be effectively used for the quantitative assessment of the segmentation algorithms using classic quality metrics.

To benefit from the 3D mesh GT representation capturing the sub-pixel vessel characteristics, we extract the straightened representation of the GT directly from the 3D mesh. For each point $\mathcal{P}_{CL}^i$, we obtain the 2D plane (as discussed in Sect. 2.1), and the intersection between the plane and the mesh is determined. Since the intersections will include all vessels on the 2D plane, we select those intersection points which are the closest to CL (Fig. 2). To create the corresponding 2D mask from the vessel's contour in an input 3D space, the contour points are translated relatively to $\mathcal{P}_{CL}^i$, and then rotated using the plane basis vectors. As a result, their z-values are zeroed, while the relative positions are maintained, which effectively converts 3D points to 2D. The entire anatomical structure of interest can be represented either as a tree or as a collection of partially overlapping CLs, originating from each vessel, and ending in the common root of the vessel tree. We exploit the latter approach, as such partial overlaps and different views of the vessels can help deal with the most challenging branching areas of the scan which are often under-represented, thus not representative enough to train a machine learning model that would generalize well over the unseen data.

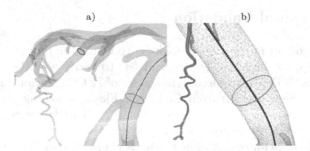

Fig. 2. To create the straightened representation of vessels from a 3D mesh, we a) determine the intersection between the 2D plane and the mesh in $\mathcal{P}_{CL}^i$ (in light blue and green), and b) select the vessel's contour closest to CL (green). (Color figure online)

2.3   Segmentation of Vessels Using U-Nets in Upsampled CTTA

The quality of vessel segmentation notably affects the blood flow simulation, and may significantly deteriorate its performance [20]. Here, we hypothesize that utilizing a sub-pixel segmentation mask can be beneficial, as it would allow us to exploit a more detailed vessel's architecture. Using our method (Sect. 2.2), we extract the straightened representation in the resolution 3× higher than the original CTTA scan. Along with the straightened segmentation mask, we extract the straightened image, also upsampled 3×, using Gaussian interpolation.

For segmentation, we employ a 3D U-Net network with six levels, each containing two convolutional layers with the $(3 \times 3 \times 3)$ kernels. The model is trained over the 3D training patches of size $(p_x,\ p_y,\ p_z)$. We utilize the loss function composed of the soft DICE and binary cross-entropy, taken with equal weights. Finally, we deploy the morphological closing as post processing, to close the "gaps" which may be introduced during the reconstruction of the 3D data in the original coordinate space, due to the relative angles of the 2D images.

2.4   Blood Flow Simulation

We simulate the blood flow in the coronary tree using the Lattice Boltzmann Method (LBM). It is an alternative technique to solve the Navier-Stokes equation with an excellent computational efficiency on massively parallel architectures [21]. Given the velocity boundary conditions, we focus on the steady flow of $100 \frac{ml}{min}$, and the coronary tree is cut at a diameter of 1.5 mm. At the outlets, the constant pressure is applied, and the simulation is run with a regulatory mechanism that increases pressure on side branches, so that the flux scaling law is fulfilled [7]. Ultimately, we extract the ratio of the pressure (p_i) along i points positioned on the vessel of interest to the inlet pressure (p_0).

3   Experimental Validation

The objectives of our study are two-fold: (i) to assess the proposed models and confront them with the nnU-Nets [8], and (ii) to verify how the segmentation quality impacts CFD. We acquired a clinical set of 72 CCTA scans (256-slice dual source scanner, Siemens Somatom Definition Flash; re-sampled to $0.35\,mm^3$) which were manually segmented by three readers (1, 3, and 6 years of experience, YOE), and reviewed by a senior reader (15 YOE). We utilize 57 random scans for training, and 15 ones for testing. The methods were coded in TensorFlow 2.6 (we used the native LBM implementation [10]), and run (all models for 500 epochs) on an NVIDIA A100 GPU (40 GB VRAM). We investigate U-Net (3×): a 3D U-Net with 3× upscaling, trained over the patches with the centers capturing the vessel mask, and the 3D U-Nets with 3× upscaling, trained over the patches drawn along CL, without and with straightened representation (SR): U-Net (3×, CL) and U-Net (3×, CL, SR). The upsampling architectures operate on the $(64 \times 64 \times 64)$ patches to produce the output $(192 \times 192 \times 192)$ ones. The nnU-Nets process ($160 \times 160 \times 96$) patches—they can benefit from a larger spatial context. For evaluation, we use DICE, Intersection over Union (IoU), precision, and recall (IoU penalizes single instances of wrong segmentation more than DICE). The inter-algorithm agreement for CFD parameters (for ground-truth vs. automatic segmentation) was evaluated by Intraclass Correlation Coefficient (ICC). For simulations, we set the spatial resolution to $75\,\mu m$, for which they are already convergent (relative error was below 1% when compared with the resolution of $50\,\mu m$). The number of fluid nodes ranged from 4 to 5 million, and we constrain the maximal numerical lattice velocity on an inlet to be $\mu_{lb} = 0.015$. Thus, we keep the Mach number low in the numerical scheme and stay within an incompressible limit of the LBM. We analyze the pressure to the proximal (first 60 mm) left anterior descending (LAD) coronary artery, as it is most relevant for CAD prognosis [16], and we sample pressure values along the ground-truth CL.

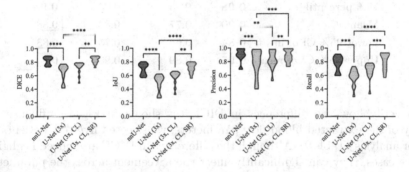

Fig. 3. The distribution of all test metrics for all models. The results of the tests (Friedman's test with post-hoc Dunn's) verifying if the differences are statistically significant are shown as: ** ($p < 0.01$), *** ($p < 0.001$), **** ($p < 0.0001$).

The distributions of the segmentation results (Fig. 3) obtained over the unseen test set of 15 unseen patients indicate that the models exploiting CL sampling and SR significantly outperform 3D U-Nets (Friedman's with post-hoc Dunn's), and U-Net ($3\times$, CL, SR) delivers the same-quality delineations as nnU-Nets. Those observations are further manifested in Table 1—U-Net ($3\times$, CL, SR) consistently outperformed the other architectures in DICE, IoU, and recall, while offering precision which is competitive with nnU-Nets. The low precision values obtained for U-Net ($3\times$) shows that it tends to over-segment the scans, thus it results in false-positive regions which are effectively pruned in the other models. It is of note that the inter-rater disagreement in vessel's tree segmentation is significant—for a selected patient, the agreement across the three raters ranged from 0.74 to 0.84 (DICE). Therefore, the quality metrics are not only directly affected by the quality of the ground truth, but it also shows an urgent need of deploying an automated segmentation approach which would be free from human bias, in order to maintain reproducibility of the analysis process.

Table 1. The results quantified by DICE and precision (for all metrics, see https://bitbucket.org/fphealthcare/amai2022/src/master/). The best results are boldfaced, whereas the second best are underlined.

Quality metric		nnU-Net	U-Net (3×)	U-Net (3×, CL)	U-Net (3×, CL, SR)
DICE	25% percentile	0.75	0.56	0.71	**0.80**
	Median	0.84	0.71	0.76	**0.85**
	75% percentile	**0.87**	0.73	0.78	**0.87**
	Mean	0.82	0.65	0.72	**0.83**
	Lower 95% CI of mean	0.79	0.57	0.67	**0.80**
	Upper 95% CI of mean	0.85	0.72	0.77	**0.86**
Precision	25% percentile	**0.87**	0.63	0.77	0.82
	Median	**0.91**	0.80	0.81	0.89
	75% percentile	**0.98**	0.95	0.93	**0.98**
	Mean	**0.90**	0.77	0.83	0.88
	Lower 95% CI of mean	**0.84**	0.66	0.75	0.83
	Upper 95% CI of mean	**0.95**	0.89	0.90	0.94

To verify how the differences in DICE (as shown in Fig. 4) influence the quality of the extracted blood flow parameters, we selected five test patients for further analysis (Table 2). Although the differences in DICE are indeed negligible in some cases, they can significantly affect the agreement across the parameters extracted for the ground-truth and automated delineations—see e.g., P2, where the difference in DICE amounts to 0.01 between nnU-Net and U-Net (3×, CL, SR), whereas ICC is notably larger for the latter model (our U-Nets delivered the best agreement across P1–P5). It shows that the segmentation quality should be also validated indirectly, as the CFD parameters are ultimately the biomarkers which may influence further clinical pathway. Finally, the Bland-Altman plots (Fig. 5) indicate that the discrepancy within the blood flow parameters' estimation accumulates across the vessel (the largest ratio is captured near the inlet).

Table 2. The DICE and ICC values for the selected test patients (P1–P5). The best results are boldfaced, whereas the second best are underlined.

Patient	nnU-Net		U-Net (3x)		U-Net (3x, CL)		U-Net (3x, CL, SR)	
	DICE	ICC	DICE	ICC	DICE	ICC	DICE	ICC
P1	**0.87**	0.949	0.75	0.796	0.76	0.979	**0.87**	**0.980**
P2	0.85	0.918	0.77	0.658	0.79	**0.978**	0.86	0.972
P3	**0.88**	0.493	0.73	**0.850**	0.78	0.495	0.87	0.758
P4	**0.89**	0.956	0.44	0.632	0.79	**0.975**	**0.89**	0.437
P5	0.86	0.810	0.62	0.850	0.76	0.559	**0.89**	**0.935**

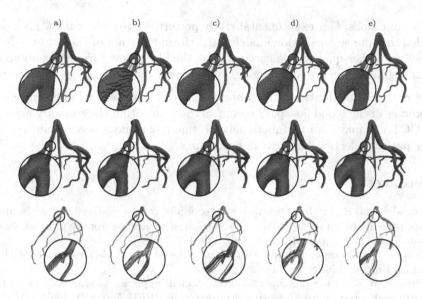

Fig. 4. Example a) ground truth, b) nnU-Net (DICE: 0.86), c) U-Net (3×) (DICE: 0.62), d) U-Net (3×, CL) (DICE: 0.76), e) U-Net (3×, CL, SR) (DICE: 0.89) segmentations (for P5). Voxel and mesh visualizations are given in the first and second row, and the last row renders the blood flow (blue and red correspond to small and large values of velocity, respectively) which is notably impacted by minor differences in the segmentation (note that the blood flow view is rotated). (Color figure online)

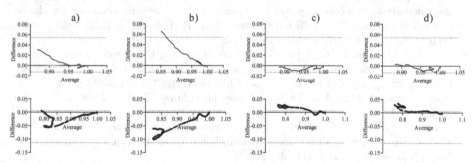

Fig. 5. The disagreement for P1 (top) and P2 (bottom) between the blood flow parameters obtained for the ground truth and automated segmentation by a) nnU-Net, b) U-Net (3×), c) U-Net (3×, CL), and d) U-Net (3×, CL, SR).

4   Conclusions and Future Work

Providing early diagnosis and effective monitoring of CAD is critical in ensuring its effective treatment. We introduced an end-to-end pipeline for extracting the blood flow parameters within the coronary arteries which benefits from deep learning and CFD. Such patient-specific models built solely on CCTA can not only accelerate the clinical procedures, but may also reduce the number of invasive examinations. Our experimental study performed over clinical CCTA scans revealed that our segmentation models outperform the state-of-the-art nnU-Nets and deliver higher-quality delineations. Also, the blood flow parameters obtained for our segmentation are in strong agreement with those for the ground truth.

Prospect of Application: Our approach may be utilized to fully automate the process of the blood flow parameters' extraction within the coronary arteries from CCTA. It may improve functional assessment of stenosis severity and enable better patient selection for invasive procedures.

References

1. Alizadehsani, R., et al.: Non-invasive detection of coronary artery disease in high-risk patients based on the stenosis prediction of separate coronary arteries. Comput. Methods Programs Biomed. **162**, 119–127 (2018)
2. Briand, T., Monasse, P.: Theory and practice of image B-spline interpolation. Image Process. Line **8**, 99–141 (2018)
3. Cheung, W.K., et al.: A computationally efficient approach to segmentation of the aorta and coronary arteries using deep learning. IEEE Access **9**, 108873–108888 (2021)
4. Gu, L., Cai, X.C.: Fusing 2D and 3D convolutional neural networks for the segmentation of aorta and coronary arteries from CT images. Artif. Intell. Med. **121**, 102189 (2021)
5. van Hamersvelt, R.W., Zreik, M., Voskuil, M., Viergever, M.A., Išgum, I., Leiner, T.: Deep learning analysis of left ventricular myocardium in CT angiographic intermediate-degree coronary stenosis improves the diagnostic accuracy for identification of functionally significant stenosis. Eur. Radiol. **29**(5), 2350–2359 (2018). https://doi.org/10.1007/s00330-018-5822-3
6. Hoe, J.W.M., Toh, K.H.: A practical guide to reading CT coronary angiograms–How to avoid mistakes when assessing for coronary stenoses. Int. J. Cardiovasc. Imaging **23**(5), 617–633 (2007). https://doi.org/10.1007/s10554-006-9173-9
7. Huo, Y., Kassab, G.S.: A scaling law of vascular volume. Biophys. J. **96**(2), 347–353 (2009)
8. Isensee, F., Jaeger, P.F., Kohl, S.A.A., Petersen, J., Maier-Hein, K.H.: nnU-Net: a self-configuring method for deep learning-based biomedical image segmentation. Nat. Methods **18**(2), 203–211 (2021)
9. Itu, L., et al.: A machine-learning approach for computation of fractional flow reserve from coronary computed tomography. J. Appl. Physiol. **121**(1), 42–52 (2016)
10. Januszewski, M., Kostur, M.: Sailfish: a flexible multi-GPU implementation of the lattice Boltzmann method. Comput. Phys. Commun. **185**(9), 2350–2368 (2014)
11. Johnson, C., et al.: The benchmark of rural health: the top 10 leading causes of death in rural Texas. Texas Public Health J. **70**(1), 18–23 (2018)
12. Ko, B.S., et al.: Combined CT coronary angiography and stress myocardial perfusion imaging for hemodynamically significant stenoses in patients with suspected coronary artery disease: a comparison with fractional flow reserve. JACC Cardiovasc. Imaging **5**(11), 1097–1111 (2012)
13. Liu, C.Y., et al.: Deep learning powered coronary CT angiography for detecting obstructive coronary artery disease: the effect of reader experience, calcification and image quality. Eur. J. Radiol. **142**, 109835 (2021)

14. Ma, G., Yang, J., Zhao, H.: A coronary artery segmentation method based on region growing with variable sector search area. Technol. Health Care **28**, 463–472 (2020). s1
15. Mirunalini, P., et al.: Segmentation of coronary arteries from CTA axial slices using deep learning techniques. In: Proceedings of TENCON, pp. 2074–2080. IEEE (2019)
16. Neumann, F.J., et al.: 2018 ESC/EACTS guidelines on myocardial revascularization. Eur. Heart J. **40**(2), 87–165 (2018)
17. Pan, L.S., et al.: Coronary artery segmentation under class imbalance using a U-Net based architecture on computed tomography angiography images. Sci. Rep. **11**(1), 1–7 (2021)
18. Schaap, M., et al.: Robust shape regression for supervised vessel segmentation and its application to coronary segmentation in CTA. IEEE Trans. Med. Imaging **30**(11), 1974–1986 (2011)
19. Taylor, C.A., Fonte, T.A., Min, J.K.: Computational fluid dynamics applied to cardiac computed tomography for noninvasive quantification of fractional flow reserve: scientific basis. J. Am. Coll. Cardiol. **61**(22), 2233–2241 (2013)
20. Tesche, C., et al.: Coronary CT angiography-derived fractional flow reserve. Radiology **285**(1), 17–33 (2017)
21. Tölke, J., Krafczyk, M.: TeraFLOP computing on a desktop PC with GPUs for 3D CFD. Int. J. Comput. Fluid Dyn. **22**(7), 443–456 (2008)
22. Tonino, P.A., et al.: Fractional flow reserve versus angiography for guiding percutaneous coronary intervention. New Engl. J. Med. **360**(3), 213–224 (2009)
23. Updegrove, A., Wilson, N.M., Merkow, J., Lan, H., Marsden, A.L., Shadden, S.C.: SimVascular: an open source pipeline for cardiovascular simulation. Ann. Biomed. Eng. **45**(3), 525–541 (2016). https://doi.org/10.1007/s10439-016-1762-8
24. Virzì, A., et al.: Comprehensive review of 3D segmentation software tools for MRI usable for pelvic surgery planning. J. Digit. Imaging **33**(1), 99–110 (2019). https://doi.org/10.1007/s10278-019-00239-7
25. Xiong, G., Kola, D., Heo, R., Elmore, K., Cho, I., Min, J.K.: Myocardial perfusion analysis in cardiac computed tomography angiographic images at rest. Med. Image Anal. **24**(1), 77–89 (2015)
26. Zreik, M., et al.: A recurrent CNN for automatic detection and classification of coronary artery plaque and stenosis in coronary CT angiography. IEEE Trans. Med. Imaging **38**(7), 1588–1598 (2019)
27. Zreik, M., et al.: Deep learning analysis of coronary arteries in cardiac CT angiography for detection of patients requiring invasive coronary angiography. IEEE Trans. Med. Imaging **39**(5), 1545–1557 (2020)

Machine Learning for Dynamically Predicting the Onset of Renal Replacement Therapy in Chronic Kidney Disease Patients Using Claims Data

Daniel Lopez-Martinez[✉], Christina Chen, and Ming-Jun Chen

Google Research, Palo Alto, USA
dlmocdm@google.com

Abstract. Chronic kidney disease (CKD) represents a slowly progressive disorder that can eventually require renal replacement therapy (RRT) including dialysis or renal transplantation. Early identification of patients who will require RRT (as much as 1 year in advance) improves patient outcomes, for example by allowing higher-quality vascular access for dialysis. Therefore, early recognition of the need for RRT by care teams is key to successfully managing the disease. Unfortunately, there is currently no commonly used predictive tool for RRT initiation. In this work, we present a machine learning model that dynamically identifies CKD patients at risk of requiring RRT up to one year in advance using only claims data. To evaluate the model, we studied approximately 3 million Medicare beneficiaries for which we made over 8 million predictions. We showed that the model can identify at risk patients with over 90% sensitivity and specificity. Although additional work is required before this approach is ready for clinical use, this study provides a basis for a screening tool to identify patients at risk within a time window that enables early proactive interventions intended to improve RRT outcomes.

Keywords: Dialysis · Kidney transplant · Chronic kidney disease · Claims data · Dynamic modeling

1 Introduction

Chronic kidney disease (CKD) is defined by decreased kidney function for three or more months and is classified based on the severity of kidney damage. As CKD is not reversible, the natural course is progression over time with the most severe form being end-stage renal disease (ESRD). When disease progresses to ESRD, residual kidney function is no longer able to meet the body's needs without the aid of life-sustaining chronic renal placement therapy (RRT), which includes chronic dialysis (hemodialysis or peritoneal dialysis) and kidney transplant. CKD affects approximately one-seventh of US adults above the age of 20 years and constitutes one of the major public health problems globally [3]. In the United States, there are 37 million patients with CKD and over 700,000 who have progressed to ESRD [1,3].

S. Wu et al. (Eds.): AMAI 2022, LNCS 13540, pp. 18–28, 2022.
https://doi.org/10.1007/978-3-031-17721-7_3

The development of ESRD is associated with significant morbidity and mortality, and the Kidney Disease Outcomes Quality Initiative (KDIGO) [21] has emphasized the importance of an individualized approach to patient care, taking into account life expectancy, comorbidities, individual vascular characteristics, as well as individual patient circumstances, needs, and preferences. Ideally, these multidisciplinary discussions should start at least 9–12 months prior to RRT initiation to allow time for adequate discussion and if appropriate, dialysis access (arteriovenous fistula or graft or peritoneal dialysis catheter) creation and maturation, and kidney transplant evaluation and listing. Dialysis access requires surgical intervention and takes time before it is ready for use; patients who do not receive adequate preparation require placement of central venous catheters for dialysis, and may be exposed to complications like severe infections [11].

Identifying patients at risk of developing ESRD and requiring RRT would enable care teams to target these populations to initiate multidisciplinary discussions, which have been associated with improved survival, lower hospitalization rates, improved uptake of dialysis and better access to kidney transplant waiting lists [7,10,17,18]. Unfortunately, it is difficult to predict the development of ESRD and most patients do not receive the recommended clinical care before RRT initiation [6,13]. Despite substantial efforts (e.g. Fistula First Catheter Last [12]), there has been virtually no reduction in central venous catheter use at initiation of hemodialysis over the last decade [9,12]. Only 20% of patients start dialysis through the recommended type of access, an arteriovenous fistula [12].

While there have been efforts to build predictive algorithms to identify at risk patients, there remains no standardized nationally implementable prediction models. Some prior studies that have modeled CKD progression include linear models based on static variables at single points in time, such as the Tangri et al. model [20], which have been evaluated in multiple studies [19,20]. While promising and well studied, these static models do not take into account the temporal progression of disease. Only a limited number of studies have focused on predicting disease deterioration with prediction horizons in the order of months [14]. While these studies have yielded promising results, they relied on medical record data, including laboratory values, which are not as widely available as claims data. To this end, Dovgan et al. [5] developed a model based solely on the comorbidities data from the National Health Insurance in Taiwan to predict initiation of RRT 3, 6, and 12 months from the time of the patient's first diagnosis with CKD. While this study showed promising results, predictions were only rendered once at incident diagnosis of CKD without any additional evaluation of subsequent disease progression.

To address the aforementioned limitations, in this study we describe a time-bucketed linear machine learning model to predict RRT initiation in patients with a diagnosis of CKD in a format that is structured to be deployable at a large scale: 1) Use of nationally available Medicare claims; 2) Integrating temporal information; 3) A linear model that is easy to interpret; 4) Monthly predictions to match the realistic cadence of care management groups. We evaluate the performance of our model on prediction windows of up to 365 days. In addition to this, we also evaluate the potential impact our model may have on improving timely dialysis access prior to initiation of RRT.

2   Methods

2.1   Dataset Description

We used the Limited Dataset (LDS) Standard Analytic Files (SAFs) sample of Medicare beneficiaries from the Centers for Medicare & Medicaid Services (CMS), the largest insurer of people aged 65 years and older in the USA. This dataset contains a 5% random sample of beneficiaries enrolled in the fee-for-service Medicare program that is representative of the overall Medicare population, and their corresponding Part A (inpatient/hospital coverage) and Part B (outpatient/medical coverage) fee-for-service administrative claims from January 1, 2011 to December 31, 2016. We included all patients who at any point after turning 65 had a fee for service claim, regardless of the original enrollment reason, whether they switched from a non fee for service plan, or they died.

2.2   Task Definition

Our goal was to identify patients at risk of requiring renal replacement therapy, specifically (1) chronic dialysis, (2) kidney transplant, and (3) any renal replacement therapy (RRT) defined as either of the previous two. We specifically sought to predict the onset of these three therapy categories within the following clinically relevant time horizons: 30, 60, 90, 180, 365 days.

The definitions of chronic dialysis, renal transplant, and RRT are derived from Healthcare Common Procedure Coding Systems (HCPCS) procedure codes, which are included in the claims data. A first occurrence in a beneficiary's claims record of any of the corresponding procedure codes would denote initiation of the corresponding therapy.

2.3   Data Representation and Processing

Data Assembling. The dataset described in Sect. 2.1 contains claims of the following types: inpatient, outpatient, home health, skilled nursing, and non-institutional (i.e. carrier). For each beneficiary in the dataset, we assembled these to produce a temporally ordered list of claims. This list was sampled periodically to generate machine learning training samples and render predictions. We call this process "triggering". In order to simulate care management workflows, eligible predictions for all beneficiaries were triggered on the first of every month between January 1, 2012 and December 1, 2015. This provides one year of buffer after the last potential trigger, as the dataset ended in December 31, 2016.

For each trigger, we assembled the entire sequence of claims up to the first of the month. Each trigger time was associated with a binary label for each of the three tasks (dialysis, kidney transplant, renal replacement) and the five time horizons (30, 60, 90, 180, 365 days). If any of the procedure codes corresponding to the task (see Sect. 2.2) was found in the beneficiary's claims within the corresponding time horizon from trigger time, a positive label was generated. Otherwise, it was negative.

Prediction Triggering Eligibility Criteria. Because of how the machine learning problem was formulated, not all possible triggers were used by the model. Candidate triggers were eligible for predictions if at the time of triggering all the following criteria were met: the patient (1) was 65 years or greater; (2) had diagnosis of CKD on any previous claim; (3) had not initiated RRT; (4) had at least a year of historical claims; (5) had a healthcare claim within the last 30 days (to avoid rendering new predictions for patients whose claims data does not contain any new information since the last prediction). Only triggers that met the aforementioned conditions were used by the model for either training or testing. This trigger filtering process is depicted in Fig. 1.

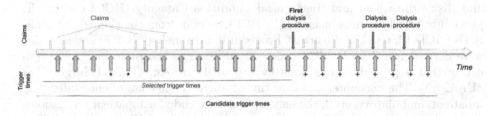

Fig. 1. Example triggers events for a patient. Triggering occurs on the first of every month as represented by the lower blue and red arrows. Claim events, including claims correlated with chronic dialysis procedures, are represented by the gray upper arrows. If all inclusion criteria are met for a patient at the time of triggering, a prediction of dialysis risk within the horizon window (next 30, 60, 90, 180, or 365 days) will be generated (blue arrow: prediction generated, red arrow: prediction not generated). For example, predictions are not generated if no claims have been filed in the previous 30 days (red arrows marked with *). Triggers after the first chronic dialysis procedure will not generate a prediction (red arrows marked with a +). (Color figure online)

Feature Extraction. We implemented a data representation that has been shown to accurately predict multiple medical events while requiring minimal data processing for improved generability and ease of implementation [15].

For each beneficiary, we extracted demographic data from the initial enrollment into Medicare. Specifically, recorded sex, reported race, and birth-year which was then converted to bucketed age (with 10-year buckets) at each trigger time. In addition to this, for each calendar day, we extracted information about the conditions, procedures, encounter types, and administered medications from the inpatient, outpatient, home health, skilled nursing, and non-institutional (i.e.

carrier) claims. This information was used to develop a total of 23 features with one-hot encoding, indicated in Table 1.

Table 1. List of the 23 features used in the model grouped by type, together with the number of features in each group.

Feature group (# feat.)	Features
Patient characteristics (3)	sex, race, bucketed age (10-year buckets)
Conditions (4)	ICD9, ICD10, CCS, HCC
Procedures (6)	ICD9, ICD10, CCS, CPT, hcpcs.alpha, performer role
Encounters (8)	class, hospitalization admit source, discharge disposition, ICD9, ICD10, CCS, HCC, code revenue type
Medications (2)	HCPCS, rxnorm

The condition-based features used all the raw ICD-9 and ICD-10 codes associated with each claim as well as the Clinical Classification Software (CCS) and Risk Adjustment and Hierarchical Condition Category (HCC) codes. The procedure-based features included the HCPCS codes from the claims, as well as ICD-9, ICD-10, CCS, and Current Procedural Terminology (CPT) codes, which were derived from the HCPCS codes, in addition to the performer role (indicating that a procedure was done by a provider in e.g. "General Surgery" or "Urology"). The encounter-based features indicated the class of encounter (e.g. inpatient, ambulatory, etc.), the encounter source code for inpatient admissions, the discharge disposition of the encounter, the ICD-9 or ICD-10 principal diagnosis in the encounter, and the revenue center codes. Finally, the medication administration features included HCPCS codes as well as RXNorm codes, which were derived from the National Drug Codes (NDCs).

Note that during the time period covered in this dataset, there was a gradual transition from ICD-9 to the updated ICD-10 billing codes and therefore both coding schemes were included.

With the exception of the demographic data, all feature values that occurred within a time range were aggregated into a new feature. We refer to this process as time-bucketing. In this work, we used the following non-overlapping disjoint time buckets: [0, 30 days), [30 days, 90 days), [90 days, 1 year), [1 year, 10 years).

Dataset Split. To generate train, validation, and test datasets for modeling we split the entire dataset by beneficiary using a random split of 80%/10%/10% respectively. There is no overlap of beneficiaries in these three groups.

2.4   Model Description

Using the features described in Sect. 2.3, we designed independent logistic regression machine learning models to render predictions for each of the three tasks (chronic dialysis, kidney transplant, and RRT) for each beneficiary on the 1st day of every month (if eligible based on the triggering eligibility criteria; see Sect. 2.3) using the data available up to that point.

At training time, we cast the problem as multiclass by dividing our overlapping prediction windows (0–30, 0–60, 0–90, 0–180, 0–365 days from trigger time) into disjoint windows (0–30, 30–60, 60–90, 90–180, 180–365 days from trigger time). In this setting, only the disjoint window that contained the event is positive, while all others are negative. Additionally, we append one extra output to explicitly represent the negative class (i.e. examples in which no adverse event occurred in any prediction window). For example, with 30/60/90/180/365-day windows, the label for an example with an event at day 50 would be [0, 1, 0, 0, 0, 0], whereas the label for an example with no events within 365 days of prediction would be [0, 0, 0, 0, 0, 1]. In this setting, we compute scores as softmax(logits) and train the model using a softmax cross-entropy loss. However, at inference time, we recover predictions for the overlapping windows by computing cumulative sum probabilities: for window i, we compute its probability as $p_i = \sum_{j=0}^{i} s_j$, where $s_j = \text{softmax}(\text{logits}[j])$. This constraint ensures that the output probabilities monotonically increase over successive prediction windows.

All models were implemented and trained with TensorFlow in Python [2]. Model hyperparameters, including L1 regularization coefficient and the parameters of an exponential learning rate decay, were tuned by minimizing loss on the validation set.

2.5 Model Evaluation

We measured the performance of the model on an independent held out test set comprising 10% of the available beneficiaries. No beneficiaries in the test set were used for model training or validation. For each prediction horizon, we calculated the receiver operating characteristic area under the curve (ROC-AUC) and the precision-recall AUC (PR-AUC). Note that given the low prevalence of triggers with positive labels, the PR-AUC is more informative [16]. In addition to this, we also computed the sensitivity and specificity by selecting the threshold that maximized the geometric mean.

Finally, we evaluated the potential impact of our model in improving rates of dialysis access creation (arteriovenous fistula creation, arteriovenous graft placement, and peritoneal dialysis catheter placement). Dialysis access creation was defined by the corresponding list of procedure codes. Specifically, we determined the number of patients we identified using a 1 year prediction horizon who had not undergone dialysis access creation before dialysis initiation, at three target sensitivities: 60%, 70%, 80%.

3 Experiments and Results

3.1 Study Population and Dataset

A total of 2,978,542 individuals were present in the dataset. Their gender and race statistics are shown in Table 1. Of these, 572,319 (19.22%) received a diagnosis with CKD at some point as indicated by the corresponding ICD9 and ICD10 codes in their claims history. We used these codes to build a cohort of CKD patients in which to render predictions for the onset of RRT. The statistics for the CMS dataset and the cohort of CKD patients is shown in Table 2.

Table 2. Statistics of the development (train and validation) and test datasets. Note that the train, validation and test split were done according to beneficiary id on the entire dataset to accomplish an 80/10/10 distribution. Here, we include the distribution of patients after triggering has been performed, which may exclude some patients if none of their triggers meet the trigger eligibility criteria.

	Development set	Test set
Patients	325,851	36,077
Female, n (%)	174,851 (53.66%)	19,357 (53.65%)
Race, n (%)		
Asian	7,007 (2.15%)	786 (2.18%)
Black	36,155 (11.10%)	4,042 (11.20%)
Hispanic	6,572 (2.02%)	789 (2.19%)
Native American	1,508 (0.46%)	161 (0.45%)
White	268,652 (82.45%)	29,656 (82.20%)
Other	4,600 (1.41%)	486 (1.35%)
Unknown	1,357 (0.42%)	157 (0.44%)
Predictions	7,772,847	704,983
Female, n (%)	4,244,917 (54.61%)	387,741 (55.00%)
Race, n (%)		
Asian	155,521 (2.00%)	14,414 (2.04%)
Black	826,666 (10.64%)	74,413 (10.56%)
Hispanic	147,134 (1.89%)	14,419 (2.05%)
Native American	33,532 (0.43%)	3,058 (0.43%)
White	6,484,990 (83.43%)	587,145 (83.28%)
Other	102,687 (1.32%)	9,114 (1.29%)
Unknown	22,317 (0.29%)	2,420 (0.34%
Age, n (%)		
65–74 years	2,019,746 (31.83%)	225,559 (31.99%)
75–84 years	2,602,663 (41.01%)	286,072 (40.58%)
85 years or more	1,723,650 (27.16%)	193,352 (27.43%)

3.2   Model Performance

Table 4 compares the performance of all tasks for 5 overlapping windows: 30, 60, 90, 180, 365 days from trigger time. The best performance was achieved for the

Table 3. Label prevalence for the three prediction tasks and each prediction horizon.

Prediction horizon	RRT	Chronic dialysis	Kidney transplant
30d	0.09%	0.09%	0.01%
60d	0.18%	0.18%	0.01%
90d	0.27%	0.26%	0.02%
180d	0.53%	0.52%	0.04%
365d	1.06%	1.05%	0.07%

Table 4. Comparison of ROC-AUC, PR-AUC, sensitivity, and specificity for the three prediction tasks in the cohort of CKD patients. Sensitivity and specificity was computed by choosing the threshold that maximized the geometric mean.

Task	Metric	Next 30d	Next 60d	Next 90d	Next 180d	Next 365d
Renal replacement procedure	ROC-AUC	0.971	0.963	0.953	0.942	0.928
	PR-AUC	0.311	0.285	0.261	0.262	0.280
	Sensitivity	0.927	0.906	0.885	0.870	0.865
	Specificity	0.940	0.922	0.910	0.887	0.855
Dialysis procedure	ROC-AUC	0.974	0.964	0.951	0.941	0.927
	PR-AUC	0.172	0.148	0.131	0.119	0.117
	Sensitivity	0.904	0.921	0.882	0.862	0.845
	Specificity	0.951	0.895	0.894	0.880	0.858
Kidney transplant procedure	ROC-AUC	0.975	0.975	0.975	0.972	0.961
	PR-AUC	0.006	0.011	0.014	0.032	0.047
	Sensitivity	0.930	0.919	0.937	0.923	0.903
	Specificity	0.939	0.941	0.922	0.923	0.018

Table 5. Percentage of beneficiaries identified by our model using a 1 year prediction horizon that had not undergone dialysis access creation procedures before dialysis initiation, for three target sensitivities and their corresponding specificities.

Sensitivity	Specificity	% of patients
80%	91.62%	35.36%
70%	95.18%	33.49%
60%	97.32%	31.80%

renal replacement task, which was similar to the chronic dialysis task as most patients in the dataset are dialysis patients. However, merging the chronic dialysis and kidney transplant tasks did improve the model performance slightly. The kidney transplant task had the lowest model performance, which is explained by only 0.71% patients on the CKD cohort having a kidney transplant (versus 4.88%) and the overall low label prevalence for all predictions across all horizons (see Table 3). Performance of all metrics decreased with increasing prediction horizons, reflecting the increased difficulty in accurately predicting onset of therapy for large prediction horizons. Note that given the low prevalence of triggers with positive labels, the PR-AUC is more informative [16].

In addition to this, Table 5 shows the percentage of beneficiaries that had been identified correctly to start dialysis within the 1 year prediction horizon that had not undergone dialysis access creation procedures before dialysis initiation, hence illustrating the potential impact of the model.

4   Conclusions

We developed a machine learning model for dynamically identifying those patients with high likelihood of starting RRT up to a year in advance. Our study has limitations. First, it was conducted with a subset of CMS patients and therefore this approach should be tested in other health systems. Second, the model used claims data only. While this may help with adoption as this information is generally available, access to laboratory data (e.g. glomerular filtration rate or albuminuria), patient's characteristics such as weight or the complete electronic health record could significantly improve the model. Thirdly, we recognize that models based on claims are intrinsically reliant on healthcare billing patterns which may be associated with racial biases due to unequal historical access. Until recently, definitions of CKD were based on race-based formulae; the new guidelines recommend a race agnostic formula [4,8]. Further work is needed to characterize and mitigate potential biases in the CKD use-case. Finally, this was a retrospective study, and therefore the model should be evaluated in a prospective study with a heterogeneous group of patients before adoption in clinical practice.

In addition to this, note that model performance may be improved by implementing more complex modeling architectures (e.g. neural networks), addressing class imbalance by upsampling the unrepresented classes or using weighted loss functions, and reducing the dimensionality of the feature space by including only the most relevant features. These can be identified through feature attribution methods, which can also be used to improve the interpretability of complex models such as neural networks.

Prospect of Application: It is difficult for providers to predict when patients with chronic kidney disease will need renal replacement therapy. Emergency renal replacement therapy initiations increase morbidity and mortality and cause significant stress. Our AI model identifies patients at risk of progression and can help care management groups systemically focus on these patients to physically and emotionally prepare them for dialysis initiation.

References

1. Comprehensive ESRD care model. https://innovation.cms.gov/innovation-models/comprehensive-esrd-care. Accessed 9 Mar 2022

2. Abadi, M., et al.: TensorFlow: a system for large-scale machine learning. In: 12th USENIX Symposium on Operating Systems Design and Implementation (OSDI 16), pp. 265–283 (2016)
3. Coresh, J., et al.: Prevalence of chronic kidney disease in the united states. JAMA **298**(17), 2038–2047 (2007)
4. Delgado, C., et al.: A unifying approach for GFR estimation: recommendations of the NKF-ASN task force. J. Am. Soc. Nephrol. **79**, 268–288 (2021)
5. Dovgan, E., et al.: Using machine learning models to predict the initiation of renal replacement therapy among chronic kidney disease patients. PLoS One **15**(6), e0233976 (2020)
6. Huang, X., Carrero, J.J.: Better prevention than cure: optimal patient preparation for renal replacement therapy. Kidney Int. **85**(3), 507–510 (2014)
7. Hurst, D.J., Waits, S., Burwell, L., Murawska, A.: In patients with chronic kidney disease, does early referral to a nephrologist improve outcomes? Evid. Based Pract. **23**(9), 45 (2020)
8. Inker, L.A., et al.: Chronic kidney disease epidemiology collaboration: new creatinine- and cystatin C-based equations to estimate GFR without race. N. Engl. J. Med. **385**(19), 1737–1749 (2021)
9. Johansen, K.L., et al.: US renal data system 2020 annual data report: epidemiology of kidney disease in the united states. Am. J. Kidney Dis. **77**(4 Suppl 1), A7–A8 (2021)
10. Koyner, J.L., Carey, K.A., Edelson, D.P., Churpek, M.M.: The development of a machine learning inpatient acute kidney injury prediction model. Crit. Care Med. **46**(7), 1070–1077 (2018)
11. Kusminsky, R.E.: Complications of central venous catheterization. J. Am. Coll. Surg. **204**(4), 681–696 (2007)
12. Lee, T.: Fistula first initiative: historical impact on vascular access practice patterns and influence on future vascular access care. Cardiovasc. Eng. Technol. **8**(3), 244–254 (2017)
13. Mehrotra, R., Marsh, D., Vonesh, E., Peters, V., Nissenson, A.: Patient education and access of ESRD patients to renal replacement therapies beyond in-center hemodialysis. Kidney Int. **68**(1), 378–390 (2005)
14. Norouzi, J., Yadollahpour, A., Mirbagheri, S.A., Mazdeh, M.M., Hosseini, S.A.: Predicting renal failure progression in chronic kidney disease using integrated intelligent fuzzy expert system. Comput. Math. Methods Med. **2016**, 6080814 (2016)
15. Rajkomar, A., et al.: Scalable and accurate deep learning with electronic health records. NPJ Digit. Med. **1**, 18 (2018)
16. Saito, T., Rehmsmeier, M.: The precision-recall plot is more informative than the ROC plot when evaluating binary classifiers on imbalanced datasets. PLoS One **10**(3), e0118432 (2015)
17. Smart, N.A., Dieberg, G., Ladhani, M., Titus, T.: Early referral to specialist nephrology services for preventing the progression to end-stage kidney disease. Cochrane Database Syst. Rev. (6), CD007333 (2014). https://doi.org/10.1002/14651858.CD007333.pub2. https://pubmed.ncbi.nlm.nih.gov/24938824/
18. Smart, N.A., Titus, T.T.: Outcomes of early versus late nephrology referral in chronic kidney disease: a systematic review. Am. J. Med. **124**(11), 1073–80.e2 (2011)
19. Tangri, N., et al.: The CKD prognosis consortium: multinational assessment of accuracy of equations for predicting risk of kidney failure: a meta-analysis. JAMA **315**(2), 164–174 (2016)

20. Tangri, N., et al.: A predictive model for progression of chronic kidney disease to kidney failure. JAMA **305**(15), 1553–1559 (2011)
21. Wavamunno, M.D., Harris, D.C.H.: The need for early nephrology referral. Kidney Int. Suppl. **94**, S128–32 (2005)

Uncertainty-Aware Geographic Atrophy Progression Prediction from Fundus Autofluorescence

Qi Yang[1,2](✉), Neha Anegondi[2,3], Verena Steffen[2,4], Simon S. Gao[2,3], Julia Cluceru[2,3], Christina Rabe[2,4], Jian Dai[1,2], and Daniela Ferrara[1,2]

[1] Data Science Imaging, Genentech, Inc, South San Francisco, CA, USA
yang.qi@gene.com
[2] Roche Personalized Healthcare, Genentech, Inc, South San Francisco, CA, USA
[3] Clinical Imaging Group, Genentech, Inc, South San Francisco, CA, USA
[4] Biostatistics, Genentech, Inc, South San Francisco, CA, USA

Abstract. Geographic atrophy (GA) is an advanced form of age-related macular degeneration leading to progressive visual loss. The ability to accurately predict GA progression over time based on a single baseline visit can improve clinical trials in GA, as well as support patient counseling in current clinical practice. The feasibility of using baseline fundus autofluorescence (FAF) images to predict GA progression with end-to-end deep learning models has been demonstrated. However, for black-box models, there is a need to increase trust for clinical practice applications and estimate the prediction uncertainty. In this paper, we applied and evaluated both non-parametric and parametric deep ensemble approaches for the prediction uncertainty estimation using both simulated and clinical study data in a multitask regression setting. The results not only show promising performance in detecting near and far out-of-distribution data cases, but may also suggest the improved performance in predicting GA growth rate for in-distribution data.

Keywords: Geographic atrophy · Uncertainty · Out-of-distribution · Multitask learning · Fundus autofluorescence · Disease prediction

1 Introduction

Geographic atrophy (GA) is an advanced form of age-related macular degeneration (AMD) that affects approximately 5 million people globally [1]. It is characterized by the progressive loss of photoreceptors, retinal pigment epithelium, and choriocapillaris that leads to vision loss [2]. There are no approved therapies to prevent the onset and progression of GA secondary to AMD, indicating significant unmet medical need. Slowing GA growth rate is the primary objective of interventional trials [3]. However, GA growth rate demonstrates large interpatient variability [2, 4, 5] that poses a challenge for the design and interpretation of interventional clinical trials, particularly smaller phase II studies. Models predicting the GA growth rate can be powerful tools for covariate adjustment in clinical trials by increasing the precision of the treatment effect estimate

S. Wu et al. (Eds.): AMAI 2022, LNCS 13540, pp. 29–38, 2022.
https://doi.org/10.1007/978-3-031-17721-7_4

and hence increasing power [6]. In the future, GA progression predictions may also be used to support patient counseling or treatment management when approved therapies become available at the point of care.

The GA lesion can be visualized by various imaging modalities. A two-dimensional fundus autofluorescence (FAF) image that shows topographic mapping of intrinsic fluorophores within lipofuscin granules in the retinal pigment epithelium [7] is used to quantify the GA area (Fig. 1) and is considered the gold standard for GA diagnosis and area measurement. The change in FAF-derived GA area over a defined period of time (ie, the GA growth rate) has been used as the primary endpoint for GA clinical trials [3]. Findings from studies on FAF have suggested that lesion shape-descriptive features, surrounding abnormal autofluorescence patterns, and previous progression rate were prognostic of GA growth rate [8–13]. However, the precise mechanisms underlying GA development and progression remain unknown. Therefore, extracting image features that accurately predict the individual GA growth rate remains challenging. This presents an opportunity to apply deep learning techniques for which no prior feature extraction or selection by human examiners is needed. Attempts have been made in using deep learning algorithms to predict individual GA growth rate from baseline retinal images [14–16].

Our previous work has demonstrated a significant performance improvement with baseline FAF using a multitask convolutional neural network approach, compared with a linear benchmark model with clinical features [16]. However, due to the prognostic nature of the algorithm and the inherent "black-box" behavior of deep learning models, it may be difficult for clinical scientists and retina specialists to fully understand, accept, and apply the model's predictions in clinical trials and clinical practice. Therefore, it is desired that the model can output uncertainty estimates to alert users for the out-of-distribution data, contributing to model trustworthiness and appropriate adoption. In recent years, researchers have shown an increased interest in estimating uncertainty in deep learning applications [17, 18]. Various uncertainty estimation methods have been developed or experimented for classification or segmentation tasks, but few regression task applications were reported in the medical application field as listed in the survey table for a review paper [17]. Among all proposed methods, deep ensemble [19] is a simple and powerful method that has shown promising results in both simulated and real-world tabular data for a prediction regression task. The results demonstrated that the proposed deep ensemble method outperformed probabilistic backpropagation and Monte Carlo dropout methods in terms of negative log likelihood (NLL), a proper scoring rule and a popular metric for evaluating predictive uncertainty. Therefore, for this GA FAF image based prediction regression task study, we evaluated the feasibility of applying deep ensemble approaches with or without parametric uncertainty [19] for the uncertainty estimation and further explored the benefit of multitask uncertainty estimation.

2 Method

In this study, the GA progression prediction task is formulated as a multitask regression problem. Let $\left\{(X_i, (y_1, y_2)_i)\right\}_{i=1}^{N}$ be the training data set, where X_i, y_i denote the i-th FAF image and its corresponding GA lesion area (y_1) and growth rate (y_2) labels; N

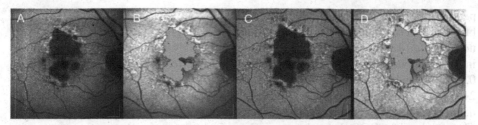

Fig. 1. Example FAF images for the same eye: (A) baseline visit, (B) corresponding GA lesion area grading, (C) week 48 visit, and (D) corresponding GA lesion area grading. In (B) and (D), GA areas were filled in and nonconfluent lesions were represented in different colors, eg, 4 nonconfluent lesions were labeled in the FAF image at the week 48 visit.

denotes the total number of samples. The model takes as input a baseline FAF image and predicts the current GA lesion area and the annualized lesion growth rate.

2.1 Data

The prediction models were developed and tested on retrospective study data from study eyes of patients with bilateral GA enrolled in Lampalizumab phase III clinical trials (Chroma [NCT02247479]; Spectri [NCT02247531]) [5] or in an observational study (Proxima A [NCT02479386]) [4]. The study eye inclusion criteria were the same in all three trials and have been described previously [4, 5]. The trials adhered to the Declaration of Helsinki and were Health Insurance Portability and Accountability Act compliant. Protocols were approved by the institutional review board at each study site before the trials started. All patients provided written informed consent for future medical research and analyses.

The field 2 macular 30-degree FAF images (768 × 768 pixels) captured using the SPECTRALIS® HRA + OCT (Heidelberg Engineering Inc., Heidelberg, Germany) were analyzed. Only study eye images from the baseline visit were used. Because no treatment effect was observed in the phase III trials, all treatment arms were pooled for this analysis [5]. GA lesion areas collected at all study visits were graded on FAF images in a central reading center by 2 trained readers, with an adjudicator if necessary. For model development, GA growth rate (mm^2/year) was derived from a linear model fitted using all available FAF measurements for each patient who underwent FAF and OCT imaging every 24 weeks over 2 years because the GA growth rate has in general been found to be linear [2, 20]. Although the annualized growth rate was chosen as the modeling endpoint, the model can be used to predict the GA area at any time point. The full image data set (1279 patients/eyes) was split into 80% training data and 20% test data. The training data set was further split into 5 folds for cross-validation (CV). Baseline characteristics of patients and eyes included in the analyses were well balanced across the data set splits. Thus, these 20% test data are considered as in-distribution data.

To evaluate the uncertainty estimation performance, an additional simulated shifted or near out-of-distribution (near OOD) data set, a real-world (RW) near OOD data set, and a simulated far out-of-distribution (far OOD) data set were prepared. Simulated near OOD data sets were generated by applying the following typical corruptions and perturbations [21] with library Albumentations [22] (Fig. 2A): Gaussian noise, Gaussian blur, random sun flare, random shadow, and coarse dropout. These perturbations were not used for data augmentation in training and possibly mimic RW low-quality FAF images. Among them, Gaussian noise was added for different degrees (0.01, 0.02, 0.04, 0.06, 0.07) and Gaussian blur kernel sizes were increased stepwise from 7 to 41 (7, 15, 21, 31, 41). The field 1 optic disc 30-degree FAF images (Fig. 2G) were used as a RW near OOD data set as the training data were all field 2 macular FAF images (Fig. 2F). The simulated far OOD data set were random pixel value images.

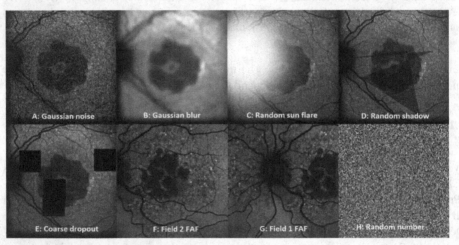

Fig. 2. Simulated near OOD cases: (A) Gaussian noise, (B) Gaussian blur, (C) random sun flare, (D) random shadow, and (E) coarse dropout; (F) shows a training data field 2 FAF image, with (G) a RW near OOD case of a field 1 FAF image; and (H) a simulated far OOD case (image generated from random numbers).

2.2 Model Development

Two convolutional neural network (CNN) models were developed to simultaneously predict baseline GA lesion area and annualized GA growth rate (Fig. 3). The multitask model was expected to find a representation capturing the information for both tasks with less chance of overfitting on the growth rate prediction task and to possibly improve the performance as the lower feature-extracting CNN layers are provided with additional information [23]. The model takes baseline FAF images as input. FAF images were resized to 512×512 pixels, and pixel values ranging from 0 to 255 were normalized between 0 and 1 by dividing all pixel values by 255. Offline data augmentation was performed on the development data set, including horizontal flip, rotation (range, − 5 to 5 degrees), and random brightness and contrast limit (range, −0.2 to 0.2). The first model only predicts lesion area and growth rate. In the second model, prediction uncertainty or variance is modeled along with the prediction as one of the outputs. The joint loss of mean squared errors of GA lesion area prediction and GA growth rate prediction was used for training for the first model. The second model adopted the negative log-likelihood function [18] as the base cost function where variance terms were included as the following Eq. (1) (θ are the parameters of the CNN, α is the weight for each term in joint loss of lesion area and growth rate, μ_1 predicted mean of lesion area, μ_2 predicted mean of growth rate, σ_1^2 predicted variance of lesion area, σ_2^2 predicted variance of growth rate). The uncertainty being modeled here is data uncertainty (aleatoric uncertainty). We call the first model non-parametric and the second model parametric in terms of uncertainty modeling.

$$\alpha \times (\frac{1}{2} \log \sigma_{1\theta}^2(x) + \frac{(y_1 - \mu_{1\theta}(x))^2}{2\sigma_{1\theta}^2(x)}) + (1 - \alpha) \times (\frac{1}{2} \log \sigma_{2\theta}^2(x) + \frac{(y_2 - \mu_{2\theta}(x))^2}{2\sigma_{2\theta}^2(x)})$$

(1)

The best hyperparameter setting was selected with 5-fold CV in training data. The hyperparameters tuned were learning rate (0.0001, 0.0002, 0.0005), optimizer (Adam, stochastic gradient descent), and dropout (0.1, 0.5, 0.9). The weight for each term in joint loss of lesion area and growth rate was fixed as 0.5. Batch size was also kept constant at 16. The CNN transfer learning model choice was also determined in a similar way; Inception v3 had the best performance compared with VGG16, ResNet50, DenseNet121, and EfficientNets. After selecting the best hyperparameter setting, the model was retrained with these hyperparameters on the full training data set and used to predict the test data set.

The prediction performance of each model was evaluated by calculating r^2, which was defined as the square of the Pearson correlation coefficient (r) between observed and predicted values. The uncertainty estimation performance was evaluated by negative log likelihood [18].

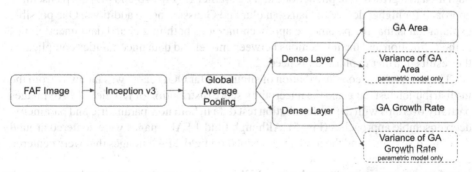

Fig. 3. Detailed architecture for the non-parametric model (solid line blocks) and parametric uncertainty model (dashed line blocks)

2.3 Uncertainty Estimation Using Deep Ensemble

For the uncertainty estimation, we evaluated the feasibility of applying the deep ensemble technique to both non-parametric and parametric uncertainty models for the regression task. For the non-parametric model, the standard deviation from the predictions of five models with randomly initialized weights was used as the uncertainty score. These models were trained on the full training data with the same hyperparameter setting selected from model development on 5-fold CV. Similarly, for the parametric model, the average of variance from the predictions of five random initial weights models (non-parametric part) was calculated and added to the average of variance predictions from these five parametric models (parametric variance part) to generate the joint variance. This joint variance was then applied with a square root serving as final uncertainty scores in the parametric deep ensemble approach. The uncertainty estimated by the non-parametric deep ensemble is model uncertainty (epistemic uncertainty), while the parametric deep ensemble uncertainty estimation combines both data and model uncertainties. We hypothesized that the parametric deep ensemble would have a better uncertainty estimation performance. The final prediction outcomes of the lesion area and growth rate were the average of five models' predictions. The averaged predicted GA area and growth rate were then used to calculate the performance matrix r^2 with the area and growth rate derived from reading center graders.

3   Results

All five non-parametric and parametric models were tested on in-distribution test data, simulated and RW near OOD data, and simulated far OOD data. The prediction results and uncertainty estimation performance were evaluated for both GA area and growth rate predictions and compared between two approaches. The results in general show the expected trend of increased uncertainty score and decreased prediction performance as the data shift degree increased for simulated near OOD cases (Gaussian blur Fig. 4A and 4B, Gaussian noise Fig. 4C and 4D). It is noted that the uncertainty score plateaued for both area and growth rate predictions in the parametric (Fig. 4B and 4D) deep ensemble approach for higher degree of Gaussian blur and Gaussian noise additions. One possible explanation is that the parametric approach includes both model and data uncertainties in the estimation and the interactions between model and data uncertainties complicated the results. Further exploration is needed.

The uncertainty score distribution of simulated far OOD cases was far away from the in-distribution test data, and the uncertainty score distribution of RW field 1 FAF images partially overlaps with the in-distribution test data in both non-parametric and parametric deep ensemble approaches (Fig. 5). Although field 1 FAF images were centered around the optic disc region and the model was trained on field 2 FAF images that were centered around the macular region, the field 2 FAF images sometimes still included partial or even full optic nerve head, and the field 1 FAF images included partial and even full GA lesion. Therefore, it is not surprising to see the uncertainty score distribution overlapped. It would give additional insights to look into the relationship between prediction errors and uncertainty scores for near-OOD cases. However, many field 1 FAF images only have partial lesions, therefore the ground truth is unavailable.

The results in Fig. 5 show that GA area prediction uncertainty scores could provide a better separation from the uncertainty score distribution of in-distribution test data compared with GA growth rate prediction. In this specific multi-task setting where area and growth rate have joint loss function, leveraging both area and growth rate uncertainties might help better identify out-of-distribution cases by applying different uncertainty score thresholding for each (Fig. 6). For different perturbations and approaches, one uncertainty score could be more sensitive than the other uncertainty score.

In general, the prediction and uncertainty estimation performance were very close on the data we tested for non-parametric and parametric uncertainty deep ensemble approaches. The deep ensemble with parametric uncertainty approach may suggest slightly better prediction performance in terms of square of the Pearson correlation coefficient (r^2), greater uncertainty estimation performance in terms of negative log likelihood (NLL, the smaller the better) (Table 1) and more balanced uncertainty estimation performance in the lesion area and growth rate performance (Fig. 6). However, given that the non-parametric deep ensemble uncertainty can be readily adopted without any additional modifications or re-training, the non-parametric deep ensemble might be practically recommended with the current data experiment results.

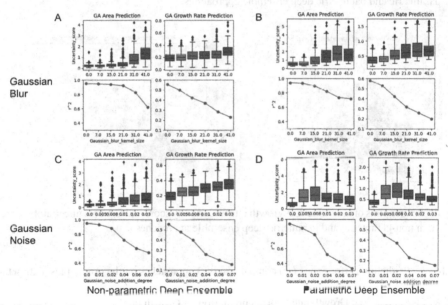

Fig. 4. Uncertainty score and prediction accuracy performance changes in different degrees of Gaussian blur and Gaussian noise perturbations with both non-parametric and parametric uncertainty deep ensemble approaches.

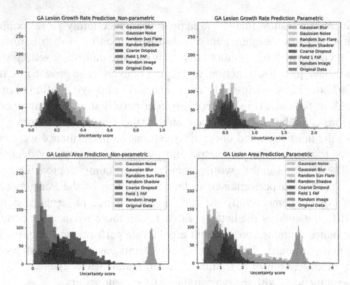

Fig. 5. Uncertainty score histogram of GA lesion area and growth rate predictions with both non-parametric and parametric deep ensemble approaches.

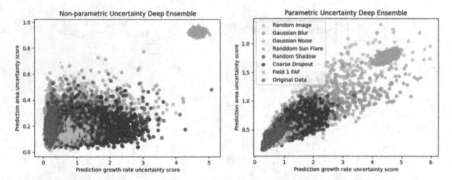

Fig. 6. Scatter plots of individual GA growth rate uncertainty score and GA area uncertainty score with both non-parametric and parametric deep ensemble approaches.

Table 1. Prediction performance (r^2) comparison of 3 approaches on the original test data set.

	Growth rate prediction	Area prediction	Growth rate prediction NLL	Area prediction NLL
Non-parametric single model	0.53	0.94	N/A	N/A
Non-parametric deep ensemble	0.55	0.94	13.11	11.80
Parametric deep ensemble	0.58	0.94	1.12	1.45

4 Conclusions

This study is the first attempt to explore both non-parametric and parametric uncertainty deep ensemble approaches for uncertainty estimation on the multitask CNN model of a regression task. The promising results on both approaches demonstrated the feasibility of detecting both near and far OOD cases leveraging uncertainty scores on GA area prediction and GA growth rate prediction and showed the uncertainty scores indicated the deviation degrees of the simulated near OOD data.

Prospect of Applications: This work could potentially enhance the trust from clinical users and improve the clinical adoption of the disease progression prediction tool. In the future, additional RW data are needed to further validate and improve the effectiveness of proposed approaches, analyze the relationship of prediction performance/errors and uncertainty scores, as well as set applicable thresholds of uncertainty scores toward implementation.

References

1. Boyer, D.S., Schmidt-Erfurth, U., van Lookeren Campagne, M., et al.: The pathophysiology of geographic atrophy secondary to age-related macular degeneration and the complement pathway as a therapeutic target. Retina **37**(5), 819–835 (2017)
2. Fleckenstein, M., Mitchell, P., Freund, K.B., et al.: The progression of geographic atrophy secondary to age-related macular degeneration. Ophthalmology **125**(3), 369–390 (2018)
3. Holz, F.G., Sadda, S.R., Staurenghi, G., et al.: Imaging protocols in clinical studies in advanced age-related macular degeneration: recommendations from classification of atrophy consensus meetings. Ophthalmology **124**(4), 464–478 (2017)
4. Holekamp, N., Wykoff, C.C., Schmitz-Valckenberg, S., et al.: Natural history of geographic atrophy secondary to age-related macular degeneration: results from the prospective Proxima A and B clinical trials. Ophthalmology **127**(6), 769–783 (2020)
5. Holz, F.G., Sadda, S.R., Busbee, B., et al.: Efficacy and safety of lampalizumab for geographic atrophy due to age-related macular degeneration: chroma and spectri phase 3 randomized clinical trials. JAMA Ophthalmol. **136**(6), 666–677 (2018)
6. Colantuoni, E., Rosenblum, M.: Leveraging prognostic baseline variables to gain precision in randomized trials. Stat Med **34**(18), 2602–2617 (2015)
7. Schmitz-Valckenberg, S., Holz, F.G., Bird, A.C., et al.: Fundus autofluorescence imaging: review and perspectives. Retina **28**(3), 385–409 (2008)
8. Batıoğlu, F., Gedik Oğuz, Y., Demirel, S., et al.: Geographic atrophy progression in eyes with age-related macular degeneration: role of fundus autofluorescence patterns, fellow eye and baseline atrophy area. Ophthalmic Res. **52**(2), 53–59 (2014)
9. Bearelly, S., Khanifar, A.A., Lederer, D.E., et al.: Use of fundus autofluorescence images to predict geographic atrophy progression. Retina **31**(1), 81–86 (2011)
10. Holmen, I.C., Aul, B., Pak, J.W., et al.: Precursors and development of geographic atrophy with autofluorescence imaging: age-related eye disease study 2 report number 18. Ophthalmol. Retina **3**(9), 724–733 (2019)
11. Pfau, M., Lindner, M., Goerdt, L., et al.: Prognostic value of shape-descriptive factors for the progression of geographic atrophy secondary to age-related macular degeneration. Retina **39**(8), 1527–1540 (2019)

12. Schmitz-Valckenberg, S., Sahel, J.A., Danis, R., et al.: Natural history of geographic atrophy progression secondary to age-related macular degeneration (geographic atrophy progression study). Ophthalmology **123**(2), 361–368 (2016)
13. Friesenhahn, M., Rabe, C., Gao, S.S., et al.: Initial lesion growth rates and other baseline prognostic factors can improve the design of clinical trials in geographic atrophy (GA). Invest Ophthalmol. Vis. Sci. **61**, 2988 (2020)
14. Normand, G., Quellec, G., Danno, R., et al.: Prediction of geographic atrophy progression by deep learning applied to retinal imaging. Invest Ophthalmol. Vis. Sci. **60**, 1452 (2019)
15. Bogunovic, H., Lachinov, D., Mai, J., et al.: Predictive identification of the fastest progressing geographic atrophy lesions based on deep learning in the phase 2 FILLY clinical trial of pegcetacoplan. Invest Ophthalmol. Vis. Sci. **62**, 129 (2021)
16. Anegondi, N., Yang, Q., Kawczynski, M., et al: Predicting geographic atrophy growth rate from fundus autofluorescence images using deep neural networks. Proceedings Volume 11634, Multimodal Biomedical Imaging XVI.https://doi.org/10.1117/12.2575898 (2021)
17. Abdar, M., Pourpanah, F., Hussain, S., et al: A review of uncertainty quantification in deep learning: techniques, applications and challenges. Inf. Fusion **76**(C), 243–297 (2021)
18. Gawlikowski, J., Tassi, C.R.N., Ali, M., et al: A survey of uncertainty in deep neural networks. arXiv:2107.03342 (2021)
19. Lakshminarayanan, B., Pritzel, A., Blundell, C.: Simple and scalable predictive uncertainty estimation using deep ensembles. Adv. Neural Inf. Process. Syst. **30**, 6405–6416 (2017)
20. Lindblad, A.S., Lloyd, P.C., Clemons, T.E., et al.: Change in area of geographic atrophy in the age-related eye disease study: AREDS report number 26. Arch. Ophthalmol. **127**(9), 1168–1174 (2009)
21. Hendrycks, D., Dietterich, T.: Benchmarking neural network robustness to common corruptions and perturbations. arXiv:1903.12261 (2019)
22. Buslaev, A., Parinov, A., Khvedchenya, E., et al: Albumentations: fast and flexible image augmentations. arXiv:1809.06839 (2018)
23. Ruder, S.: An overview of multi-task learning in deep neural networks. arXiv preprint arXiv: 1706.05098 (2017)

Automated Assessment of Renal Calculi in Serial Computed Tomography Scans

Pritam Mukherjee[1]([✉]), Sungwon Lee[1], Perry J. Pickhardt[2], and Ronald M. Summers[1]

[1] Imaging Biomarkers and Computer-Aided Diagnosis Laboratory, Department of Radiology and Imaging Sciences, National Institutes of Health Clinical Center, Bethesda, MD, USA
pritam.mukhrejee@nih.gov

[2] Department of Radiology, School of Medicine and Public Health, The University of Wisconsin, Madison, WI, USA

Abstract. An automated pipeline is developed for the serial assessment of renal calculi using computed tomography (CT) scans obtained at multiple time points. This retrospective study included 722 scans from 330 patients chosen from 8544 asymptomatic patients who underwent two or more CTC (CT colonography) or non-enhanced abdominal CT scans between 2004 and 2016 at a single medical center. A pre-trained deep learning (DL) model was used to segment the kidneys and the calculi on the CT scans at each time point. Based on the output of the DL, 330 patients were identified as having a stone candidate on at least one time point. Then, for every patient in this group, the kidneys from different time points were registered to each other, and the calculi present at multiple time points were matched to each other using proximity on the registered scans. The automated pipeline was validated by having a blinded radiologist assess the changes manually. New graph-based metrics are introduced in order to evaluate the performance of our pipeline. Our method shows high fidelity in tracking changes in renal calculi over multiple time points.

Keywords: Renal calculi · Serial assessment · Deep learning · Registration

1 Introduction

CT colonography (CTC) is a nonenhanced CT of the abdomen and pelvis for detecting colorectal polyps but can be used for the opportunistic screening for kidney stones. Indeed, CT can be considered the diagnostic "gold standard", with accuracy close to 100% due to the higher attenuation of renal calculi compared to the surrounding tissue [1, 2]. Studies [3–5] have found the presence of asymptomatic kidney stones in 5–8% of CTC scans. Though considered a less significant finding, patients with asymptomatic kidney stones are known to be at increased risk of future symptomatic stone events [6] as more than half of the stones are reported to grow on longitudinal follow-up [7]. Fortunately, once stones are detected, suitable medications and dietary interventions have proven very effective, with dramatic reductions of more than 50% in recurrence rates [8]. Given the high clinical and financial burden of kidney stones (and urinary

S. Wu et al. (Eds.): AMAI 2022, LNCS 13540, pp. 39–48, 2022.
https://doi.org/10.1007/978-3-031-17721-7_5

stones, in general) with nearly 200,000 hospitalizations and an estimated annual cost exceeding $2 billion in 2000 [9], opportunistic detection and tracking of kidney stones can be vital.

Unfortunately, kidney stones, especially small asymptomatic ones, are often not reported or measured [10, 11]. Even when they are measured, inter-reader variability due to various factors such as CT window level etc.[12], and movement of the stones in the kidney during the follow-up interval tends to make serial assessment of stones difficult, time consuming and unreliable. Despite the importance and widespread use of serial imaging in clinical decision making [13], few machine learning studies to date have focused on the analysis of serial scans. Here, we propose a fully automated computing pipeline to detect and track stones on CTC over multiple follow-up scans.

1.1 Our Contributions

While several kidney stone detectors (deep learning based or otherwise) have been presented in the literature, to the best of our knowledge, tracking and serial assessment of kidney stones has largely remained unexplored. This work is a first step in that direction. Our main thrust in this paper is the tracking of stones over multiple scans – we leverage an existing deep learning based kidney stone detector [14] for the detection and segmentation step. The tracking step uses computationally cheap affine registration of bounding boxes containing the kidney – this enables accurate kidney registration while avoiding unintended deformations that may occur with deformable registration due to the relative movement of organs in the vicinity of the kidney. We evaluate an integrated software pipeline that combines both stone detection and stone tracking components and show that it is quite accurate despite its conceptual simplicity.

We also introduce new graph-based metrics for evaluating the performance of stone tracking. Existing multiple object tracking (MOT) metrics like multiple object tracking precision (MOTP) and multiple object tracking accuracy (MOTA)[15] may be inadequate for our task. MOTP measures the tracker's ability to precisely estimate the objects position independent of its skill at correctly matching the objects; while this is an important metric in near-real-time tracking in videos, this does not apply in our offline case with only 2–3 "frames" (corresponding to the scan time points), where the error in localizing the stones is zero if the stone is detected on the scan. MOTA, on the other hand does apply – it accounts for the total number of misses, false positives and mismatches over all frames and averaged over the total number of objects over all frames – and we use it to evaluate our full pipeline. However, MOTA is a patient-level metric and does not adequately capture the performance at the level of individual stone trajectories. Therefore, we introduce new graph-based metrics that capture the fidelity of tracking individual stones across multiple time points.

2 Materials and Methods

2.1 Data

This Health Insurance Portability and Accountability Act (HIPAA) compliant retrospective study was approved by the Institutional Review Board, and the need for signed informed consent was waived. The initial cohort comprised asymptomatic patients who underwent CT colonography (CTC) screening or follow-up between 2004 and 2016 at a single medical center. We only included patients who had nonenhanced CT scans with slice thickness less than 2 mm. We excluded (a) patients with no follow-up scans, (b) patients who exhibited stone-related symptoms in the follow-up interval, and (c) patients who underwent stone intervention such as extracorporeal shock wave lithotripsy (ESWL) between scans. A description of the indications for the cohort is in [16].

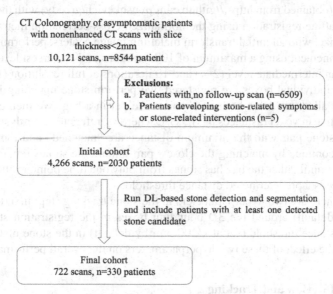

Fig. 1. Cohort selection

2.2 Calculi Detection and Segmentation

The first step of the pipeline is the detection and segmentation of the calculi within the kidney. To that end, we use the model and method in [14] First, a 3D U-Net is used to segment the kidneys, followed by denoising and thresholding at the de facto standard 130 HU to identify candidate stones within the kidney. Finally, a CNN is used to predict if the candidate is truly a stone. The final output is a labeled volume with segmentations of each stone identified by the model. We use the pretrained model from [14] to identify and segment the stones in our dataset. The patients for which stones were detected by the model for at least one time point constituted our final cohort.

2.3 Registration and Stone Matching

For a given patient, and scans from two consecutive time points, we used affine registration to approximately align the kidneys and match the stones by location. The CT scans were first windowed (level: 50, width: 450) and normalized to the range [0, 1].

Registering the full abdominal CT scans is both computationally expensive and sensitive to the deformations of the large abdominal organs. We first extracted 3D "kidney boxes" – padded bounding boxes containing the kidney – from the CT scans. This was done by first labeling the kidney segmentation obtained from the model in the previous step using connected component analysis and assigning "left" and "right" designations based on their relative position in the axial images. Then the left and right kidney boxes from the first time point were individually registered to the left and right kidney boxes from the second time point. For the registration, we used the "greedy" registration software[17] (obtained from https://github.com/pyushkevich/greedy) with the following settings: 3D affine registration using the normalized cross-correlation metric with $4 \times 4 \times 4$ patch size, with an initial transform matching image centers, performing a multi-resolution refinement using a maximum of 100 iterations at the coarsest level ($4 \times$), 50 iterations at an intermediate level ($2 \times$) and 10 iterations at full resolution ($1 \times$).

Once the individual boxes are registered, we perform stone matching in a greedy manner. First all stones from both time points are put in a bag. We then compute all pairwise Euclidean voxel distances $d(s_{1i}, s_{2j})$, where s_{tk} refers to the k th stone at time point i. The stone pair with the minimum distance are "matched" and removed from the bag. We continue by matching the closest pair among the stones remaining in the bag, and so on until either the bag has stones from only one time point, or the minimum distance exceeds a predetermined distance threshold.

Overall, there are two hyperparameters in the stone tracking step: first, the padding (set at 0 by default) around the 3D bounding boxes in the registration step and the maximum distance threshold (set at $\sqrt{200}$ mm by default) in the stone matching step. We evaluate the effect of these two hyperparameters on the overall performance.

2.4 Manual Review and Tracking

The results of the stone detection and tracking were manually reviewed by a board-certified radiologist with 13 years of experience. The true stones were identified and tracked across the follow-ups.

2.5 Evaluation of Performance

We first evaluated the performance of the stone detection algorithm. Using the ground truth from manual review, we computed the precision and recall of the model.

Next, we evaluated the performance of registration and stone tracking. We did this in several ways. First, we used the widely used multiple object tracking accuracy (MOTA)[15] metric to evaluate the performance at the patient level. We also introduce several stone level performance metrics. We consider each stone (or candidate stone) identified in any scan as a vertex in a graph and add a directed edge (v_i, v_j) between two vertices v_i and v_j if they are determined to be the same stone from two time points i and j, and $i < j$. . We can thus construct a graph based on the ground truth stones and another on the predicted stones (see Fig. 2a for an example where both graphs have been merged). Using these graphs, we computed the following metrics:

(a) The precision and recall of the predicted edges. Heuristically, given the predicted edges (i.e., our pipeline determined that two stones from two consecutive time-points are the same stone), precision computes the fraction of them that are present in the ground-truth graph; conversely recall computes the fraction of edges in the ground-truth graph that are also present in the predicted graph. These metrics evaluate the tracking performance across two time points.

(b) The precision and recall of the predicted connected components. Each connected component represents a unique stone. Here, we are interested in evaluating how well we reproduce the full trajectory of the stones across all time points (possibly more than two). As before, precision computes the fraction of predicted stone trajectories that are present in the ground-truth graph, and recall computes the fraction of ground-truth stone trajectories that are present in the predicted graph. Note that a correctly predicted trajectory entails: (i) the stones being detected by the deep learning model in all time points, and (ii) the stones are correctly matched to each other across all consecutive time points. We also evaluate this metric for non-singleton connected components (stones or candidate stones that appear in the scans from only one time point).

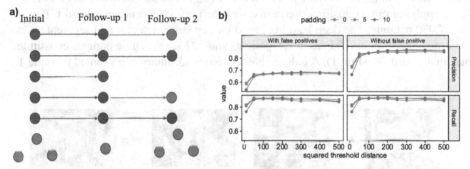

Fig. 2. (a.) Combined ground truth and predicted graphs for a patient. Each node is a stone. Blue indicates correct detection or tracking, orange indicates false positive predictions, red misses. (b.) Precision and recall of connected component retrieval with changing padding and threshold distance. It also shows the increase in precision when false positive stones are removed from the prediction graph before evaluating tracking. (Color figure online)

To disentangle the effect of stone detection and stone tracking, we repeat the above analysis by removing the false positive stone candidates. Further, after removing the false positive stone candidates, we consider two vertex-based metrics:

(a) The accuracy of retrieving a predecessor. Given a stone, we retrieve its predecessor from the previous time point. If the retrieved predecessor is the same for both the ground-truth graph and the predicted graph, we consider it correct. Stones from the initial scan necessarily do not have a predecessor; we remove these stones while computing this metric. However, new stones in follow-up scans may also lack predecessors – if both the ground-truth graph and the predicted graph agree, we consider it correct.

(b) The accuracy of retrieving a successor. Given a stone, we retrieve its successor from the next time point. If the retrieved successor is the same for both the ground-truth graph and the predicted graph, we consider it correct. Note that stones from the last follow-up scan do not have a successor; we remove these stones while computing this metric. However, stones that disappear in follow-up scans may also lack successors – if both the ground-truth graph and the predicted graph agree, we consider it correct.

2.6   Statistical Analysis

We use bootstrapping with 1000 iterates of patient sets randomly sampled with replacement from the original cohort to obtain confidence intervals, and the empirical quantiles at 2.5% and 97.5% are used as the 95% confidence intervals.

3   Results

3.1   Cohort Characteristics

Based on our inclusion criteria, 10,121 scans from 8544 patients were initially identified. After applying our exclusion criteria, we were left with 4266 nonenhanced CT scans from 2030 patients. The deep learning based kidney stone detector and segmenter [14] identified 837 stone candidates in 330 patients and 722 scans. These patients constituted our final cohort (see Fig. 1). A cohort characteristics summary is presented in Table 1.

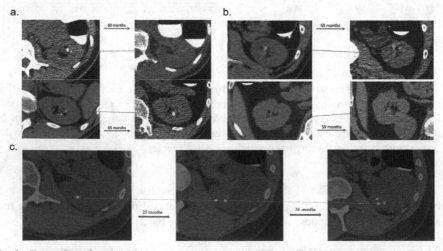

Fig. 3. Examples of registration. a. Inconclusive ground truth b. Incorrect stone matching. The red line shows the predicted matching. c. Correct matching over 3 time points

3.2 Performance of the Stone Detection and Segmentation

We evaluate the performance of the stone detection and segmentation based on the manual review by the radiologist. Out of 837 stone candidates, 149 (17.8%) of them belonging to 99 patients are determined to be false positives. The median number of false positives per scan is 1 (maximum: 8, IQR: [1]). Additionally, 13 stones from 12 patients were missed by the model. Common false positives included artifacts (beam hardening from contrast media, for example), atherosclerotic plaque in the renal sinus or renal artery and calcification or debris related to renal cysts.

3.3 Performance of Stone Tracking

Figure 3 shows three examples of stone tracking, one where the ground truth was inconclusive and another where the predictions were incorrect, and a third where the tracking was correct across 3 time points. Our pipeline achieved a mean MOTA of 0.91 with the 95% confidence interval (0.91, 0.92) on our dataset using our default parameters. Note that in computing MOTA, we only consider patients who have a true stone in at least one scan. In terms of metrics at the stone level, our pipeline achieves edgewise precision and recall rates of 0.82 (0.74, 0.93) and 0.85 (0.81, 0.91), respectively; the precision increased to 0.95 when false positive stones were removed before tracking. In tracking the full trajectory via connected components, we achieve a precision of 0.68 (0.64, 0.73) and recall of 0.88 (0.86, 0.92). The relatively low precision is largely due to false positive singleton stones – removing either all singletons or removing the false positive candidate stones increases the precision to 0.87 (0.83, 0.92), or 0.86 (0.82, 0.91), respectively. In terms of the vertex-based metrics, our method retrieves the correct predecessor with an accuracy of 0.91 (0.88, 0.94) and the correct successor (same stone in the following scan if it exists) with an accuracy of 0.91 (0.88, 0.95).

We also highlight that the performance is quite robust to a wide range of hyperparameter (padding and distance threshold) values, see for example, Fig. 2b – barring the very low range of distance threshold, the performance remains quite stable.

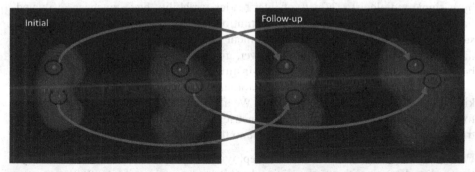

Fig. 4. 3D visualization of matched calculi between the initial and follow-up scans with the follow-up interval of 23 months. The kidney and calculi segmentations as well as the stone matching (indicated by the blue arrows) was performed by our pipeline.

4 Discussion

We have presented a fully automated pipeline to detect and track kidney stones on CTC scans of asymptomatic patients. First, the stones are detected and segmented separately on each scan using a pre-trained deep learning model, and second, the stones found on scans from two different time points are matched to each other using affine registration and greedy matching based on distance in the registered scans Fig. 4. By using affine registration of patches around the kidney, we avoid issues due to relative movement of large organs near the kidney, and unintended deformations due to changes in the stone.

Among existing work, perhaps [18], which introduced the Deep Lesion Tracker to track lesions in the DeepLesion [19] dataset is the closest to ours in spirit. In [18], the tracking problem is cast as a prediction problem: given an object (lesion in their case) in the scan from time point 1, the objective is to predict the location of the same object in the scan from time point 2. The end-to-end method leverages both appearance and anatomical information – the anatomical information helps avoid mistakes when the object looks like other objects in the background. Fortunately, kidney stones are typically quite different from the surrounding kidney tissue. Our approach has several advantages. First, our pipeline is modular; for example, we can easily plug in a different (possibly better) kidney stone detector. Uncoupling the two steps also allows for easier training without any serial training datasets. Second, the pipeline is highly explainable and can easily incorporate human-in-the-loop; the output of the detector can be easily reviewed by the radiologist, and corrected, if necessary. Removing the false positive stones improves the tracking performance significantly (see Fig. 2b).

One of the key contributions in this paper is that we introduce new metrics to evaluate performance of tracking. Unlike the CLEAR MOT metrics, these metrics are tailored to the typical tracking use case in medical imaging – 3D images, only a few "frames" or time points, no requirement for near-real-time processing, and unpredictable relative movement of objects during the long follow-up interval. The vertex-based metrics on retrieving a predecessor or a successor are relevant in the clinic where a physician may want to review the stone in multiple time points to make decisions.

Our study has several limitations. First, the ground truth assessments were performed by a single radiologist – effects of inter-reader variability have not been evaluated. Second, the data came from a single institution, and the number and location of the stones were relatively stable without treatment or interventions; the generalizability of the method has not been assessed. However, given the modularity of our pipeline, we believe our method will be robust to inter-institutional effects.

In conclusion, we have presented an automated pipeline to detect, segment and track kidney stones across multiple time points. We also introduced new graph-based metrics to evaluate tracking performance. These metrics decouple detection, segmentation and tracking errors and are particularly suitable to the medical image domain.

Prospect of Application: We envision deploying the proposed automated stone detection and tracking algorithm to the clinic where it can be used to monitor the progression of kidney stones in both asymptomatic and symptomatic patients. We hope it will reduce the burden on radiologists, reduce inter-reader variability and facilitate more accurate serial assessment of kidney stones.

Table 1. Patient characteristics in the final cohort. The numbers represent Median (IQR). *Missing information for 22 patients

Number of patients with stones (n = 330)	Male (n = 191)	Female (n = 117)
Age at first visit*	57 (52, 63)	57 (52, 60)
Height (cm)*	177.8 (175.2, 182.9)	162.6 (160.0, 167.6)
Weight (kg)*	90.7 (81.7, 101.8)	68.0 (56.7, 81.6)
BMI (kg/m^2)*	28.7 (25.7, 31.7)	25.8 (22.7, 30.3)
Number of scans per patient	2 (2, 2)	
Number of scans with stones	510	
Scan date	2004–2016	
Scan interval (months)	63 (60, 73)	

Acknowledgements. This research was supported by the Intramural Research Program of the National Institutes of Health, Clinical Center, and we utilized the computational resources of the National Institutes of Health high-performance computing Biowulf cluster.

References

1. Smith, R.C., et al.: Acute flank pain: comparison of non-contrast-enhanced CT and intravenous urography. Radiology **194**, 789–794 (1995)
2. Preminger, G.M., Vieweg, J., Leder, R.A., Nelson, R.C.: Urolithiasis: detection and management with unenhanced spiral CT–a urologic perspective. Radiology **207**, 308–309 (1998)
3. Rajapaksa, R.C., Macari, M., Bini, E.J.: Prevalence and impact of extracolonic findings in patients undergoing CT colonography. J. Clin. Gastroenterol. **38**, 767–771 (2004)
4. Hara, A.K., Johnson, C.D., MacCarty, R.L., Welch, T.J.: Incidental extracolonic findings at CT colonography. Radiology **215**, 353–357 (2000)
5. Boyce, C.J., Pickhardt, P.J., Lawrence, E.M., Kim, D.H., Bruce, R.J.: Prevalence of urolithiasis in asymptomatic adults: objective determination using low dose noncontrast computerized tomography. J. Urol. **183**, 1017–1021 (2010)
6. Kang, H.W., et al.: Natural history of asymptomatic renal stones and prediction of stone related events. J. Urol **189**, 1740–1746 (2013)
7. Koh, L.T., Ng, F.C., Ng, K.K.: Outcomes of long-term follow-up of patients with conservative management of asymptomatic renal calculi. BJU Int. **109**, 622–625 (2012)
8. Curhan, G.C.: Epidemiology of stone disease. Urol. Clin. North Am. **34**, 287–293 (2007)
9. Pearle, M.S., Calhoun, E.A., Curhan, G.C.: Urologic diseases of America, P.: urologic diseases in America project: urolithiasis. J. Urol. **173**, 848–857 (2005)
10. Gluecker, T.M., et al.: Extracolonic findings at CT colonography: evaluation of prevalence and cost in a screening population. Gastroenterology **124**, 911–916 (2003)
11. Kampa, R.J., Ghani, K.R., Wahed, S., Patel, U., Anson, K.M.: Size matters: a survey of how urinary-tract stones are measured in the UK. J. Endourol. **19**, 856–860 (2005)
12. Lidén, M., Andersson, T., Geijer, H.: Making renal stones change size—impact of CT image post processing and reader variability. Eur. Radiol. **21**, 2218–2225 (2011)

13. Acosta, J.N., Falcone, G.J., Rajpurkar, P.: The need for medical artificial intelligence that incorporates prior images. Radiology, 212830
14. Elton, D.C., Turkbey, E.B., Pickhardt, P.J., Summers, R.M.: A deep learning system for automated kidney stone detection and volumetric segmentation on noncontrast CT scans. Med. Phy. **49**, 2545–2554 (2022)
15. Bernardin, K., Stiefelhagen, R.: Evaluating multiple object tracking performance: the clear MOT metrics. EURASIP J. Image Video Process. **2008**(1), 1 (2008). https://doi.org/10.1155/2008/246309
16. Pickhardt, P.J., et al.: Computed tomographic virtual colonoscopy to screen for colorectal neoplasia in asymptomatic adults. N Engl J Med **349**, 2191–2200 (2003)
17. Yushkevich, P.A., Pluta, J., Wang, H., Wisse, L.E.M., Das, S., Wolk, D.: IC-P-174: Fast automatic segmentation of hippocampal subfields and medial temporal lobe subregions in 3 tesla and 7 tesla T2-weighted MRI. Alzheimers Dement. **12**, P126–P127 (2016)
18. Cai, J., et al.: Deep lesion tracker: monitoring lesions in 4d longitudinal imaging studies. In: 2021 IEEE/CVF Conference on Computer Vision and Pattern Recognition (CVPR), IEEE (2021)
19. Yan, K., Wang, X., Lu, L., Summers, R.M.: DeepLesion: automated mining of large-scale lesion annotations and universal lesion detection with deep learning. J. Med. Imaging **5**, 1 (2018)

Prediction of Mandibular ORN Incidence from 3D Radiation Dose Distribution Maps Using Deep Learning

Laia Humbert-Vidan[1,2]([✉]), Vinod Patel[3], Robin Andlauer[4], Andrew P King[4], and Teresa Guerrero Urbano[5]

[1] Department of Medical Physics, Guy's and St Thomas' NHS Foundation Trust, London, UK
[2] School of Cancer and Pharmaceutical Sciences, Comprehensive Cancer Centre, King's College London, London, UK
laia.humbert-vidan@kcl.ac.uk
[3] Department of Oral Surgery, Guy's Dental Hospital, London, UK
Vinod.Patel@gstt.nhs.uk
[4] School of Biomedical Engineering and Imaging Sciences, King's College London, London, UK
robin.andlauer@web.de, andrew.king@kcl.ac.uk
[5] Department of Clinical Oncology, Guy's and St Thomas' NHS Foundation Trust, London, UK
Teresa.GuerreroUrbano@gstt.nhs.uk

Abstract. *Background.* Absorbed radiation dose to the mandible is an important risk factor in the development of mandibular osteoradionecrosis (ORN) in head and neck cancer (HNC) patients treated with radiotherapy (RT). The prediction of mandibular ORN may not only guide the RT treatment planning optimisation process but also identify which patients would benefit from a closer follow-up post-RT for an early diagnosis and intervention of ORN. Existing mandibular ORN prediction models are based on dose-volume histogram (DVH) metrics that omit the spatial localisation and dose gradient and direction information provided by the clinical mandible radiation dose distribution maps. *Methods.* We propose the use of a binary classification 3D DenseNet121 to extract the relevant dosimetric information directly from the 3D mandible radiation dose distribution maps and predict the incidence of ORN. We compare the results to a Random Forest ensemble with DVH-based parameters. *Results.* The 3D DenseNet121 model was able to discriminate ORN vs. non-ORN cases with an average AUC of 0.71 (0.64–0.79), compared to 0.65 (0.57–0.73) for the RF model. *Conclusion.* Obtaining the dosimetric information directly from the clinical radiation dose distribution maps may enhance the performance and functionality of ORN normal tissue complication probability (NTCP) models.

Keywords: Head and neck cancer · Radiotherapy · Mandibular osteoradionecrosis · NTCP · Toxicity

A. P. King and T. Guerrero Urbano—Joint last authors.

S. Wu et al. (Eds.): AMAI 2022, LNCS 13540, pp. 49–58, 2022.
https://doi.org/10.1007/978-3-031-17721-7_6

1   Introduction

Radiotherapy (RT), either alone or combined with surgery and/or chemotherapy, is typically the primary treatment for head and neck cancer (HNC). With the introduction of modern RT techniques, we are able to irradiate the target volume with high precision and dose conformity. However, due to the nature of energy deposition of photons in tissue, non-target organs inevitably absorb ionising radiation, potentially resulting in normal tissue toxicity. Acute and late radiation-induced toxicities have a significant effect on the patient's quality of life and can also jeopardise treatment compliance, potentially impacting treatment outcome.

Osteoradionecrosis (ORN) of the mandible is a rare but severe radiation-induced toxicity observed in 4–8% [1] of patients after HNC RT. Radiation damages the vascularisation of the mandible. Consequently, necrosis of the bone can develop either spontaneously or be triggered by trauma to the mandible bone (e.g. dental extractions, surgery, implants). Necrosis occurs because the bone is not able to heal due to reduced blood supply, hypoxia or hypo-cellularity caused by exposure to radiation [2]. The severity of ORN can vary between patients with the most severe cases experiencing significant pain levels and even pathological fracture of the mandible (Fig. 1).

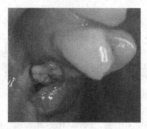

Fig. 1. Example of a recent mandibular ORN case at our centre. This image shows exposed bone in line with ORN of the upper right second premolar tooth socket.

Quality of life can be greatly affected in patients who develop mandibular ORN. Moreover, the management of ORN is often complex and requires costly clinical interventions [3]. Being able to identify patients that are at a higher risk of developing ORN will contribute to more individualised treatment and follow-up regimes potentially resulting in a reduced incidence probability or early management with improved prognosis.

The amount of an organ irradiated to a certain dose level is typically described in the clinical setting using a 2D dose-volume histogram (DVH), where the horizontal axis is divided into dose bins and the vertical axis represents the percentage or absolute volume of the organ receiving each of the dose levels on the horizontal axis. Thus, in a DVH the 3D radiation dose distribution map of an organ is reduced to a 2D representation with the resulting loss of clinically relevant spatial localisation as well as dose gradient and direction information. Spatial dosimetric information is of great interest in the investigation of radiation damage to the mandible, where there are regions that are more vulnerable to ORN development such as the posterior molar segment [4]. In addition, it has previously been observed [5] that the ORN region within the mandible may actually develop far from the high dose region.

Normal tissue complication probability (NTCP) models are used as a clinical decision support system to reduce the incidence of a given toxicity by identifying the patients who are at a higher risk of developing it. Existing ORN NTCP models are based on DVH data [6,7]. The use of spatial dose features in NTCP models may provide more comprehensive information than the typically used DVH-based metrics such as mean or maximum doses. Other HNC studies [8–11] have included spatial dose metrics into NTCP models by manually extracting dosiomic features on a voxel-by-voxel basis. An alternative method for incorporating spatial dose metrics into NTCP models is the use of deep learning (DL) [12,13].

To the best of our knowledge, this is the first study to investigate the use of DL methods in mandibular ORN NTCP models with clinical 3D radiation dose distribution maps as input.

2   Methods and Materials

2.1   Data

Patient Selection: A cohort of 70 ORN cases and 70 control cases was retrospectively selected from a database of HNC cases treated at our hospitals with radical intensity-modulated RT (IMRT) between 2011 and 2019. During the time span considered, a total 187 patients were diagnosed with ORN. From the entire ORN population, 36 cases were treated with 3D conformal RT instead of IMRT, 9 cases were not treated for HNC, for 32 cases the RT dose and/or RT plan DICOM files were unavailable and 40 additional patients were excluded either due to previous irradiation of the HN region, the ORN being located in the maxilla or receiving a palliative treatment. Only control cases with a minimum follow up time of 3 years following completion of RT were included. Controls were matched to the selected ORN cases based on primary tumour site whenever corresponding controls where available. Table 1 provides the demographic and clinical characteristics and compares the ORN and control cohorts.

At our institution ORN is graded according to its severity following the Notani grading system, which classifies ORN severity into three categories [14]. However, for the purpose of binary classification in this study, any grade of ORN was considered as an event.

3D Mandible Dose Distribution Maps: The data preparation workflow is illustrated in Fig. 2. The mandible was manually segmented from the patients'

Table 1. Demographic and clinical characteristics.

	ORN	Control	p-value
Gender			
Male/Female (%)	70.0/30.0	80.0/20.0	0.15/0.15
Age (median (IQR))	61.5 (13.3)	60.5 (13.5)	0.49
Primary tumour site			
Oropharynx (%)	60.0	52.1	0.35
Oral cavity (%)	30.0	21.4	0.23
Larynx (%)	2.9	12.9	0.04
Hypopharynx (%)	0.0	2.9	0.37
Salivary glands (%)	1.4	3.6	0.66
Nasopharynx (%)	0.0	1.4	0.80
Paranasal sinus (%)	1.4	0.0	0.72
Unknown primary (%)	4.3	2.1	0.66
Smoking			
Current/Previous (%)	44.3/27.1	32.1/36.4	0.12/0.23
Alcohol			
Current/Previous (%)	62.9/10.0	63.6/9.3	0.96/0.93
Chemotherapy (%)	65.7	62.1	0.72
Pre-RT dental extractions (%)	64.3	63.6	0.96
Pre-RT surgery (%)	32.9	32.1	0.96

CT volumes by a single observer in the treatment planning system (TPS) including the mandible sockets and excluding the maxilla and teeth. The 3D radiation dose maps, mandible segmentations and CT images were exported as DICOM files from the RT TPS. All data were resampled to a common slice thickness of 2 mm and slice size of 512 pixels × 512 pixels using 3-D Slicer (http://www.slicer.org). All mandible segmentations were rigidly registered to a common reference space using ITKSnap (www.itksnap.org) in order to reduce inter-patient positional variation. The patient with the largest number of mandible segmentation slices was selected as the reference patient and smaller mandibles were padded with empty slices. The dose maps were transformed using the same rigid transformations to maintain alignment. The 3D mandible dose distribution maps used by the model were obtained by multiplying the normalised dose maps by the binary mandible segmentation masks. Finally, the 3D mandible dose distribution maps were normalised as follows: normalised intensity = (intensity − Dmin)/(Dmax − Dmin), where Dmin and Dmax are the global minimum and maximum intensities across the entire dataset.

DVH Metrics: The cumulative DVH of the mandible structure was exported in relative volume and absolute dose (Gy) from the TPS. Maximum (Dmax and

D2%), minimum (Dmin and D98%), Dmean and Dmedian (D50%) dose metrics were extracted from the DVH using the DVHmetrics package in R statistical software (https://www.R-project.org/). Dose-volume data were converted to an equivalent dose in 2 Gy fractions assuming an alpha-beta ratio of 3 for late effects [15].

2.2 Prediction Models

A 3D densely-connected 121-layer (DenseNet121) [16] convolutional neural network (CNN) was implemented with the MONAI (https://monai.io/) Pytorch-based framework for the purpose of binary classification of ORN vs. control cases. A softmax activation layer was added at the end of the network to obtain the predicted probability for each class. The categorical cross entropy objective loss function was used. The 3D DenseNet121 was trained on the 3D mandible dose distribution maps. Small 3D random rotation (-0.1 to 0.1 rad) and zoom (0.8 to 1.2) augmentations were applied to the training images. The prediction performance of the 3D DenseNet121 was compared to a Random Forest (RF) trained with DVH metrics only (maximum, minimum, mean and median doses).

2.3 Model Evaluation

In both models, a stratified nested cross-validation (CV) approach with ensemble learning was followed (Fig. 3). The data were split into training, validation and test sets following a nested CV approach. In the outer loop of this procedure, a stratified 5-fold CV was applied by randomly splitting the data into training (80%) and test (20%) sets repeatedly. Hyperparameter optimisation was performed using a stratified 5-fold inner CV on the training set of the outer CV folds. For each of the outer folds, the entire training set was used for training using the optimised hyperparameters and the prediction accuracy calculated on the held-out fold. For the final training, an ensemble of models was trained to improve generalisation performance and to reduce the sensitivity of the model performance to stochastic noise of the training. In this study, our ensemble model was created by randomly initialising each model five times and each time, training the model on the training set of the outer fold. Due to the stochastic randomness of the weight initialisation and the selection of mini-batches during training, this created five slightly different models for each outer fold. To calculate the prediction of this ensemble model, the predicted softmax probabilities of each of the five individual models were averaged for each class (i.e. soft voting).

2.4 Statistical Analysis

The predictive performance of the models was assessed in terms of their discriminative ability using the area under the receiver operating characteristic curve (ROC AUC). The DeLong nonparametric statistical test [17] was performed to compare the AUC of the two models using the pROC package [18] with the statistical software R.

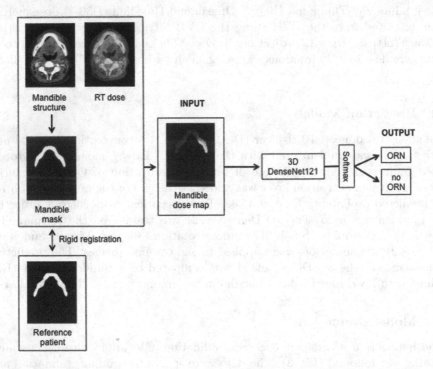

Fig. 2. Schematics of the data preparation workflow and deep-learning pipeline used.

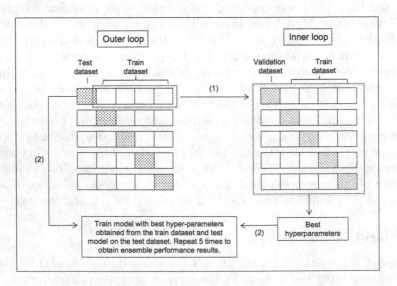

Fig. 3. Model evaluation workflow. A stratified nested CV approach with ensemble training was followed.

3   Results

Table 2 summarises the model discrimination performance results obtained from the two models: a 3D DenseNet121 model trained with mandible dose distribution maps and a RF model trained with DVH metrics. When comparing the two ROC curves with the DeLong test, the difference in AUC (0.71 vs. 0.65) was not found to be statistically significant with a p-value of 0.24 (significance level of 0.05).

Table 2. Model discrimination performance.

	3D DenseNet121 (dose map)	Random forest (DVH metrics)
ROC AUC (95% CI)	0.71 (0.64−0.79)	0.65 (0.57−0.73)
Sensitivity	0.70	0.66
Specificity	0.73	0.64
Precision	0.72	0.65

4   Discussion

In this study, we have explored the use of DL models to predict mandibular ORN in HNC using clinical 3D radiation dose distribution maps. This is a novel approach to NTCP modeling for mandibular ORN as it uses the actual RT dose distribution rather than the more traditionally used DVH parameters.

4.1   ORN Prediction

Our results show that the 3D DenseNet121 model was able to discriminate well between ORN and control cases based on the 3D mandible dose distribution maps. However, we found that the performance of the model was dependent on the test-train data split (i.e. classification performance varied between the outer loop CV folds). This may be due to the high variability in the anatomical localisation of the radiation dose distribution of our cohort, suggesting that training using a larger cohort will lead to improved classification accuracy and robustness. Moreover, in some of the outer loop CV folds, there was a large variation between the ensemble models, i.e. there was stochastic noise in the model training process for a given test-train data split.

Although the difference in model performance was not found to be statistically significant, the average discriminative performance of the RF model using DVH data was 9% lower than that of the 3D DenseNet121. This could be due to the fact that the entire DVH was not included in this model, i.e. only maximum, minimum, mean and median doses were included as variables, although we note that these are the variables typically used in clinical NTCP models. However, it is likely that the inclusion of the spatial information in the dose maps may contribute to an improved performance. Furthermore, there are features such as the mandible volume that can be extracted from the mandible dose distribution maps but are not DVH dosimetric parameters that have previously been associated with ORN incidence [5,19].

4.2   Study Limitations and Future Work

Due to mandibular ORN being a rare toxicity, the case numbers are naturally low. Although we have tried to mitigate this with data augmentation in the DL model, planned work will consider a larger multi-institutional ORN population that will enable us to more thoroughly evaluate the potential of CNNs in ORN prediction as well as to perform an external validation of the models.

Radiation dose, in particular maximum dose, has typically been associated with ORN incidence. There are, however, other risk factors for mandibular ORN to be considered [20,21]. In this study we have focused on radiation dose as the only risk factor but the inclusion of non-dosimetric clinical parameters into the model would be of great clinical value. Moreover, there are cases where ORN develops away from the high radiation dose region within the mandible and the correlation between ORN incidence and intermediate or high radiation doses is less obvious. Particularly in such cases, non-dosimetric parameters may play an important role in the development of ORN. We will investigate including such clinical parameters in our CNN framework in future work.

Finally, in this study we have not included information on ORN region localisation. To take full advantage of a DL model using dose distribution maps, knowledge of the actual ORN region or at least the ORN localisation within the mandible may be included into the model. Predicted ORN incidence could then be analysed, for instance, with regards to proximity of the ORN localisation to the tumour volume or the high radiation dose region within the mandible. With regards to model interpretability, qualitative methods such as saliency maps could also be compared to the ORN localisation data.

5   Conclusion

With the methods proposed in this study, we are contributing towards a more individualised treatment of HNC. This study is, to the best of our knowledge, the first to investigate the use of a deep CNN in mandibular ORN NTCP modeling. Our results suggest that it is not only possible to predict mandibular ORN incidence from 3D radiation dose distribution maps but that a deep CNN model may even outperform the more traditional DVH-based models. Obtaining the dosimetric information directly from the clinical radiation dose distribution maps rather than the DVH may enhance the performance and functionality of the ORN NTCP models.

Prospect of Application. This is a novel application of DL for a HNC clinical decision support system. The individual prediction of patients that are more likely to develop mandibular ORN prior to RT will guide the RT treatment planning optimisation process and also help to identify which patients would benefit from a closer follow-up post-RT for an early diagnosis and intervention of ORN.

Acknowledgements. This work was supported by NVIDIA Corporation with the donation of the Titan Xp GPU and by Cancer Research UK.

References

1. Frankart, A.J., Frankart, M.J., Cervenka, B., Tang, A.L., Krishnan, D.G., Takiar, V.: Osteoradionecrosis: exposing the evidence not the bone. Int. J. Radiat. Oncol. Biol. Phys. **109**(5), 1206–1218 (2021)
2. Chen, J.A., et al.: Osteoradionecrosis of mandible bone in patients with oral cancer-associated factors and treatment outcomes. Head Neck **38**, 762–768 (2016)
3. Patel, V., Ormondroyd, L., Lyons, A., McGurk, M.: The financial burden for the surgical management of osteoradionecrosis. Br. Dent. J. **222**, 177–180 (2017)
4. Habib, S., Sassoon, I., Thompson, I., Patel, V.: Risk factors associated with osteoradionecrosis. Oral Surg. **14**, 227–35 (2021)
5. Humbert-Vidan, L., et al.: PH-0387 Mandible osteoradionecrosis: a dosimetric study (poster presented at ESTRO 2021, Madrid, Spain). Radiother. Oncol. **161**, S285–S286 (2021)
6. Van Dijk, L.V., et al.: Normal tissue complication probability (NTCP) prediction model for osteoradionecrosis of the mandible in patients with head and neck cancer after radiation therapy: large-scale observational cohort. Int. J. Radiat. Oncol. Biol. Phys. **111**(2), 549–558 (2021)
7. Humbert-Vidan, L., Patel, V., Oksuz, I., King, A.P., Guerrero Urbano, T.: Comparison of machine learning methods for prediction of osteoradionecrosis incidence in patients with head and neck cancer. Br. J. Radiol. **94** (2021)
8. Beasley, W., et al.: Image-based data mining to probe dosimetric correlates of radiation-induced trismus. Int. J. Radiat. Oncol. Biol. Phys. **102**(4), 1330–1338 (2018)
9. Jiang, W., et al.: Machine learning methods uncover radiomorphologic dose patterns in salivary glands that predict xerostomia in patients with head and neck cancer. Adv. Radiat. Oncol. **4**(2), 401–412 (2019)
10. Gabryś, H.S., Buettner, F., Sterzing, F., Hauswald, H., Dangert, M.: Design and selection of machine learning methods using radiomics and dosiomics for normal tissue complication probability modeling of xerostomia. Front. Oncol. **8**(25), 35 (2018)
11. Dean, J., et al.: Incorporating spatial dose metrics in machine learning-based normal tissue complication probability (NTCP) models of severe acute dysphagia resulting from head and neck radiotherapy. Clin. Trans. Radiat. Oncol. **8**, 27–39 (2018)
12. Ibragimov, B., Toesca, D., Chang, D., Yuan, Y., Koong, A., Xing, L.: Development of deep neural network for individualized hepatobiliary toxicity prediction after liver SBRT. Med. Phys. **45**(10), 4763–4774 (2018)

13. Men, K., Geng, H., Zhong, H., Fan, Y., Lin, A., Xiao, Y.: A deep learning model for predicting xerostomia due to radiotherapy for head-and-neck squamous cell carcinoma in the RTOG 0522 clinical trial. Int. J. Radiat. Oncol. Biol. Phys. **105**(2), 440–447 (2019)

14. Notani, K., et al.: Osteoradionecrosis of the mandible-factors influencing severity. Asian J. Oral Maxillofac. Surg. **14**(1), 5–9 (2002)

15. Williams, M.V., Denekamps, J., Fowler, J.F.: A review of alpha/beta ratios for experimental tumours: implications for clinical studies of altered fractionation. Int. J. Radiat. Oncol. Biol. Phys. **11**, 87–96 (1985)

16. Huang, G., Liu, Z., Van Der Maaten, L., Weinberger, K.Q.: Densely connected convolutional networks. In: Proceedings of the IEEE Conference on Computer Vision and Pattern Recognition, pp. 4700–4708 (2017)

17. DeLong, E.R., DeLong, D.M., Clarke-Pearson, D.L.: Comparing the areas under two or more correlated receiver operating characteristic curves: a nonparametric approach. Biometrics **44**, 837–845 (1988)

18. Robin, X., et al.: pROC: an open-source package for R and S+ to analyze and compare ROC curves. BMC Bioinform. **12**, 77 (2011)

19. Patel, V., et al.: Radiotherapy quadrant doses in oropharyngeal cancer treated with intensity modulated radiotherapy. Fac. Dent. J. **11**, 166–72 (2015)

20. Aarup-Kirstensen, S., Hansen, C.R., Forner, L., Brink, C., Eriksen, J.G., Johansen, J.: Osteoradionecrosis of the mandible after radiotherapy for head and neck cancer: risk factors and dose-volme correlations. Acta. Oncol. **58**(10), 1373–1377 (2019)

21. MDA Hnc symptom working group: dose-volume correlates of mandibular osteoradionecrosis in oropharynx cancer patients receiving intensity-modulated radiotherapy: results from a case-matched comparison. Radiother. Oncol. **124**, 232–239 (2017)

Analysis of Potential Biases on Mammography Datasets for Deep Learning Model Development

Blanca Zufiria[1,2]($\boxtimes$), Karen López-Linares[1,3], María J. García[1],
Kristin M. Rebescher[1], Iván Lalaguna[4], Esther Albertín[4],
Maria B. Cimadevila[5], Javier Garcia[5], Maria J. Ledesma-Carbayo[2],
and Iván Macía[1,3]

[1] Vicomtech, Basque Research and Technology Alliance, San Sebastián, Spain
[2] Universidad Politécnica de Madrid, Madrid, Spain
blanca.zufiria@gmail.com
[3] Biodonostia Health Research Institute, San Sebastián, Spain
[4] Instrumentación y Componentes SA, Inycom, Zaragoza, Spain
[5] Servicio Gallego de Salud, Galicia, Spain

Abstract. The development of democratized, generalizable deep learning applications for health care systems is challenging as potential biases could easily emerge. This paper provides an overview of the potential biases that appear in image analysis datasets that affect the development and performance of artificial intelligence algorithms. Especially, an exhaustive analysis of mammography data has been carried out at the patient, image and source of origin levels. Furthermore, we summarize some techniques to alleviate these biases for the development of fair deep learning models. We present a learning task to classify negative and positive screening mammographies and analyze the influence of biases in the performance of the algorithm.

Keywords: Bias · Deep learning · Mammography · Breast cancer

1 Introduction

Recent advances in artificial intelligence (AI) in the medical field enable transforming large sets of images together with their annotations into predictive models using deep learning techniques. Such a model is expected to behave in an unbiased way to produce fair, objective decisions, without basing them on spurious attributes. However, AI algorithms can be biased towards certain input patterns, deriving unfair decisions dependent on the domain and not on the task to be solved. Biases may come from several origins, among which data-related biases frequently appear [1,2]. Thus, to prevent from a biased behavior and ensure a good generalization of deep learning models in real-world environments, special care must be taken during the creation of training datasets and the design and development of the models [3,4]. There are recent studies in the literature that

S. Wu et al. (Eds.): AMAI 2022, LNCS 13540, pp. 59–67, 2022.
https://doi.org/10.1007/978-3-031-17721-7_7

analyze bias in deep learning algorithms applied to medical images [2,3,5,6]. [7,8] perform an analysis of the impact of bias related to sociological factors such as sex, age, race or type of health insurance. [9] describe a methodology to clinically evaluate AI technology on medical images. [10] found a source of bias in patient age, which they mitigated with adversarial training. Similarly, [11] apply a multi-task strategy together with an adversarial training scheme to simultaneously detect and mitigate bias (sex and skin tone) in a skin lesion detection scenario. [8,12–15] analyze selection biases in chest X-ray datasets and [8,14,15] emphasize on how acquisition equipment-related biases and domain shifts affect a pneumonia detection algorithm. Regarding mammography solutions, [2] comments that the presence of an image marker could interfere in the performance of the algorithm. [16,17] develop a deep learning algorithm to predict breast cancer risk and they use adversarial training to discriminate image origin, even if the variability in the manufacturers used during training is scarce. Furthermore, [18] developed an screening algorithm to predict cancer probability from a mammogram view using a wide variety of manufacturers. Nevertheless, they do not mention preprocessing techniques or data cleaning, which could derive into biases.

This paper aims at highlighting the relevance of performing an analysis of potential data-related biases before deep learning model development. Here, data bias is defined as gathered data that does not represent the phenomenon to predict. It can also contain characteristics produced by humans that may lead algorithms to solve a different task from the desired one and to fail when tested on properly selected independent data. In Sect. 2, we provide an overview on bias detection and mitigation techniques using a mammography dataset, with a high variability in manufacturers and models, as an example. Also, we show the influence of data related bias on classification experiments, together with possible solutions to reduce the impact of the bias. In Sect. 3, results from experiments are discussed. Finally, conclusions are provided in Sect. 4.

2   Materials and Methods

This section describes the input mammography dataset and our approach to analyze biases. We also present some techniques that can be used to mitigate these biases. Finally, some experiments were carried out to evaluate the influence of biases in deep learning algorithms.

2.1   Mammography Dataset

The dataset is composed of 1727 mammography studies provided by the Galician health care system. Since the goal was to provide democratized deep learning solutions for the health area, the main criterion to gather the data from the picture archiving and communication system (PACS) was to contemplate all the available manufacturers. Mammograms from Fujifilm Corporation, Hologic Inc, Philips Medical Systems, and Siemens were obtained and filtered so that only those containing two views, i.e. bilateral craniocaudal (CC) and mediolateral oblique (MLO), for each breast were considered. Finally, a selection according to the following breast cancer screening clinical categories was performed: 1) **Negative screening**: mammograms where radiologist did not detect signs of cancer and from women that were not derived for further tests and 2) **Positive screening**: mammograms where radiologists detected a sign of cancer and women were derived to further tests in the diagnostic departments. The distribution of exams in these categories, shown in Table 1, was balanced for most equipment manufacturers except for Philips scans, which were not used to acquire the mammography prior to further tests in any case.

Table 1. Number of studies distributed by manufacturers and clinical categories.

	Fujifilm	Hologic	Philips	Siemens	Total
Negative screening	277	263	271	270	1081
Positive screening	262	197	0	187	646
Total	539	460	271	457	1727

2.2 Bias Analysis

An in-depth analysis of the dataset for AI model development is an important step to detect potential biases and to ensure model performance in real world applications. Especially, datasets containing medical images are ideally built gathering information from different hospitals, different devices and several protocols to fulfill the needs of the whole health care system. Socio-technological analysis is crucial in these cases to detect potential biases, some of which can be discussed at the DICOM metadata level or at the content or pixel data level.

DICOM Metadata Analysis: Some information about the patient and the imaging studies can be directly extracted from standard DICOM tags (Fig. 1-a). In general, there are relevant differences between negative and positive studies. Specially, images are acquired with different scanners (Device ID) and acquisition parameters (WW/WC) between negative and positive exams. Furthermore, differences in the Patient Age and Institution tags induce a very important bias in the dataset. Hence, suggesting that negative studies may come from hospitals where a breast cancer screening program is carried out, whereas positive exams may come from diagnostic departments. Thus, when designing algorithms, the global performance of the network could be unfairly biased towards some specific devices, which should be detected and considered.

Histogram Analysis: Understanding the distribution of image intensity values across different categories is another approach to measure bias in the dataset and to decide appropriate preprocessing methods. Mean and standard deviation histograms are calculated (Fig. 1-b) for positive and negative screening exams independently. Differences are observed, probably related to the different scanners and acquisition parameters previously discussed and shown in Fig. 1-a.

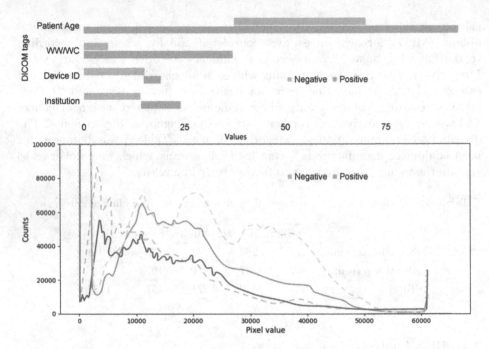

Fig. 1. a) Distribution positive and negative screening studies with respect to the different DICOM tags. b) Mean (continuous line) and standard deviation (dotted line) histograms for the different clinical categories in the dataset.

2.3   Bias Correction Techniques

Based on the analysis previously described, we identified some methods to mitigate the biases. The techniques can be divided into modification of image appearance or modification of model training and architecture to guide the learning towards the desired features.

Image Appearance Bias Correction: Some manufacturers introduce text marks in the image, e.g. labels indicating the view (CC, MLO) or the breast (left, right) and deletion of this markers is important to avoid biases. Furthermore, changing window width (WW) and window center (WC) values according to the VOI LUT DICOM tag of the study equalizes appearance between different manufacturers, devices and acquisition protocols.

Model Training Bias Correction: Domain-Adversarial training performs a domain transfer where final predictions must be made based on features that cannot discriminate the domain from which the images are obtained [19]. It could be a good solution to mitigate domain biases, derived from the distribution of the different mammography units and hospitals found in the dataset. Furthermore, data augmentation during training can be used to mitigate biases by increasing the number of training samples with different appearances applying, for example, random Gaussian noise, elastic deformations and modifying the contrast and the brightness.

2.4 Experimental Setup

To show the influence of data-related bias, we carried out a classification task using a deep learning approach. Especially, we aim at building a model that differentiates between normal mammograms (negative screening) and mammograms from patients derived to further tests in the diagnostic departments of the hospital (positive screening).

We employ a network architecture based on [18] using the DenseNet121 architecture where the four instances (right CC, right MLO, left CC, left MLO) are used to decide whether a study is a negative or positive screening exam. The model combines features between breast views and it is trained to minimize a binary cross-entropy loss, with a learning rate of $1e^{-5}$, batch size of 4 and Adam optimizer. The dataset is divided into training (70%), validation (20%) and test (10%) for each class to train the network (manufacturers and clinical categories are balanced between subsets). First, images are rescaled between 0 and 1 and normalized dividing each image by the mean and the standard deviation of the intensities, calculated beforehand for the whole rescaled dataset. Studies acquired with inverted gray scale values are modified so all images have a dark background. Instances corresponding to the left breast are flipped to the right side to facilitate the learning process. Finally, the training dataset is balanced according to the clinical categories to avoid a bias towards the majority class. Several experiments are performed to evaluate the influence of the bias for the screening classification task:

Baseline: the neural network is trained with the preprocessed dataset and parameters as described above. The aim is the classification of mammography studies into positive and negative screening focusing on breast tissues.

WW/WC: from the baseline, this experiment aims at adjusting WW and WC values of the mammograms to homogenize the images across the acquisition devices (Fig. 3-f) as described in Sect. 2.4.

Data Augmentation: data augmentation is included to the WW/WC experiment as described in Sect. 2.4.

Domain-Adversarial Training: the goal is to obtain device independent features to mitigate the image type bias and focus more on the clinical classification task (Sect. 2.4). Based on the fact that a model could be trained to differentiate between devices (Fig. 3-e, upper figure), a domain-adversarial training that extracts intermediate features independent on the device could be developed. We introduce a domain-discriminator to classify features from different devices according to the Device ID DICOM tag and thereby, encourage similar feature extraction for all the domains to solve the actual screening classification task

(Fig. 3-e). The training procedure minimizes the loss of the classifier differentiating between negative and positive samples while maximizing the loss of the domain classifier.

Unbiased Data Addition: the inclusion of additional unbiased data could help the network focusing on the desired clinical task by ignoring previous biases. Hence, a new dataset was requested from screening units with balanced manufacturers and devices (Fig. 2) for 1179 screening negative and 393 screening positive mammograms. Furthermore, all these patients belong to the breast cancer screening program so the age range is fixed (Fig. 2). Preprocessing (with WW/WC modifications) of the images and data augmentation were applied in this experiment.

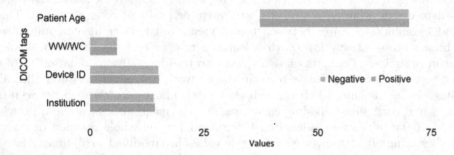

Fig. 2. Distribution positive and negative screening studies with respect to the different DICOM tags for the unbiased dataset. The distribution of the tags is balanced unlike in Fig. 1-a.

3   Results and Discussion

Trained models are evaluated on a subset of 188 mammography studies (104 negative screening and 84 positive screening) separated from the dataset and on a subset of 156 studies (125 negative screening and 31 positive screening) from the additional unbiased dataset. The experiments yield similar results, as shown in Table 2, where models achieve a high performance on test studies but metrics worsen for the unbiased test dataset, suggesting that the bias is not overcome (Table 2). Positive screening studies are misclassified as negative screening studies, probably influenced by its origin of acquisition (scanners and hospitals).

An extra verification of the models performance was carried out by visualizing their learning with heatmap explanations applying the Grad-CAM algorithm [20] (Fig. 3). Grad-CAM produces a coarse localization map that highlights the important regions in the image used to predict a specific class. Results shown in Fig. 3 suggest that screening models are not classifying studies according to the desired clinical task, as they focus more on the type of image than on breast

Table 2. Evaluation metrics on test and unbiased test subsets (separated before experiments training)

	Test dataset (188 exams)			Unbiased test dataset (156 exams)		
	ROC-AUC	Sensitivity	Specificity	ROC-AUC	Sensitivity	Specificity
Baseline	0.997	0.988	0.961	0.501	0.064	0.968
WW/WC	0.996	0.976	0.961	0.503	0.032	0.992
Data augmentation	0.982	0.988	0.923	0.525	0.064	0.944
Domain adversarial	0.995	0.952	0.971	0.551	0.032	1.0
Unbiased data addition	0.995	0.964	0.961	0.658	0.032	1.0

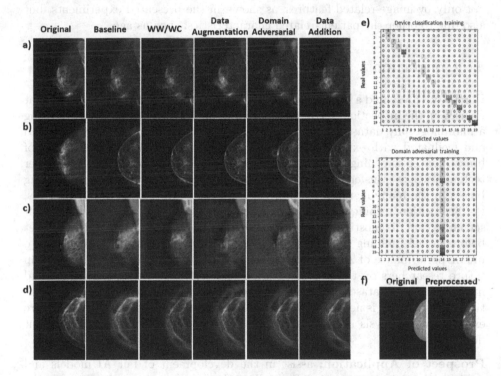

Fig. 3. (a–d) Grad-CAM computed for correctly classified mammography studies from the test subset. a) Right MLO view of a negative Siemens study. b) Left CC view of a negative Hologic stud. c) Left MLO view of a positive Fujifilm study. d) Left CC view of a positive Philips study. e) Confusion matrices of the device classifier (upper figure) and the domain discriminator classifier during the domain-adversarial training (lower figure). f) Preprocessed instance modifying the window width (WW) and window center (WC) values according to the function defined in the VOI LUT DICOM tag (Sect. 2.4).

tissues to find abnormalities. This is visible in Fig. 3-d, where a mass is present but models focus on the curvature of the breast. Furthermore, such explanations are highlighted on other parts of the images outside the breast like illuminated borders(Figure 3-b) or background (Fig. 3-c). Adding unbiased data mitigates the bias in some cases, where the trained algorithm focuses on the tissues inside the breast and not on the background or other characteristics derived from the device (Fig. 3-c). However, such mitigation is not enough to train a fair algorithm as seen in the quantitative results on the unbiased test subset (Table 2). Finally, domain-adversarial training results show that the discriminator is not able to differentiate between mammography devices (Fig. 3-e, upper figure) but metrics on the unbiased dataset (Table 2) and Grad-cam visualizations (Fig. 3) demonstrate that the bias still persists. Hence, based on the quantitative results and the Grad-CAM visualizations on test studies, we assume that models are biased not only by image-related features, as shown in the presented experiments, but also due to other the patient-related characteristics, such as age.

4   Conclusions

Hereby, we presented a bias analysis approach for deep learning applications that focuses on the inspection of DICOM metadata and pixel data distribution, using a mammography dataset as use case. Bias correction techniques were proposed and evaluated with experiments proving that, for the specific clinical task of breast cancer screening, results are biased toward the source of origin. Further techniques, like transfer learning, should be implemented to mitigate the existing biases in the mammography dataset. Such biases could be the age of patients, the acquisition techniques or other characteristics present in the two different screening and diagnostic departments. A careful initial inspection of the dataset before model building is essential to detect potential biases that may lead to unfair performance of AI algorithms. Hence, the proposed approach could help future researchers on the implementation of fair deep learning algorithms and methodology for dataset extraction and generation for medical imaging applications. Future work is needed to further investigate this potential issue with more experiments, analysis and techniques and to expand the research to different datasets.

Prospect of Application: assist in the development of fair AI models and unbiased database construction. Specially, in breast cancer screening scenario the robustness of AI models would increase for a fair performance at different health care systems, mammographers and acquisition protocols. Thus, all professionals and patients, regardless of the hospital they are in, would have access to the system equally.

Acknowledgments. This work has been partially funded by FEDER "Una manera de hacer Europa". This research has been done within the project CADIA - Sistema de Detecciónn de Diversas Patologíss Basado en el Analisis de Imagen con Inteligencia Artificial (DG-SER1-19-003) under the Codigo100 Public Procurement and Innovation Programme by the Galician Health Service - Servizo Galego de Saude (SERGAS) cofunded by the European Regional Development Fund (ERDF).

References

1. Hammer, G.P., du Prel, J.B., Blettner, M.: Avoiding bias in observational studies: part 8 in a series of articles on evaluation of scientific publications. Dtsch Arztebl Int. **106**, 664 (2009)
2. Yu, A.C., Eng, J.: One algorithm may not fit all: how selection bias affects machine learning performance. Radiographics **40**, 1932–1937 (2020)
3. Varoquaux, G., Cheplygina, V.: How I failed machine learning in medical imaging - shortcomings and recommendations. Electr. Eng. Syst. Sci. (2021)
4. Tong, S., Kagal, L.: Investigating bias in image classification using model explanations. Comput. Sci. Comput. Vis. Pattern Recogn. (2020)
5. Oakden-Rayner, L., Dunnmon, J., Carneiro, G., Re, C.: Hidden stratification causes clinically meaningful failures in machine learning for medical imaging. Comput. Sci. Mach. Learn. (2019)
6. K. Winkler, et al.: Association between surgical skin markings in dermoscopic images and diagnostic performance of a deep learning convolutional neural network for melanoma recognition. JAMA Dermatol (2019)
7. Pot, M., Kieusseyan, N., Prainsack, B.: Not all biases are bad: equitable and inequitable biases in machine learning and radiology. Insights Imaging **12**, 1–10 (2021)
8. Larrazabal, A.J., Nieto, N., Peterson, V., Milone, D.H., Ferrante, E. Gender imbalance in medical imaging datasets produces biased classifiers for computer-aided diagnosis. In: Proc. Natl. Acad. Sci. USA , **117**, 12592–12594 (2020)
9. Park, S.H., Han, K.: Methodologic guide for evaluating clinical performance and effect of artificial intelligence technology for medical diagnosis and prediction. Radiology **286**, 800–809 (2003)
10. Zhao, Q., Adeli, E., Pohl, K.M.: Training confounder-free deep learning models for medical applications. Nat. Commun. **11**, 1–9 (2020)
11. Li, X., Cui, Z., Wu, Y., Gu, L., Harada, T.: Stimating and improving fairness with adversarial learning. Comput. Sci. Comput. Vis. Pattern Recogn. (2021)
12. Seyyed-Kalantari, L., Zhang, H., McDermott, M., Chen, I.Y., Ghassemi, M.: Underdiagnosis bias of artificial intelligence algorithms applied to chest radiographs in under-served patient populations. Nat. Med. **27**, 2176–2182 (2021)
13. Catala, O.D.T., et al.: Bias analysis on public x-ray image datasets of pneumonia and Covid-19 patients. IEEE Access. **9**, 42370–42383 (2021)
14. E. H. P. Pooch, P. L. Ballester, R. C. Barros: Can we trust deep learning based diagnosis? the impact of domain shift in chest radiograph classification. Electr. Eng. Syst. Sci. Image Video Process. (2020)
15. Zech, J.R., Badgeley, M.A., Liu, M., Costa, A.B., Titano, J.J., Oermann, E.K.: Variable generalization performance of a deep learning model to detect pneumonia in chest radiographs: a cross-sectional study. PLoS Med. **15**, e1002683 (2018)
16. Yala, A., et al.: Toward robust mammography-based models for breast cancer risk. Sci Transl. Med. **13**, eaba4373 (2021)
17. Mayer McKinney, S., et al.: International evaluation of an AI system for breast cancer screening. Nature **577**, 89–94 (2020)
18. Wu, N., et al.: Deep neural networks improve radiologists' performance in breast cancer screening. IEEE Trans. Med. Imaging **39**, 1184–1194 (2020)
19. Ganin, Y., et al.: Domain-adversarial training of neural networks. Stat. Mach. Learn. **17**, 2096–2130 (2016)
20. Selvaraju, R.R., Cogswell, M., Das, A., Vedantam, R., Parikh, D., Batra, D.: Visual explanations from deep networks via gradient-based localization. In: IEEE International Conference on Computer Vision (ICCV). (2017)

ECG-ATK-GAN: Robustness Against Adversarial Attacks on ECGs Using Conditional Generative Adversarial Networks

Khondker Fariha Hossain[1]([✉]), Sharif Amit Kamran[1], Alireza Tavakkoli[1], and Xingjun Ma[2]

[1] Department of Computer Science and Engineering, University of Nevada, Reno, NV, USA
khondkerfarihah@nevada.unr.edu
[2] School of Computer Science, Fudan University, Shanghai, China

Abstract. Automating arrhythmia detection from ECG requires a robust and trusted system that retains high accuracy under electrical disturbances. Many machine learning approaches have reached human-level performance in classifying arrhythmia from ECGs. However, these architectures are vulnerable to adversarial attacks, which can misclassify ECG signals by decreasing the model's accuracy. Adversarial attacks are small crafted perturbations injected in the original data which manifest the out-of-distribution shifts in signal to misclassify the correct class. Thus, security concerns arise for false hospitalization and insurance fraud abusing these perturbations. To mitigate this problem, we introduce the first novel Conditional Generative Adversarial Network (GAN), robust against adversarial attacked ECG signals and retaining high accuracy. Our architecture integrates a new class-weighted objective function for adversarial perturbation identification and new blocks for discerning and combining out-of-distribution shifts in signals in the learning process for accurately classifying various arrhythmia types. Furthermore, we benchmark our architecture on six different white and black-box attacks and compare them with other recently proposed arrhythmia classification models on two publicly available ECG arrhythmia datasets. The experiment confirms that our model is more robust against such adversarial attacks for classifying arrhythmia with high accuracy.

Keywords: ECG · Adversarial attack · Generative Adversarial Network · Electrocardiogram · Deep learning

1 Introduction

ECG is a crucial clinical measurement that encodes and identifies severe electrical disturbances like cardiac arrhythmia and myocardial infractions. Many artificial intelligence and machine learning approaches have been proposed to detect different types of ECGs accurately [11,19,25]. Recently, deep convolutional neural networks (CNNs) [1,2,20,30,32] has become the norm for achieving near-human-level performance for classifying cardiac arrhythmia and other cardiac abnormalities. Popular systems such as Medtronic LINQ II ICM [27], iRhythm Zio [31], and Apple Watch Series 4 [17]

S. Wu et al. (Eds.): AMAI 2022, LNCS 13540, pp. 68–78, 2022.
https://doi.org/10.1007/978-3-031-17721-7_8

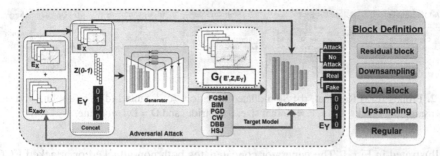

Fig. 1. Proposed ECG-ATK-GAN consisitng of a generator and a discriminator. The discriminator is utilized for generating the six attacked signals $E_{x_{adv}}$, namely FGSM, BIM, PGD, CW, HSJ, and DBB. These are then added with the non-attacked signals E_x to create the training dataset E'_x. Contrarily, the generator takes both attacked and non-attacked ECG signals, E'_x, a noise vector z, and the class labels E_y as input.

use embedded DNN models to analyze cardiac irregularities by monitoring the signals. Accurately detecting arrhythmia in real-time enables an immediate referral of the patient to appropriate medical facilities. In addition to providing the patient with timely medical help, this will benefit the insurance companies by potentially reducing long-time consequences of delayed healthcare. Despite all these benefits, state-of-the art systems used to predict arrhythmia are vulnerable to adversarial attacks. These vulnerabilities are crucial as they can result in false hospitalization, misdiagnosis, patient data-privacy leaks, insurance fraud, and negative repercussion for healthcare companies [12,17].

Although these vulnerabilities are highly studied [9,23], a comprehensive solution is yet to be devised. Adversarial attacks misclassify ECG signals by introducing small perturbations that inject the out-of-distribution signal into the classification path. The perturbations could be introduced to the data by accessing the model parameters (White-box attack) or inferring the bad prediction outputs for a given set of input (Black-box attack) [7]. Current deep learning [1,20,30] and GAN-based [13–15,18] classifiers are not specifically designed to utilize the objective function to identify and mitigate adversarial attacked ECGs. Although recent works [9,17] illustrated the vulnerability of deep learning architectures to adversarial attacks, our work proposes a first-of-its-kind defense strategy against six different adversarial attacks for ECGs using a novel conditional generative adversarial networks. Additionally, we incorporate a class-weighted categorical loss function for identifying out-of-distribution perturbations and emphasizing the class-specific features. Both qualitative and quantitative benchmarks on two publicly available ECG datasets illustrate our proposed method's robustness.

2 Methodology

2.1 Generator and Discriminator

We propose a novel GAN based on a class-conditioned generator and a robust discriminator for categorical classification of both real and adversarial attacked ECG signals

Fig. 2. Proposed (a) Residual, (b) Skip-dilated attention, (c) Regular, (d) Upsampling and, (e) Downsampling blocks. Here, K = Kernel size, S = Stride, and D = Dilation rate.

as illustrated in Fig. 1. The generator concatenates both non-attacked or attacked ECG signals E'_x, label E_y, and a noise vector z as input and generates $G(E'_x, Ey, z)$. We use a Gaussian filter with $\sigma = 3$ to generate the smoothed noise vector, z. The label vector E_y in our model is utilized so that generated signal is not random. Rather it imitates class-specific ECG representing an arrhythmia. The noise vector, z ensures that the generated signal has small perturbations so that it does not fully imitate the original ECG signal and helps in overall training in extrapolation of generated signals. The generators incorporate Residual, Downsampling, Upsampling, and Skip-Dilated Attention (SDA) block as visualized in Fig. 1. The generator uses Sigmoid activation as output, so the synthesized signal is constrained within 0–1 as a continuous value.

The discriminator takes attacked/non-attacked real ECG, x and GAN synthesized ECG, $G(E'_x, E_y, z)$ signals sequentially while training. The discriminator consists of three regular blocks and three downsampling blocks (Fig. 1). The discriminator utilizes three losses: 1) Class-weighted Categorical cross-entropy for identifying adversarial attacked/non-attacked ECGs, 2) Categorical cross-entropy for normal and arrhythmia beat classification and 3) Mean-squared Error for GAN adversarial training. So we use three output activations: Sigmoid (GAN training), and two Softmax for adversarial attack and arrhythmia/normal beat classification.

- **Residual Block:** For extracting small perturbations in the attacked ECG signals, we use convolution with a small kernel, $k = 3$ and stride, $s = 1$ in the residual block in the Generator, illustrated in Fig. 2(a). This residual block is capable of extracting fine features that extrapolate the original signal to contain small perturbations and make it out-of-distribution. Specifically, the residual skip connection retains important signal-specific information that is added with more robust features extracted after the batch-normalization and leaky-ReLU activation.
- **Skip-Dilated Attention Block:** We use skip-dilated attention (SDA) block with kernel size, $k = 2$, dilation rate, $d = 2$ and stride, $s = 1$, as illustrated in Fig. 2(b). By utilizing dilated convolution, our receptive fields become larger, covering larger areas of the attacked signals [33].
- **Regular Block:** We use the regular block for discriminators, containing convolution ($k = 3, s = 1$), batch-norm, and leaky-ReLU layers, as visualized in Fig. 2(c). Our main objective here is to encode the signals to meaningful classification outputs for two tasks, which is to 1) classify the type of arrhythmia and, 2) distinguish between non-attacked/attacked signals. Therefore, we avoid using any complex block for feature learning and extraction.
- **Downsampling and Upsampling Blocks:** The generator consist of both downsampling and upsampling blocks, whereas the discriminator consist of only downsam-

pling blocks to get the desired feature maps and output. The upsampling block consists of a transposed-convolution layer, batch-norm, and Leaky-ReLU activation layer successively and is given in Fig. 2(d). In contrast, The downsampling block comprises of a convolution layer, a batch-norm layer and a Leaky-ReLU activation function consecutively and is illustrated in Fig. 2(e).

2.2 Objective Function and Individual Losses

To distinguish non-attacked and attacked signals with out-of-distribution perturbations and emphasize the class-specific features even under significant perturbations, we propose a class-weighted categorical cross-entropy loss. The loss function is given in Eq. 1, where $m = 2$, for attacked/non-attacked signal and κ is the class weight for the ground-truth, E_y and predicted class-label, $E_{y'}$.

$$\mathcal{L}_{atk}(D) = -\sum_{i=0}^{m} \kappa^i E_y^i \log(E_{y'}^i) \tag{1}$$

For classification of normal and different arrhythmia signals, we use categorical cross-entropy loss. Here, $k = $ distinct normal/arrhythmia beats, depending on the dataset.

$$\mathcal{L}_{ary}(D) = -\sum_{i=0}^{k} E_y^i \log(E_{y'}^i) \tag{2}$$

For ensuring that the synthesized signal contains representative features of both adversarial examples and adversarial attacks, our generator incorporates the mean-squared error (MSE) as shown in Eq. 3. This helps the generator output signals with small perturbations that guarantee the signal to misclassify. As the generator, G is class-conditioned, it takes distinct ground truth class-label E_y, along with the attacked/non-attacked ECGs, E_x' and Gaussian noise vector z as input.

$$\mathcal{L}_{mse}(G) = \frac{1}{N} \sum_{i=1}^{N} (G(E_x', E_y, z) - E_x)^2 \tag{3}$$

We use Least-squared GAN [26] for calculating the adversarial loss and training our GAN. The cost function for our adversarial loss is given in Eq. 4. The discriminator takes real ECG signal, E_x and generated ECG signal, $G(E_x', E_y, z)$ in two iterations. The adversarial loss quadratically penalizes the error while stabilizing the min-max game between the generator and discriminator.

$$\mathcal{L}_{adv}(D) = \left[(D(E_x', E_y) - 1)^2 \right] + \left[(D(G(E_x', E_y, z), E_y) + 1))^2 \right] \tag{4}$$

By incorporating Eqs. 1, 2, 3 and 4, we can formulate our final loss function as given in Eq. 5. Here, λ_{mse}, λ_{atk}, and λ_{ary} denote different weights, that are multiplied with their corresponding losses. We want our generator to synthesize realistic ECGs to fool the Discriminator, while classifying the types of arrhythmia with high accuracy. So, the final goal is to maximize the adversarial loss and minimize other losses.

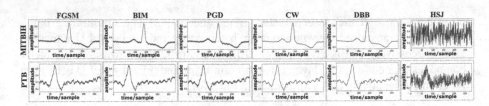

Fig. 3. The non-attacked and attacked signals (white and black-box attacks) overlapped on each other signified by Red and Blue lines. (Color figure online)

$$\min_{G, D_{ary}, D_{atk}} \left(\max_{D_{adv}} (\mathcal{L}_{adv}(D)) + \lambda_{mse} \left[\mathcal{L}_{mse}(G) \right] + \lambda_{atk} \left[\mathcal{L}_{atk}(D) \right] + \lambda_{ary} \left[\mathcal{L}_{ary}(D) \right] \right) \quad (5)$$

2.3 Adversarial Attacks

We incorporated six established adversarial attacks (shown in Fig 3) that target our discriminator model as it is responsible for classifying different types of arrhythmia and normal beats in ECG signals. The reason for choosing these state-of-the-art attacks is to make our model more robust for intrusive perturbations in real-world applications. Four of these attacks are white-box, meaning detailed knowledge of the network architecture, the parameters, and the gradient w.r.t to the input is utilized to corrupt the data [6]. The other two are black-box attacks, meaning no knowledge of the underlying architecture or parameter is needed; instead, some output is observed for some probed inputs [6]. Moreover, the attack corrupts the data by estimating the gradient direction using the information at the decision boundary of the output [4, 10]. We experimented with perturbation values, ϵ ranging from 0.001 to 0.1, and selected the value which looked visually realistic and harder to discern. So, the visually realistic perturbations for FGSM, BIM, PGD and DBB is, $\epsilon = 0.01$ and for CW, $\epsilon = 0.1$.

- **Fast Gradient Sign Method (FGSM):** This white-box attack creates attacked ECGs, $E_{X_{adv}}$ by perturbing the original signal, E_X. For this, it calculates the gradients of the loss, $\mathcal{L}_{ary}$ (Eq. 2) based on the input signal to create new adversarial signals that maximize the loss [16].
- **Basic Iterative Method (BIM):** This is an improved white-box attack, where the FGSM attack is iteratively updated in a smaller step size and clips the signals values of intermediate results to ensure the ϵ-neighborhood of the original signal, E_X [22].
- **Projected Gradient Descent (PGD):** This white-box attack is considered the most decisive first-order attack. Though similar to BIM, it varies in initializing the example to a random point in the ϵ-ball of interest (decided by the L_∞ norm) and does random restarts. In contrast, BIM initializes in the original point [24].
- **Carlini-Wagner (CW):** This is an optimization-based white-box attack [5]. It resolves the unboundedness issue by using line search to optimize the attack objective. We utilized the version with the L_∞ norm, i.e., for maximum perturbation applied to each point in the signal.

– **Decision-Based Boundary Attack (DBB):** This is a decision-based black-box attack that starts from querying a large adversarial perturbation and then seeks to reduce the perturbation while staying adversarial [4]. It only requires the final class prediction of the model.

– **Hop Skip Jump Attack (HSJ):** A powerful black-box attack that only requires the final class prediction of the model [10]. And it is an advanced version of the boundary attack, requiring significantly fewer model queries than Boundary Attack.

3 Experiments

3.1 Data Set Preparation

We used the PhysioNet MIT-BIH Arrhythmia dataset for our experiment [28]. We divided the dataset into four categories, **N** [Normal beat, Left and right bundle branch block beats, Atrial and Nodal escape beat], **S** [Atrial premature beat, Aberrated atrial, Supraventricular and Nodal premature beat], **V** [Premature ventricular contraction, Ventricular escape beat], and **F** [Fusion of the ventricular and regular beat]. We first find the R-peak for every signal, use a sampling rate of 280 centering on R-peak, and then normalize the amplitude between $[0, 1]$. In the benchmarking, we combine and split the samples into 80% and 20% sets of train and test data. So we end up having train samples of N: 69958, S: 4766, V: 1965, F:617, and test samples of N: 17571, S: 1126, V: 473, and F: 157. To overcome the lack of minority class samples, we use Synthetic Minority Over-sampling Technique (SMOTE) [8] to increase the number of samples for S, V, and F to 10,000 each. We do not use SMOTE on test data. Next, we use the train and test ECG signals to create the six types of adversarial attacked ECGs (using Adversarial Robustness toolbox [29]). So we end up having same number attacked ECGs as non-attacked ones for each adversarial attacks. Next, we combine the original and adversarial ECGs to create our whole training dataset, $E_x + E_{xadv} = E'_x$ (Fig. 1). We use 5-fold cross validation and select the model with the best validation score.

We also benchmark on PTB Diagnostic ECG Database [3], which consists of Normal and Myocardial Infraction beats. For each category, we use 10,000 samples, meaning we end up having 20,000 ECGs in total. We split them into 80% training and 20% test data. In similar manner to MITBH, we apply six adversarial attacks on these ECG signals. For training we end up having 32,000 (16,000 non-attacked and 16,0000 attacked) signals for each attack types. We use the same 5-fold cross-validation method.

3.2 Hyper-parameters

We chose $\lambda_{atk} = 10$ (Eq. 1), $\lambda_{ary} = 10$ (Eq. 2), and $\lambda_{mse} = 1$ (Eq. 3), to give more weight to classification losses than to adversarial loss. We give more weight to attacked signals than non-attacked ones by using $\kappa = [1, 1.05]$ (Eq. 1). We used Adam optimizer [21] with a learning rate of $\alpha = 0.0001$, $\beta_1 = 0.5$ and $\beta_2 = 0.999$. We used Tensorflow 2.0 to train the model with batch size, $b = 128$ for 100 epochs taking 4 h to train on NVIDIA P100 GPU. We initialized the noise vector, z with float values between $[0, 1]$. Code repository is provided in this link.

Table 1. MIT-BIH dataset : Comparison of architectures trained and evaluated on **non-attacked/attacked** ECGs for normal and three arrhythmia beat classification.

	Model	Accuracy	N		S		V		F	
			Sensitivity	Specificity	Sensitivity	Specificity	Sensitivity	Specificity	Sensitivity	Specificity
No attack	**Proposed method**	**99.2**	**98.8**	95.2	83.7	**99.8**	97.9	**99.7**	92.4	99.3
	Shaker et al. [30]	98.6	97.4	**98.1**	**93.0**	98.7	**99.2**	99.0	87.2	**99.6**
	Kachuee et al. [20]	98.1	96.8	94.5	88.7	97.6	92.5	99.6	90.4	99.3
	Acharya et al. [1]	96.4	92.8	96.2	86.2	97.0	95.9	98.8	**94.2**	97.1
FGSM	**Proposed method**	**98.7**	**97.9**	**95.0**	**82.6**	**99.2**	**99.2**	98.7	73.2	**99.8**
	Shaker et al. [30]	92.6	84.7	93.3	81.8	89.9	96.5	95.6	57.9	98.7
	Kachuee et al. [20]	86.5	73.1	82.8	68.9	83.4	73.7	97.3	**82.8**	93.2
	Acharya et al. [1]	77.2	53.3	87.9	65.7	74.1	66.2	92.3	65.6	87.9
BIM	**Proposed method**	**98.1**	**97.1**	**91.2**	**76.1**	**98.6**	95.0	**99.4**	84.1	98.9
	Shaker et al. [30]	96.2	93.1	90.1	69.1	98.2	**97.6**	94.9	55.4	**99.8**
	Kachuee et al. [20]	85.6	70.6	90.4	67.4	90.5	83.6	92.3	82.1	88.5
	Acharya et al. [1]	76.9	54.4	87.5	49.0	88.2	42.1	91.9	**87.8**	73.8
PGD	**Proposed method**	**98.4**	**97.0**	**96.1**	**89.0**	**98.0**	97.5	**99.3**	**88.5**	**99.6**
	Shaker et al. [30]	96.5	93.4	92.8	81.3	97.9	94.5	98.2	82.8	97.4
	Kachuee et al. [20]	87.2	74.0	86.9	66.3	87.6	84.7	91.8	65.6	95.2
	Acharya et al. [1]	77.2	54.0	88.8	54.1	91.3	57.8	82.0	66.2	80.6
CW	**Proposed method**	**98.8**	**97.8**	**97.0**	**91.1**	**98.8**	**98.3**	**99.5**	**91.0**	99.5
	Shaker et al. [30]	95.4	90.8	96.0	84.7	97.0	97.8	94.1	72.6	**99.7**
	Kachuee et al. [20]	91.9	84.5	83.3	74.4	89.3	79.7	99.3	61.1	96.3
	Acharya et al. [1]	81.2	61.8	89.1	64.6	81.5	67.7	94.1	83.4	86.8
DBB	**Proposed method**	**93.0**	**85.8**	**94.9**	**84.4**	**96.1**	**91.3**	**96.2**	**84.1**	**93.9**
	Shaker et al. [30]	90.1	80.6	86.7	65.1	94.2	79.4	94.9	83.4	91.7
	Kachuee et al. [20]	79.7	57.9	86.4	78.0	69.3	70.9	96.6	82.1	93.6
	Acharya et al. [1]	81.9	62.6	85.8	68.1	75.6	77.0	95.8	82.8	92.7
HSJ	**Proposed method**	**71.9**	**44.8**	**68.2**	**34.6**	78.6	35.7	**82.6**	32.4	83.8
	Shaker et al. [30]	70.5	41.2	67.4	33.0	77.1	**40.4**	81.1	37.5	83.4
	Kachuee et al. [20]	68.6	39.3	65.8	21.3	82.5	10.3	94.5	**43.9**	62.2
	Acharya et al. [1]	68.4	37.6	70.0	32.3	57.4	23.6	90.4	20.3	**90.0**

3.3 Quantitative Evaluation

We perform the quantitative evaluation by comparing our model with other state-of-the-art architectures [1,20,30] on both attacked and non-attacked data from MITBH and PTB datasets. In the first experiment, we use either only normal or adversarial attacked test data (19,327 and 4,000 for MITBH and PTB) for benchmarking the models on normal/abnormal beat classification, which is illustrated in Table 1 and Table 2. We train all the models on their respective attacked and non-attacked training samples for a fair comparison. For metrics, we use Accuracy, Sensitivity, and Specificity. We can see that for **'No Attack'**, all models achieve comparatively good results. However, for each distinct attack, the results worsen for other models compared to ours. The architecture in [1,20,30] utilizes 1D Convolution based architecture. Out of these models, Shaker et al. [30] adopt DC-GAN, a generative network for adversarial signal generation. However, their classification architecture is trained separately, and they provide results only on real ECG signals. One reason for their model's good performance for the no-attack scenario is training with GAN-generated adversarial samples, which helps to learn out-of-distribution signals. Moreover, the two 1D CNN architectures achieve better sensitivity for minority category **F** for FGSM, BIM, and HSJ attacks. Similarly, our model's performance on the minority category **F** is best for PGD, CW, and DBB attacks and second best for FGSM and BIM. Our model performs poorly against HSJ attacks because the signals have too much high noise and no clear pattern, as illustrated in Fig. 3. Besides that, our architecture's overall performance is more robust against adversarial attacks for classifying arrhythmia and myocardial infractions, as shown in Table 2.

Table 2. PTB dataset : Comparison of architectures trained and evaluated on **non-attacked/attacked** ECGs for normal and myocardial infarction beat classification.

	Methods	No Attack	FGSM	BIM	PGD	CW	DBB	HSJ
Accuracy	**Proposed method**	**99.5**	**99.4**	**99.6**	**99.6**	**99.5**	93.1	71.8
	Shaker et al. [30]	98.0	98.6	95.8	96.4	98.3	91.4	70.2
	Kachuee et al. [20]	95.2	97.1	94.4	92.2	91.3	88.6	56.5
	Acharya et al. [1]	79.8	84.1	83.2	84.1	80.9	77.4	54.7
Sensitivity	**Proposed method**	**99.3**	**99.2**	**99.6**	**99.7**	**99.2**	92.6	79.8
	Shaker et al. [30]	96.7	98.3	92.1	94.8	98.0	91.5	83.7
	Kachuee et al. [20]	98.3	96.0	95.9	92.1	95.4	86.7	85.5
	Acharya et al. [1]	82.1	93.1	93.4	90.6	90.3	88.5	**90.7**
Specificity	**Proposed method**	**99.7**	**99.5**	**99.7**	**99.5**	**99.7**	93.7	64.0
	Shaker et al. [30]	99.3	98.9	99.4	98.0	98.7	91.2	56.8
	Kachuee et al. [20]	92.1	98.2	93.0	92.2	87.3	90.3	28.1
	Acharya et al. [1]	77.7	75.3	73.2	77.8	71.6	66.5	19.4

Table 3. Generator's performance: Similarity of adversarial and attacked/non-attacked signals.

	MITBIH				PTB			
	Mean-squared-error	Structural similarity	Cross-corelation coefficiet	Normalized RMSE	Mean-squared-error	Structural similarity	Cross-corelation coefficient	Normalized RMSE
No attack	0.0129	99.90	99.86	3.487e−5	0.0184	99.87	99.93	8.152e−5
FGSM	0.0117	99.81	99.89	2.890e−5	0.0001	99.84	99.89	0.02391
BIM	0.0134	99.80	99.86	3.737e−5	0.0155	99.91	99.95	5.769e−5
PGD	0.0122	99.84	99.89	3.115e−5	0.0179	99.88	99.92	7.722e−5
CW	0.0065	99.95	99.97	9.038e−6	0.0188	99.87	99.97	8.498e−5
DBB	0.0002	99.00	99.39	0.03159	0.0007	99.19	99.29	0.05532
HSJ	0.0003	99.42	99.45	0.0393	0.0003	99.51	99.60	0.03872

3.4 Qualitative Evaluation

For finding the similarity between real and synthesized attacked/non-attacked ECG signals, we benchmarked generated adversarial signals using four different metrics, i) Mean Squared Error (MSE), ii) Structural Similarity (SSIM), iii) Cross-correlation coefficient, and iv) Normalized Mean Squared Error (NRMSE). In Table 3, We use both attacked and non-attacked signals from the test set. We score SSIM of 99.90%, 99.81% (FGSM), 99.80% (BIM), 99.84% (PGD), 99.95% (CW), 99.00% (DBB) and 99.43% (DBB) for MITBH Dataset. On the other hand we achieve SSIM of 99.87% (No Attack), 99.84% (FGSM), 99.91% (BIM), 99.84% (PGD), 99.87% (CW), 99.19% (DBB) and 99.51% (DBB) for PTB Dataset. As for cross-correlation, MSE, and NRMSE, our model generates quite realistic signals with minimal error.

4   Conclusions and Future Work

This paper presents ECG-ATK-GAN, a novel conditional Generative Adversarial Network for accurately predicting different types of arrhythmia from both regular and adversarially attacked ECGs. In addition, our architecture incorporates a new class-weighted categorical objective function for capturing out-of-distribution signals and robustly discerning class-specific features corrupted by adversarial perturbations. We provided an extensive benchmark on two publicly available datasets to prove the robustness of our proposed architecture. One future direction is to improve our architecture by defending against other types of adversarial attacks.

Prospect of Application: Detecting arrhythmia accurately and robustly in real-time will pave the way for better patient care and disease monitoring. In addition, insurance companies, contractors, partners, and many stakeholders will financially benefit from a trusted cardiac arrhythmia diagnostic system that is robust against adversarial attacks. This system can also help identify new attack types by distinguishing signal anomalies.

References

1. Acharya, U.R., et al.: A deep convolutional neural network model to classify heartbeats. Comput. Biol. Med. **89**, 389–396 (2017)
2. Ahmad, Z., Tabassum, A., Guan, L., Khan, N.: Ecg heart-beat classification using multi-modal image fusion. In: ICASSP 2021–2021 IEEE International Conference on Acoustics, Speech and Signal Processing (ICASSP), pp. 1330–1334. IEEE (2021)
3. Bousseljot, R., Kreiseler, D., Schnabel, A.: Nutzung der ekg-signaldatenbank cardiodat der ptb über das internet. Biomedical Engineering/Biomedizinische Technik (1995)
4. Brendel, W., Rauber, J., Bethge, M.: Decision-based adversarial attacks: reliable attacks against black-box machine learning models. arXiv preprint arXiv:1712.04248 (2017)
5. Carlini, N., Wagner, D.: Towards evaluating the robustness of neural networks. In: 2017 IEEE Symposium on Security and Privacy (SP), pp. 39–57. IEEE (2017)
6. Chakraborty, A., Alam, M., Dey, V., Chattopadhyay, A., Mukhopadhyay, D.: Adversarial attacks and defences: a survey. arXiv preprint arXiv:1810.00069 (2018)
7. Chakraborty, A., Alam, M., Dey, V., Chattopadhyay, A., Mukhopadhyay, D.: A survey on adversarial attacks and defences. CAAI Trans. Intell. Technol. **6**(1), 25–45 (2021)
8. Chawla, N.V., Bowyer, K.W., Hall, L.O., Kegelmeyer, W.P.: Smote: synthetic minority over-sampling technique. J. Artif. Intell. Res. **16**, 321–357 (2002)
9. Chen, H., Huang, C., Huang, Q., Zhang, Q., Wang, W.: Ecgadv: generating adversarial electrocardiogram to misguide arrhythmia classification system. In: Proceedings of the AAAI Conference on Artificial Intelligence, vol. 34, pp. 3446–3453 (2020)

10. Chen, J., Jordan, M.I., Wainwright, M.J.: Hopskipjumpattack: a query-efficient decision-based attack. In: 2020 IEEE Symposium on Security and Privacy (SP), pp. 1277–1294. IEEE (2020)

11. Faziludeen, S., Sabiq, P.: Ecg beat classification using wavelets and svm. In: 2013 IEEE Conference on Information & Communication Technologies, pp. 815–818. IEEE (2013)

12. Finlayson, S.G., Bowers, J.D., Ito, J., Zittrain, J.L., Beam, A.L., Kohane, I.S.: Adversarial attacks on medical machine learning. Science 363(6433), 1287–1289 (2019)

13. Golany, T., Freedman, D., Radinsky, K.: Ecg ode-gan: learning ordinary differential equations of ecg dynamics via generative adversarial learning. In: Proceedings of the AAAI Conference on Artificial Intelligence, vol. 35, pp. 134–141 (2021)

14. Golany, T., Radinsky, K.: Pgans: Personalized generative adversarial networks for ecg synthesis to improve patient-specific deep ecg classification. In: Proceedings of the AAAI Conference on Artificial Intelligence, vol. 33, pp. 557–564 (2019)

15. Golany, T., Radinsky, K., Freedman, D.: Simgans: simulator-based generative adversarial networks for ecg synthesis to improve deep ecg classification. In: International Conference on Machine Learning, pp. 3597–3606. PMLR (2020)

16. Goodfellow, I.J., Shlens, J., Szegedy, C.: Explaining and harnessing adversarial examples. arXiv preprint arXiv:1412.6572 (2014)

17. Han, X., Hu, Y., Foschini, L., Chinitz, L., Jankelson, L., Ranganath, R.: Deep learning models for electrocardiograms are susceptible to adversarial attack. Nat. Med. 26(3), 360–363 (2020)

18. Hossain, K.F., et al.: Ecg-adv-gan: detecting ecg adversarial examples with conditional generative adversarial networks. In: 2021 20th IEEE International Conference on Machine Learning and Applications (ICMLA), pp. 50–56. IEEE (2021)

19. Jambukia, S.H., Dabhi, V.K., Prajapati, H.B.: Classification of ecg signals using machine learning techniques: a survey. In: 2015 International Conference on Advances in Computer Engineering and Applications, pp. 714–721. IEEE (2015)

20. Kachuee, M., Fazeli, S., Sarrafzadeh, M.: Ecg heartbeat classification: a deep transferable representation. In: 2018 IEEE International Conference on Healthcare Informatics (ICHI), pp. 443–444. IEEE (2018)

21. Kingma, D.P., Ba, J.: Adam: a method for stochastic optimization. arXiv preprint arXiv:1412.6980 (2014)

22. Kurakin, A., Goodfellow, I., Bengio, S., et al.: Adversarial examples in the physical world (2016)

23. Lam, J., Quan, P., Xu, J., Jeyakumar, J.V., Srivastava, M.: Hard-label black-box adversarial attack on deep electrocardiogram classifier. In: Proceedings of the 1st ACM International Workshop on Security and Safety for Intelligent Cyber-Physical Systems, pp. 6–12 (2020)

24. Madry, A., Makelov, A., Schmidt, L., Tsipras, D., Vladu, A.: Towards deep learning models resistant to adversarial attacks. arXiv preprint arXiv:1706.06083 (2017)

25. Mahajan, R., Kamaleswaran, R., Howe, J.A., Akbilgic, O.: Cardiac rhythm classification from a short single lead ecg recording via random forest. In: 2017 Computing in Cardiology (CinC), pp. 1–4. IEEE (2017)

26. Mao, X., Li, Q., Xie, H., Lau, R.Y., Wang, Z., Paul Smolley, S.: Least squares generative adversarial networks. In: Proceedings of the IEEE International Conference on Computer Vision, pp. 2794–2802 (2017)

27. Medtronic: Linq ii, cardiac monitors. https://www.medtronic.com/us-en/healthcare-professionals/products/cardiac-rhythm/cardiac-monitors/linq-ii.html

28. Moody, G.B., Mark, R.G.: The impact of the mit-bih arrhythmia database. IEEE Eng. Med. Biol. Mag. 20(3), 45–50 (2001)

29. Nicolae, M.I., et al.: Adversarial robustness toolbox v1.2.0. CoRR 1807.01069 (2018). https://arxiv.org/pdf/1807.01069

30. Shaker, A.M., Tantawi, M., Shedeed, H.A., Tolba, M.F.: Generalization of convolutional neural networks for ecg classification using generative adversarial networks. IEEE Access **8**, 35592–35605 (2020)
31. iRhythm technologies: how could using ai impact cardiology? https://www.irhythmtech.com/providers/evidence/ai
32. Wang, B., Liu, C., Hu, C., Liu, X., Cao, J.: Arrhythmia classification with heartbeat-aware transformer. In: ICASSP 2021–2021 IEEE International Conference on Acoustics, Speech and Signal Processing (ICASSP), pp. 1025–1029 (2021)
33. Yu, F., Koltun, V.: Multi-scale context aggregation by dilated convolutions. arXiv preprint arXiv:1511.07122 (2015)

CADIA: A Success Story in Breast Cancer Diagnosis with Digital Pathology and AI Image Analysis

María Jesús García-González[1][(✉)], Rodrigo Cilla Ugarte[1],
Blanca Zufiria Gerbolés[1], Kristin May Rebescher[1], Esther Albertín Marco[3],
Iván Lalaguna[3], Javier García Navas[4], Maria Blanca Cimadevila Alvarez[4],
Iván Macía Oliver[1,2], Karen López-Linares Román[1,2],
and Valery Naranjo Ornedo[5]

[1] Vicomtech, Basque Research and Technology Alliance, San Sebastián, Spain
mjgarcia@vicomtech.org
[2] Biodonostia Health Research Institute, San Sebastián, Spain
[3] Instrumentación y Componentes S.A., Inycom, Zaragoza, Spain
[4] Servicio Gallego de Salud, Galicia, Spain
[5] Universitat Politècnica de València, Valencia, Spain

Abstract. The rise of Digital Pathology during the past few years is leading to the digitisation of the pathology field; the widespread use of Whole Slide Images (WSI) and the digitisation of the diagnostic process have allowed the introduction of AI-based methods to aid some parts of the process. In this framework, the CADIA project was raised in response to the Galician healthcare system digitisation needs. CADIA aims to develop an AI-based medical image analysis solution for the diagnosis of several pathologies and its demonstration on breast cancer diagnosis from WSIs. In this paper, we describe the development of CADIA, from the capture of requirements to the deployment and integration of the solution into the healthcare system infrastructure. We describe the opportunities, challenges and lessons learned during the project development.

Keywords: Digital Pathology · Whole Slide Images · Breast cancer diagnosis

1 Introduction

The interpretation of medical images is a subjective cognitive process that requires experience and takes a considerable amount of time to perform it correctly. The fatigue and monotony of the process may cause a decrease in the detection rates of suspicious lesions and may lower reproducibility in human assessments. Hence, developing image-based computer-aided diagnosis (CAD) systems becomes essential to assist clinicians in their work. Advances in deep learning for medical imaging, along with dedicated hardware and new training,

S. Wu et al. (Eds.): AMAI 2022, LNCS 13540, pp. 79–87, 2022.
https://doi.org/10.1007/978-3-031-17721-7_9

annotation, and adaptation strategies have resulted in a set of artificial intelligence (AI) models that achieve unprecedented results in tasks such as detection, diagnosis or treatment selection.

Lately, pathology is advancing in digitisation with the rise of Digital Pathology (DP). There are several definitions for DP, all including the digitisation of the pathology sample, resulting in a Whole Slide Image (WSI). Many studies have evaluated the performance of using WSI compared to the standard process of histological diagnosis and have proven its non-inferiority [1]. Thus, DP opens up new opportunities for telepathology or AI-based computational pathology tools. Apart from these opportunities and benefits, DP also forces the provision of infrastructure for the management and storage of digital samples, integration with the Laboratory Information System (LIS), and visualisation tools.

In 2019, the Galician Healthcare System (SERGAS) proposed CADIA, currently in its last phases, as a public innovation procurement project. It aimed at developing an AI-based medical image analysis solution for the diagnosis of several pathologies. For the past two years, the temporary business association (TBA) formed by Vicomtech and Inycom has been working on developing the required system and demonstrating its use for breast cancer diagnosis from WSIs. The multidisciplinary team formed by pathologists, computer scientists and researchers working closely together has led to the success of the project, for which a pilot is being carried out to prove the validity of the proposed solution in several Galician hospitals.

This paper aims at describing the project development process and achieved results, including the main challenges, lessons learned and milestones.

2   Methods

This section summarizes the steps followed during the project development, which are: 1) analysis of the current breast cancer diagnosis process at SERGAS, to identify the needs and define the requirements for data collection and AI model development, 2) data gathering, which comprises sample selection, anonymisation, digitalisation and annotation, and 3) WSI-based AI model development, deployment and integration.

2.1   Starting Point Analysis and Functional Requirement Collection

Together with the clinicians and healthcare administrators, we performed an analysis of the breast cancer diagnosis process at SERGAS. A breast cancer patient can arrive at the diagnosis unit from a screening program or due to the presence of signs or symptoms of the disease. In both cases, additional imaging tests are performed at the diagnostic unit and if the physician suspects breast cancer, a biopsy is performed to confirm the diagnosis.

Once the biopsy arrives at the pathology laboratory, it is fixed, sectioned, and stained with Hematoxylin and Eosin (H&E). The pathologist performs a first surface-level look at the H&E slide to retrieve morphological information (histologic type and histologic grade) about the tumour. To complete the diagnosis and decide the proper treatment, a protocol defines the IHC-stains that should be requested to enhance specific tumour features according to the histological type. A comprehensive microscopic analysis is again performed with all the information to make the final diagnostic decision.

This process constitutes the conventional analogical process, but it is now increasingly common to have some parts of the process digitised, fitting in the concept of DP. The microscope is substituted or complemented by a slide scanner and a screen, converting the samples into WSIs. The use of these images allows proposing AI tools to support multiple tasks in the diagnostic process. Concretely, within the project 3 tasks were defined after conversations with pathologists, which determined the type of models and the requirements for CADIA.

The first task consisted of using AI to provide a second opinion on histological subtyping, attempting to reduce the false-negative rate. The second task aimed at automating the request for the additional IHC slides directly from the H&E slide, to reduce the time to diagnosis. Finally, a third task to evaluate the histological grade of the tumour was proposed.

This evaluation led us to propose the development of three AI models, to support each task, respectively: 1) slide-level classifier of the histological subtype, 2) Slide-level classifier to provide the most invasive tumor type in the sample, and 3) region-level classifier to perform the sample's histological grading.

Finally, in order to fully exploit model functionalities and facilitate their adoption, models should work with imaging studies following the DICOM format and they must be deployed into a solution that ensures the storage of WSIs, the management of working orders and the visualisation of the model's inputs and outputs.

2.2 Sample Selection and Collection

A database containing digitised samples is essential for model training and validation.

The physicians selected retrospective representative physical samples for the project considering the incidence of the most common breast cancer histologic subtypes. In particular, they retrieved 1925 diagnostic breast cancer biopsy H&E-stained slides from the daily routine of the pathology laboratory of 6 different hospitals in the Galician healthcare system. In particular, 551 Fibroadenoma samples, 395 Invasive lobular carcinoma samples, 636 Invasive ductal carcinoma samples, and 343 Ductal carcinoma in situ samples were retrieved.

All these samples were transferred from their origin to the location where the scanner was deployed in order to carry out the digitisation. They pseudoanonymised all samples relabelling their patient IDs to new ones generated for the project and removing all patient-related information.

The employed equipment for digitalisation was a VENTANA DP 200 slide scanner (Roche Diagnostics, Rotkreuz, Switzerland), which is DICOM conformant, and generates many small high-resolution image tiles from the tissue slide and assembles them to make a full image of the histological section [1]; the digital images were adquired with 40x magnification. It automatically generates StudyInstanceUIDs and SeriesInstancesUIDs, and also allows filling some additional tags from the DICOM header. We included the generated pseudo-anonymized ids as accession numbers. Finally, we generated a private DICOM tag to fill with the already-known final histological classification extracted from the pathological reports, which is codified following the SnomedCT standard at Sergas.

Once DICOM WSIs were generated with the appropriate headers, all imaging studies were uploaded and stored in a Picture Archiving and Communication System (PACS) deployed for the project at Sergas. Specifically, we used Orthanc [2] to save and later retrieve the images.

2.3 Digital Image Annotation

To generate the training database, it is essential to capture pathologists' knowledge associated with breast cancer diagnosis to use it as ground truth during model training and validation. For the development of the model that determines the histological type, the required ground truth annotation was already accessible from the DICOM header, as explained in Sect. 2.2. However, for histological grade determination, gathering values for tubularity and pleomorphism grades from pathologists was required.

For that, we adapted and deployed a web-based annotation tool based on the Open Health Imaging Foundation (OHIF) open-source viewer [3]. We connected the annotation tool with the deployed Orthanc PACS to retrieve the images and we also integrated it with Sergas' access control system to ensure the annotators' access and use of the tool.

Clinicians were asked to contour representative regions of each histological type of breast cancer in the WSI and annotate the tubular and pleomorphism grades for each region. These annotations were saved associated with the StudyInstanceUID of the corresponding WSI. An overview of the annotation tool is shown in Fig. 1 (a).

A total of 15 pathologists coming from different hospitals participated in the annotation work. Three pathologists annotated each sample in order to reduce the inter-annotator variability, so each pathologist annotated approximately 520 WSIs.

2.4 Model Development

To develop the models, the digital samples and the annotations were transferred from the PACS deployed at Sergas to another PACS deployed at the TBAs premises. We deployed a model training infrastructure to ensure the models development process's quality to guarantee the traceability of the data and the experiments using open-source tools such as git (for code version control), DVC (for data version control) and MLFlow (for experiment's parameters and metrics tracking).

Then, we divided the 1925 samples that make up the database into train and test sets to perform the experiments. The test set counts with 10% of the samples, which were retrieved considering the hospital they came from; 8 examples for each hospital and each class defines the test set, equaling 168. The remaining 1757 examples comprised the train set for all the models.

We carried out the experiments using a cross-validation strategy and performed a statistical analysis to determine the average models' sensibility (recall, True Positive Rate-TPR), f1-score, and specificity (True Negative Rate-TNR).

Task 1: Histological Grading. We developed a deep learning model that leverages the Multiple Instance Learning (MIL) assumptions.

According to MIL terminology, a training bag is made up of multiple instances, but each instance's ground truth is unknown. Using this approach with WSIs means that each slide is a bag, and the tiles composing it are the instances. MIL considers that the instances' class might differ from the bag class, which perfectly fits with histopathological images due to the tissue heterogeneity found within the same slide. This way of working with WSIs is also computationally efficient. Thus, we trained a model using WSI patches and the known histological subtype of the sample as ground truth. These patches correspond to the high-resolution image tiles that make up the WSI [4].

The model was built with two architectures working together: a feature extractor and a classifier. The feature extractor takes the images as input and outputs a feature vector summarizing the information within the image; then, the features of all individual tiles of the WSI are aggregated and fed into the classifier, yielding the final histologic type.

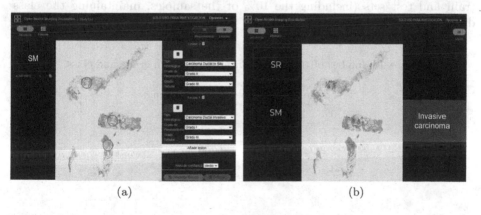

(a)   (b)

Fig. 1. (a) example of an annotation performed with the CADIA annotation tool, and (b) visualisation of the analysis result of a DICOM WSI with CADIA.

Task 2: Automatically Requesting IHC. Based on the analysis of the protocol for requesting extra IHC stainings for a sample, a model that classifies the invasiveness of the tumour in the samples is required: benign samples do not require further IHC analysis, and both in situ and invasive samples require IHC stains to make the final diagnostic decision, which is different between each group. Hence, we grouped the training examples into benign-fibroadenomas, in situ and invasive cases.

We conducted multiple experiments to determine the proper deep learning model architecture, data preprocessing method, database balance strategy and MIL aggregation method. Unlike the model for task 1, in task 2 we chased for a model able to process not only one of the previously considered histological subtypes, so a MIL multi-task classification model was developed. With it, all tissue types present in the sample are predicted, and the one that leads to diagnosis is selected as the final classification; if there are no signs of tumour, the model is able to return the class "not known".

Task 3: Pleomorphism and Tubularity Grading. Currently, a model that addresses the third task of the project, i.e. the prediction of the tubular and pleomorphism grades, is being developed to be integrated into CADIA.

For that, first, we transform the pathologists' manual annotations into training samples as follows: 1) obtain the pixel coordinates of the manual annotations, 2) retrieval of the corresponding tiles of the WSIs, and 3) label the tiles with the aggregated information of the three annotators using majority voting.

For the non-cancer samples, the tubular and pleomorphism grades are not provided, so we exclude Fibroadenoma samples for this model. The final number of training images (tiles) is displayed in Table 1. We split the dataset into train and test sets (including the 10% of the samples, maintaining the class distribution).

Table 1. Number of tiles in the database for each grade and class.

Grade	Tubularity	Pleomorphism
0	23754	582
1	5148	20550
2	17264	66766
3	53468	11736

A classification model that simultaneously predicts both grades, taking advantage of the biological relationship they have, is proposed. The model architecture has two independent classifiers, one for each grade, but they share the feature extractor.

To make a prediction, the model first processes all tiles that make up a WSI and performs the tubular and pleomorphism grading for each input tile. A heatmap is constructed for each grade by re-assembling the WSI, highlighting areas of interest in the image.

It is important to emphasise that this model is still under development, and thus, further experiments to get to the proper model architecture and pre/post-processing schemes will be performed.

2.5 Model Deployment and Integration

As an overview, tasks 1 and 2 models input a DICOM WSI and return the classification of the tumour in the sample. To ensure the visualisation and storage of the results provided by AI models, we encoded the output classification in a DICOM Structured Report (DICOM SR) file format, linked with the DICOM WSI by the StudyInstanceUID.

We have developed and integrated a web application, with access control systems and the models deployed. The CADIA application allows inspecting the status of the digital studies stored in the PACS, which may be one of the following: Pending, Analysing, or Analysed. When a pathologist launches the analysis of a sample, the application reads the WSI, feeds it into the model and stores the output Dicom SR back to the PACS. The resulting DICOM SR and the WSI can be visualised together in the application. An example of the CADIA solution results visualisation is depicted in Fig. 1 (b).

3   Results

During the development of CADIA, multiple milestones have been achieved. As a result of sample collection and annotation, a digital databank has been built, containing 1925 digitized breast cancer biopsies in DICOM WSI format.

We have successfully performed a proof of concept of an AI-driven DP work-flow at Sergas, achieved thanks to the implementation of the CADIA solution. CADIA includes digital image storage and a web-based application that enables to launch AI analyses and visualise the results.

We have performed a two-level evaluation of the solution: 1) quantitative analysis of the AI models' performance, and 2) qualitative evaluation.

Regarding the quantitative analysis, Table 2 shows the average performance of the developed models, considering the model for Task 3 is still ongoing

The qualitative evaluation of CADIA was performed by the collection of three participant pathologists' feedback using questionnaries that addressed other less technical aspects, such as usability, ease of use, and utility. The general opinion was that the developed tool is valid, agile and easy to use.

Finally, the model addressing task 2 is currently being clinically validated with new samples from some Galician hospitals' daily diagnostic process in a pilot study to prove the validity of the proposed solution in a close to real-world environment.

Table 2. True negative rate (TNR), true positive rate (TPR) and F1-score for AI models. DCIS: ductal carcinoma in-situ. IVDC: invasive ductal carcinoma. LC: lobulillar carcinoma. FD: fibroadenoma. IS: in-situ. IV: invasive. Tub: tubularity. Pleo: pleomorphism.

	Task 1					Task 2				Task 3		
	DCIS	IVDC	LC	FD	Mean	FD	IS	IV	Mean	Tub	Pleo	Mean
TNR	0.97	0.97	0.91	1.00	0.96	1	0.94	0.98	0.97	0.56	0.78	0.65
TPR	0.88	0.83	0.90	0.94	0.89	1	0.94	0.91	0.95	0.88	0.93	0.90
F1-score	0.88	0.88	0.82	0.97	0.89	1	0.87	0.94	0.94	–	–	–

4   Conclusions and Future Perspectives

This paper describes the development and results of the CADIA project, which aimed to provide a solution for the detection of several pathologies using image analysis and AI.

We have successfully developed a proof of concept introducing DP and AI into the breast cancer diagnostic process. Our project has digitised biological samples and developed a space to store and visualise these images in order to later execute our AI algorithms to aid in the current diagnostic process. The pilot study that is going to be performed to clinically validate CADIA will lay the foundation for the DP workflow in the Galician Healthcare system, facilitating the inclusion of additional AI-based models to address other tissue and tumour types.

Furthermore, CADIA yields the histological type of breast cancer from a WSI with high precision and allows a more objective grading of pleomorphism and tubularity. The current analogical process requires that the pathologist views the same slides multiple times, generating delays in the diagnostic process. Not only are there operational consequences, but there are also extensive effects on the patients and their emotional wellbeing. With our CADIA model, the healthcare system can accelerate the "time-to-diagnosis" by automatically requesting the additional IHC stainings needed to determine the final diagnostic decision, resulting in the reduction of the patient's wait time for receiving a potentially life-changing diagnosis.

One of the main issues to overcome during the project's development has been ensuring the quality control of every aspect developed. Considerable effort was taken to ensure that all experiments and testing carried out were properly documented, tracked, and verisoned before the ultimate integration into the healthcare system infrastructure.

The key to CADIA's success has been the commitment from and close collaboration with clinicians from the Galician Health System to fully understand the needs and potential usefulness of the solution during development.

Prospect of Application: Any innovation that reduces the time and resources required to properly diagnose and provide patients with the optimal treatment is essential. CADIA provides a tumor classification and recommendation for further staining of a sample when needed. A pathologist will only need to look at a slide once and will have all the information they need to make an accurate diagnosis.

Acknowledgements. This work has been partially funded by FEDER "Una manera de hacer Europa". The project CADIA (DG-SER1-19-003) has been developed under the Codigo100 Public Procurement and Innovation Programme by the Galician Healthcare System - Servizo Galego de Saúde (SERGAS) co-funded by the European Regional Development Fund (ERDF).

We would like to acknowledge the work done by the pathologists at Ferrol, Lugo, Ourense, Pontevedra, Santiago, and Vigo health service areas from the Galician Healthcare System.

References

1. Yagi, Y., Gilbertson, J.R.: Digital imaging in pathology: the case for standardization. J. Telemed. Telecare **11**(3), 109–16 (2005). https://doi.org/10.1258/1357633053688705
2. Jodogne, S.: The orthanc ecosystem for medical imaging. J. Digit. Imaging **31**(3), 341–352 (2018). https://doi.org/10.1007/s10278-018-0082-y
3. Ziegler, E., et al.: Open health imaging foundation viewer: an extensible open-source framework for building web-based imaging applications to support cancer research. JCO Clin. Cancer Inform. **4**, 336–345 (2020). https://doi.org/10.1200/CCI.19.00131
4. Amores, J.: Multiple instance classification: review, taxonomy and comparative study. Artif. Intell. **201**, 81–105 (2013). https://doi.org/10.1016/j.artint.2013.06.003

Was that so Hard? Estimating Human Classification Difficulty

Morten Rieger Hannemose[1]([⊠]), Josefine Vilsbøll Sundgaard[1],
Niels Kvorning Ternov[2], Rasmus R. Paulsen[1],
and Anders Nymark Christensen[1]

[1] Department of Applied Mathematics and Computer Science,
Technical University of Denmark, Kgs. Lyngby, Denmark
`mohan@dtu.dk`
[2] Department of Plastic Surgery, Copenhagen University,
Herlev and Gentofte Hospital, Copenhagen, Denmark

Abstract. When doctors are trained to diagnose a specific disease, they learn faster when presented with cases in order of increasing difficulty. This creates the need for automatically estimating how difficult it is for doctors to classify a given case. In this paper, we introduce methods for estimating how hard it is for a doctor to diagnose a case represented by a medical image, both when ground truth difficulties are available for training, and when they are not. Our methods are based on embeddings obtained with deep metric learning. Additionally, we introduce a practical method for obtaining ground truth human difficulty for each image case in a dataset using self-assessed certainty. We apply our methods to two different medical datasets, achieving high Kendall rank correlation coefficients on both, showing that we outperform existing methods by a large margin on our problem and data.

Keywords: Difficulty estimation · Deep metric learning · Human classification

1 Introduction

When doctors diagnose patients, not all cases have the same diagnostic difficulty. A case can be very easy if there are clear diagnostic signs. However, if the typical signs are missing or give conflicting information, a doctor will be more likely to assign an incorrect diagnosis. When doctors are trained to diagnose certain diseases, they learn faster when starting with easy cases and then gradually progressing to harder cases [22]. Knowing how hard each case is to classify is thus useful in an educational context. This concept is well-known in pedagogy [9] and applies to many other areas such as language training, mathematics, etc.

In this paper, we present a novel approach for estimating human classification difficulty using deep metric learning. In deep metric learning, high-dimensional data (in our case, images) are mapped to a lower-dimensional

---

M. R. Hannemose and J. V. Sundgaard—These authors contributed equally.

S. Wu et al. (Eds.): AMAI 2022, LNCS 13540, pp. 88–97, 2022.
https://doi.org/10.1007/978-3-031-17721-7_10

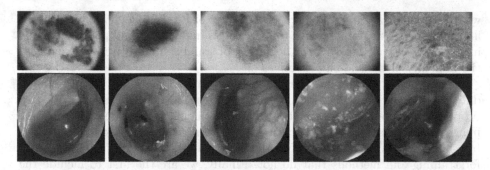

Fig. 1. Image examples from the skin lesion (top row) and eardrum (bottom row) datasets. The difficulty increases from left to right from 0 to 1 in steps of 0.25 for each image. For the skin lesion dataset, only images from the melanoma class are shown, while the eardrum images are from all three diagnostic classes, see Sect. 3.

embedding that captures similarities between the training examples: Similar images cluster together, and dissimilar images are pushed apart. In our paper, we define metrics in the embedding space that capture human classification difficulty. We evaluate our methods on two different medical datasets, one containing images of skin lesions and the other of eardrums, see Fig. 1.

The term *difficulty* is used in various ways in image analysis. Difficulty can be defined as how hard it is for machine learning to reach high accuracy on a given dataset [25], how challenging it is to automatically segment an image [16], visual complexity and clutter in the image [19], the time needed for a human to segment an image [33], or the human response time for a visual search task [31]. The latter definition was employed by Ionescu *et al.* [31], who proposed a method based on a pretrained neural network for feature extraction, followed by support vector regression to estimate the difficulty score. They presented a dataset with difficulty scores on the PASCAL VOC2012 dataset evaluated by 736 raters. They achieved a high Kendall's τ coefficient of 0.472. In contrast to our approach, they do not use any knowledge about the ground truth class of the image but instead estimate the difficulty directly from image features. By using both the ground truth class and an embedding space our approach becomes more interpretable [24]. We define human difficulty as the fraction of incorrect classifications from people familiar with the classification task. This definition was also employed by André *et al.* [1]. For one of our datasets, we use a self-evaluated certainty of all raters to obtain a less noisy estimated ground truth difficulty with few annotators.

We compare our work to methods in active learning and curriculum learning. Active learning accelerates labeling efficiency by selecting the most useful samples from an unlabeled dataset for labeling, thus reducing the labeling cost [21]. The intuition behind the most commonly used approach, the uncertainty-based approach, is that with a lower certainty on a specific example, a higher amount of informativeness will be added to the classifier when utilizing the example for training [35]. Curriculum learning is inspired by the learning process of humans, where examples are presented with increasing order of difficulty. This concept is transferred to neural networks to increase training speed and performance by introducing easy examples at the beginning of training, and to gradually increase the difficulty of the training examples [2].

In this paper, we present a new procedure for obtaining ground truth human difficulty from several annotators by including a self-evaluated certainty. We also propose a new method for estimation of human difficulty based on embeddings of images learned using deep metric learning, which outperforms existing methods by a large margin. We propose methods that both utilize ground truth difficulties for training and methods that do not. Finally, we are the first to include the ground truth class label for human difficulty estimation, which increases the performance of our methods even further.

2 Estimating Image Difficulty

Our difficulty estimation models are all based on the embedding space learned using a deep neural network, trained with metric learning. By training a model this way, instead of as a classification network, we learn the similarities in the training dataset. The output from the network is an embedding vector, mapping each individual image to the embedding space. The idea is that easy cases will be placed far from decision boundaries in the embedding space, while difficult cases will be further away from the class cluster center, and possibly closer to other cluster classes. We separate our proposed methods into two categories depending on whether or not they utilize ground truth difficulties during training. An overview of these methods is in Table 1.

Methods without ground truth difficulties are all based on embeddings of samples, extracted using a trained neural network. As our neural networks are trained using cosine similarity, our methods for estimating difficulties are thus also based on cosine similarities. As difficulties should be high for points far from their cluster, we refer to inverse similarity which is one minus the similarity. The methods still apply to neural networks trained using Euclidean distances, and in that case, one would use the Euclidean distance in the embedding space instead.

Inverse similarity is a naïve approach to estimating the difficulty, found by computing the similarity between the sample and the cluster center of its ground truth class. This is intuitive, as samples less similar to the cluster center are typically more similar to other class clusters, and thus harder to classify. To find the difficulty, and not the easiness, we report the inverse of the similarity.

Inverse softmax of similarity is an improvement of inverse similarity. Samples can have low similarity to their cluster center without being close to other classes. To handle this, we compute the similarity between the sample and all cluster centers and normalize these with softmax. The difficulty is the inverse of the softmax output corresponding to the ground truth class. This method is related to decision margin sampling in active learning [32], except we can go on both sides of the decision boundary since the ground truth *class label* is known.

Sample classification power is an alternative way of obtaining an estimate of image difficulty. Here, we evaluate how many of the neighboring points in the embedding space belong to the ground truth class of a certain sample. To do that for a single sample s from class c, we imagine classifying the closest k samples as c, and classifying the rest as not c. By varying k from one to the number of samples, we can draw a receiver operating characteristic (ROC) curve. We then use the area under the curve (AUC) of this ROC curve as our estimate of the difficulty of s. To handle class imbalance, we use the weighted ROC curve, with the weights being the inverses of the class frequencies.

Normalization is carried out on the estimated difficulties, by introducing the assumption that each class has the same average difficulty. To enforce this assumption, we propose normalizing the difficulty on a per-class basis by dividing it by the average estimated difficulty of that class. We refer to this as "norm".

Methods with ground truth difficulties are methods, where the ground truth difficulties of a training set are employed. These can also be called supervised methods. We set up a regression problem to predict the difficulty scores directly from the image embeddings. We employ the tree-based ensemble model extra trees [10] for the regression problem. In addition to only predicting from the embeddings, we also fit a model using the ground truth label as additional input. The ground truth label will allow the model to learn that samples placed close to incorrect class clusters should have a higher difficulty, than samples within their correct class cluster. Several other models were tested for this task, including support vector regression, but extra trees showed superior performance.

3   Datasets

To validate our method, we performed experiments on two medical image datasets, examples of which are shown in Fig. 1. We have obtained estimates of the human difficulty for a number of images from both datasets, which we use as our test-sets for evaluating our proposed approaches.

The skin lesion dataset consists of dermoscopic images of skin lesions divided into eight diagnoses, which include benign (nevus [NV], keratoses [BKL], vascular lesions [VASC], dermatofibromas [DF]), pre-malignant (actinic keratoses), and malignant (melanoma [MEL], squamous cell carcinoma [SCC], basal cell carcinoma [BCC]). The diagnoses were determined by histopathology or as the consensus between two to three domain experts. We have a dataset of 52 292 images from the 2019 ISIC Challenge training set [5, 6, 30][1] and our own dataset (Permission to access and handle the patients' data was granted by the Danish Patient Safety Authority (Jr.# 3-3013-2553/1) and the Data Protection Agency of Southern Denmark (Jr.# 18/53664)).

Skin lesion difficulties are obtained for 1723 images from our own dataset, based on diagnoses from 81 medical students with an interest in dermatology (Ethical waiver: Jr.#: H-20066667, data handling agreement case #: P-2019-556). On average, each student diagnosed 609 randomly sampled images. It was

---

[1] License: CC-BY-NC.

ensured that at least eight students diagnosed each case. The images were diagnosed into seven different categories, as we expected actinic keratoses would be too difficult for the medical students. We estimate the difficulty of a case as the fraction of students answering incorrectly.

The eardrum dataset contains 1409 images collected during the standard clinical routine at an Ear-Nose-and-Throat (ENT) clinic. The data was collected under the ethical approval from the Non-Profit Organization MINS Institutional Review Board (ref.# 190221). The images show the patients' eardrum captured using an endoscope and are diagnosed into three different diagnoses: acute otitis media, otitis media with effusion, and no effusion by an experienced ENT specialist. The dataset is split into a training and test set of 1209 and 204 images.

Eardrum difficulties were estimated by getting the test set of 204 equally class sampled eardrum images analyzed and diagnosed by four additional experienced ENTs. The ENTs diagnosed each case as one of the three diagnoses or "unknown", counting as an incorrect diagnosis. Furthermore, each ENT rated their certainty of each diagnosis on the scale: very low, low, medium, moderate, or high, which is converted to a scale from 0 to 1. More details on this dataset are in Sundgaard *et al.* [28]. For a case, $\mu_{correct}$ is the fraction of correct ENT answers and $\mu_{certainty}$ is the average self-evaluated certainty. The difficulty of each case is then

$$1 - \mu_{correct} \cdot \mu_{certainty}. \tag{1}$$

We evaluate the eardrum difficulties with "leave-one-annotator-out", by comparing the responses from one annotator with the difficulties estimated from the remaining annotators using Kendall's τ. This resulted in an average Kendall's τ of 0.548 based the difficulty using only on the fraction of correct ENT answers. The score increased to 0.570, corresponding to 78.5% correctly ranked cases, when including the self-evaluated certainty in the definition of difficulty, showing that this improves the estimated difficulties.

4   Experiments

The embeddings of the images in our proposed methods are computed using neural networks trained with a metric loss function. All experiments are conducted in PyTorch (v. 1.10) using the PyTorch metric learning library [18]. The neural networks are trained using the multi-similarity loss function [34] ($\alpha = 2$, $\beta = 50$, base $= 1$) and a multi similarity miner ($\epsilon = 0.1$) using cosine similarity to optimize the selection of training pairs. Our models are pretrained on the ImageNet database [8]. The fully connected layer before the final softmax of the model is replaced by a fully connected layer without an activation function, which returns the embedding space. The output embeddings are L2 normalized.

The skin lesion network is based on a ResNet-50 model [12], with a 64-dimensional embedding space. The model is trained for 350 epochs with a learning rate of 10^{-5}. The input images (256×256) are color normalized using the Minkowski norm ($p = 6$). Data augmentation consists of flips, rotations, scaling, and color jitter. We do inference with the same augmentations, and compute each prediction as the average of 64 random augmentations. The eardrum network is based on the Inception V3 network [29], with a 32-dimensional embedding space. The Inception V3 network has been used by several others for similar images [4,27]. The parameters of the first half of the network (until first grid size reduction) were frozen to avoid over-fitting. The initial learning rate (10^{-3}) is decreased by a factor of 0.1 every 50th epoch. Training is continued until the training loss has not decreased for 20 epochs, resulting in 111 training epochs. Data augmentation consists of horizontal flips, rotations, color jitter, and random erasing. Images are resized to 299×299.

We use Kendall's τ [13] to evaluate how well our methods can predict the ground truth difficulties. This is a non-parametric measurement from -1 to 1 of the correlation between two ranked variables. As it only compares how the images are ranked, it is not important to achieve the exact same difficulty as the ground truth estimate, as long as the ordering of samples is correct.

We use Extra trees [10] for supervised difficulty estimation, with five-fold cross-validation. This allows us to obtain predictions for all samples in the test set, and thus compute a single Kendall's τ for the entire test set. All our experiments with extra trees use 500 trees, with 10 as the minimum number of samples required to split an internal node.[2]

Comparisons are made between our methods and methods from both active and curriculum learning using a standard trained classification network, and with the approach proposed by Ionescu et al. [31]. The classification networks employ the same architecture as our embedding networks, but the dimension of the output is the number of classes in each dataset. The networks are trained with cross-entropy loss weighted by the inverse frequency of each class, but otherwise using the same setup as described for the embedding networks.

Visual search difficulty proposed by Ionescu et al. [31] is used for comparison. We replicate their method by passing each image (299×299) through VGG-16 [26] once and using the penultimate features to fit a ν-support vector regression.[2]

We compare to the following approaches from active learning, all based on the softmax output of a classification network: classification uncertainty, which is one minus the maximum value of the softmax [14]; entropy of the softmax probabilities [7]; and classification margin found by computing the difference between the second-highest and highest probabilities of the softmax [15].

We also compare to three approaches from curriculum learning: standard deviation of the images [23]; transfer scores obtained by running all images through a pretrained Inception V3 network using the penultimate features to train a support vector classifier to obtain the confidence of the model [11]; and one minus the softmax output of the ground truth class from our classification network [11]. These active and curriculum learning methods are only used to estimate the difficulty for each image, and have not been utilized to train the neural networks.

---

[2] Unspecified parameters are the defaults in Scikit-Learn v. 0.24.2 [20].

Table 1. Kendall's τ for all methods on both datasets. Methods with (L) use the ground truth class label for prediction, and with (D) use a training set of ground truth difficulties. Bold indicates the significantly best performance, and bold with a star indicates the methods without D performing significantly better than the rest. We used nonparametric bootstrap based testing [3] with 50 000 replicates and $\alpha = 5\%$.

Method	Uses		Skin lesion	Eardrum
Visual search difficulty [31]		D	0.142	0.117
Curriculum learning				
Std. of image [23]			−0.070	0.011
Transfer scoring [11]	L		0.115	0.213
Self-taught scoring [11]	L		0.176	0.261
Active learning				
Classification uncertainty [14]			0.094	0.217
Entropy of probabilities [7]			0.118	0.216
Classification margin [15]			0.068	0.215
Ours				
Inverse similarity	L		0.137	−0.140
Inverse softmax of similarity	L		**0.239** *	0.354
Inverse softmax of similarity norm.	L		**0.239** *	0.380
Sample classification power	L		0.201	0.143
Sample classification power norm.	L		**0.247** *	**0.440** *
Extra trees: embeddings		D	0.322	0.465
Extra trees: embeddings + label	L	D	**0.398**	**0.517**

5   Results

The Kendall's τ for all experiments is reported in Table 1. The table also gives an overview of whether the ground truth label is used for prediction, and whether a training set of ground truth difficulties has been used. The embeddings for the two datasets are shown in the top of Fig. 2. For the eardrum data, we see how most easy examples are located within the class clusters, while the difficult examples are the ones located in another class cluster, or at the edge of the clusters. The same tendencies are visible in some classes of the skin lesion embeddings. The bottom of Fig. 2 shows scatter plots of the ground truth difficulties versus predicted difficulties for both datasets.

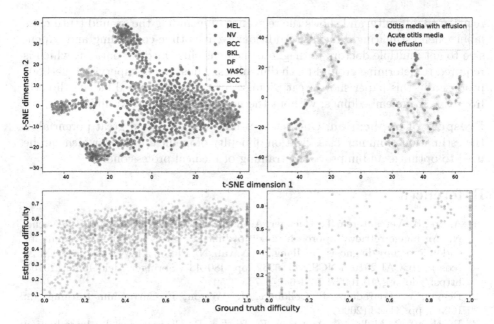

Fig. 2. Left: skin lesion dataset. **Right**: eardrum dataset. **Top**: visualization of the embeddings in two dimensions with t-SNE [17]. The transparency of each point indicates the ground truth difficulty with very transparent being the easiest. Grey points are the training samples for the eardrum data. **Bottom**: scatter plots of ground truth difficulties and difficulties estimated with the *embeddings + label* approach, together with the least squares regression lines.

6   Discussion and Conclusion

We have shown that image embeddings from neural networks trained with metric learning can be used to estimate diagnostic difficulty. Our methods for difficulty estimation outperform all existing methods in both active and curriculum learning. Ionescu *et al.* [31] report a Kendall's τ of 0.472, while their method achieves 0.142 and 0.117 on our datasets . Their method is, however, developed for a different problem, thus this drop in performance is not surprising. Our methods are significantly better, with our best achieving Kendall's τ of 0.398 and 0.517. This corresponds to 69.9% and 75.8% of pairs being ordered correctly, which is an improvement of 12.8 and 11.1% points from the best performing existing method (self-taught scoring).

Table 1 shows that our contribution of incorporating the ground truth class greatly increases performance. A similar tendency is seen in the higher performance of self-taught scoring compared to classification uncertainty, as the only difference between these two methods is the knowledge about the ground truth class. This intuition is also visible in Fig. 2, especially for the eardrum dataset, where the most difficult examples are often placed in the extremities of the clusters, or placed inside other clusters. This indicates that the embedding has a relation to difficulty, and shows the relevance of including the ground truth class label when estimating difficulty. Additionally, it is time-consuming and expensive to get multiple doctors to diagnose each case in a medical dataset, which is required to determine ground truth difficulties. Thus, the unsupervised methods proposed in this paper show great promise for estimating the difficulty directly from the image embeddings, without the need for ground truth difficulties.

Prospect of application: Our methods have demonstrated great potential in the estimation of human classification difficulty of medical images, which can be used to optimize and improve the training of medical professionals.

References

1. André, B., Vercauteren, T., Buchner, A.M., Shahid, M.W., Wallace, M.B., Ayache, N.: An image retrieval approach to setup difficulty levels in training systems for endomicroscopy diagnosis. In: Jiang, T., Navab, N., Pluim, J.P.W., Viergever, M.A. (eds.) MICCAI 2010. LNCS, vol. 6362, pp. 480–487. Springer, Heidelberg (2010). https://doi.org/10.1007/978-3-642-15745-5_59
2. Bengio, Y., Louradour, J., Collobert, R., Weston, J.: Curriculum learning. In: ICML, pp. 41–48 (2009)
3. Brockhoff, P., Møller, J., Andersen, E., Bacher, P., Christiansen, L.: Introduction to statistics - eNotes (2015)
4. Cha, D., Pae, C., Seong, S.B., Choi, J.Y., Park, H.J.: Automated diagnosis of ear disease using ensemble deep learning with a big otoendoscopy image database. EBioMedicine **45**, 606–614 (2019)
5. Codella, N.C., et al.: Skin lesion analysis toward melanoma detection: a challenge at the 2017 international symposium on biomedical imaging (isbi), hosted by the international skin imaging collaboration (ISIC). In: 2018 IEEE 15th international symposium on biomedical imaging (ISBI 2018), pp. 168–172. IEEE (2018)
6. Combalia, M., et al.: Bcn20000: dermoscopic lesions in the wild. arXiv preprint arXiv:1908.02288 (2019)
7. Dagan, I., Engelson, S.P.: Committee-based sampling for training probabilistic classifiers. In: Proceedings of the Twelfth International Conference on Machine Learning, pp. 150–157. Morgan Kaufmann (1995)
8. Deng, J., Dong, W., Socher, R., Li, L.J., Li, K., Fei-Fei, L.: Imagenet: a large-scale hierarchical image database. In: CVPR, pp. 248–255 (2009)
9. Elio, R., Anderson, J.R.: The effects of information order and learning mode on schema abstraction. Mem. Cogn. **12**(1), 20–30 (1984). https://doi.org/10.3758/BF03196994
10. Geurts, P., Ernst, D., Wehenkel, L.: Extremely randomized trees. Mach. Learn. **63**(1), 3–42 (2006)
11. Hacohen, G., Weinshall, D.: On the power of curriculum learning in training deep networks. In: ICML, pp. 2535–2544 (2019)
12. He, K., Zhang, X., Ren, S., Sun, J.: Deep residual learning for image recognition. In: Proceedings of the IEEE conference on computer vision and pattern recognition, pp. 770–778 (2016)
13. Kendall, M.G.: Rank correlation methods (1948)
14. Lewis, D.D., Gale, W.A.: A sequential algorithm for training text classifiers. In: Croft, B.W., van Rijsbergen, C.J. (eds.) SIGIR 1994, pp. 3–12. Springer, London (1994). https://doi.org/10.1007/978-1-4471-2099-5_1

15. Li, X., Guo, Y.: Active learning with multi-label SVM classification. In: Twenty-Third International Joint Conference on Artificial Intelligence (2013)
16. Liu, D., Xiong, Y., Pulli, K., Shapiro, L.: Estimating image segmentation difficulty. In: Perner, P. (ed.) MLDM 2011. LNCS (LNAI), vol. 6871, pp. 484–495. Springer, Heidelberg (2011). https://doi.org/10.1007/978-3-642-23199-5_36
17. Van der Maaten, L., Hinton, G.: Visualizing data using t-SNE. J. Mach. Learn. Res. **9**(11) (2008)
18. Musgrave, K., Belongie, S., Lim, S.N.: Pytorch metric learning (2020)
19. Nagle, F., Lavie, N.: Predicting human complexity perception of real-world scenes. Roy. Soc. Open Sci. **7**(5), 191487 (2020)
20. Pedregosa, F., et al.: Scikit-learn: machine learning in Python. J. Mach. Learn. Res. **12**, 2825–2830 (2011)
21. Ren, P., et al.: A survey of deep active learning. arXiv preprint arXiv:2009.00236 (2020)
22. Roads, B.D., Xu, B., Robinson, J.K., Tanaka, J.W.: The easy-to-hard training advantage with real-world medical images. Cogn. Res. Principles Implications **3**(1), 1–13 (2018). https://doi.org/10.1186/s41235-018-0131-6
23. Sadasivan, V.S., Dasgupta, A.: Statistical measures for defining curriculum scoring function. arXiv preprint arXiv:2103.00147 (2021)
24. Sanakoyeu, A., Tschernezki, V., Buchler, U., Ommer, B.: Divide and conquer the embedding space for metric learning. In: Proceedings of the IEEE/CVF Conference on Computer Vision and Pattern Recognition, pp. 471–480 (2019)
25. Scheidegger, F., Istrate, R., Mariani, G., Benini, L., Bekas, C., Malossi, C.: Efficient image dataset classification difficulty estimation for predicting deep-learning accuracy. Vis. Comput. **37**(6), 1593–1610 (2020). https://doi.org/10.1007/s00371-020-01922-5
26. Simonyan, K., Zisserman, A.: Very deep convolutional networks for large-scale image recognition. arXiv preprint arXiv:1409.1556 (2014)
27. Sundgaard, J.V., et al.: Deep metric learning for otitis media classification. Med. Image Anal. **71**, 102034 (2021)
28. Sundgaard, J.V., et al.: Inter-rater reliability of the diagnosis of otitis media based on otoscopic images and wideband tympanometry measurements. Int. J. Pediatr. Otorhinolaryngol. **153**, 111034 (2022)
29. Szegedy, C., Vanhoucke, V., Ioffe, S., Shlens, J., Wojna, Z.: Rethinking the inception architecture for computer vision. In: CVPR, pp. 2818–2826 (2016)
30. Tschandl, P., Rosendahl, C., Kittler, H.: The ham10000 dataset, a large collection of multi-source dermatoscopic images of common pigmented skin lesions. Sci. Data **5**(1), 1–9 (2018)
31. Tudor Ionescu, R., Alexe, B., Leordeanu, M., Popescu, M., Papadopoulos, D.P., Ferrari, V.: How hard can it be? estimating the difficulty of visual search in an image. In: CVPR, pp. 2157–2166 (2016)
32. Tuia, D., Volpi, M., Copa, L., Kanevski, M., Munoz-Mari, J.: A survey of active learning algorithms for supervised remote sensing image classification. IEEE J. Sel. Top. Signal Process. **5**(3), 606–617 (2011)
33. Vijayanarasimhan, S., Grauman, K.: What's it going to cost you?: predicting effort vs. informativeness for multi-label image annotations. In: CVPR, pp. 2262–2269 (2009)
34. Wang, X., Han, X., Huang, W., Dong, D., Scott, M.R.: Multi-similarity loss with general pair weighting for deep metric learning. In: CVPR, pp. 5022–5030 (2019)
35. Wu, J., et al.: Multi-label active learning algorithms for image classification: overview and future promise. ACM Comput. Surv. (CSUR) **53**(2), 1–35 (2020)

A Deep Learning-Based Interactive Medical Image Segmentation Framework

Ivan Mikhailov[1,2](✉), Benoit Chauveau[2,3], Nicolas Bourdel[2,3],
and Adrien Bartoli[1,2]

[1] EnCoV, Institut Pascal, Université Clermont Auvergne, Clermont-Ferrand, France
ivanmikhailov.mail@gmail.com
[2] SurgAR, Clermont-Ferrand, France
[3] CHU de Clermont-Ferrand, Clermont-Ferrand, France

Abstract. Image segmentation is an essential component in medical image analysis. The case of 3D images such as MRI is particularly challenging and time consuming. Interactive or semi-automatic methods are thus highly desirable. While deep learning outperforms classical methods in automatic segmentation, its use in interactive frameworks is still limited. The main reason is that most neural networks do not lend themselves well to the required user interaction loop. We propose a general deep learning-based interactive framework for image segmentation, which embeds a base network in a user interaction loop with a user feedback memory. We propose to model the memory explicitly as a sequence of consecutive framework states, from which the features can be learned. A major difficulty is related to training, as the network inputs include the user feedback and thus depend on the network's previous output. We propose to introduce a virtual user in the training process, modelled by simulating the user feedback from the current segmentation. We demonstrate our framework on the task of female pelvis MRI segmentation, using a new dataset. We evaluate our framework against existing work with the standard metrics and conduct a user evaluation. Our framework outperforms existing systems.

Keywords: Interactive segmentation · Deep learning · MRI · RNN

1 Introduction

Image segmentation is an essential component of many visual processing systems, which involves classifying each pixel or, equivalently, delineating the regions containing pixels of the same class. In medical image analysis, the images are often patient scans from modalities such as MRI (Magnetic Resonance Imaging) or CT (Computed Tomography). MRI segmentation is a tremendously difficult task, owing to it being 3D, low contrast, noisy, low resolution and artifacted. Existing segmentation approaches can be divided into three settings based on user involvement: manual, automatic and interactive. The manual approach is the most time-consuming, as each pixel has to be attributed a label independently, which may require hours for a single MRI. It is error-prone and infeasible in the clinical environment. At the other extreme lies the automatic approach, which works without user involvement. This strongly limits its applicability, as a clinician operator shall validate and possibly edit the result before its use in a therapeutic act. The interactive approach trades-off manual and automatic features: it typically involves an automatic part with an extent of user control. The interactive approach attempts at minimising the amount of required user interaction whilst maximising the quality of the result. It is the most adapted approach to the clinical environment.

The automatic approach is largely dominated by deep learning, which overturned classical methods over the last decade. In contrast, interactive deep learning methods present specific difficulties and have yet received limited attention. Concretely, deep learning interactive segmentation requires embedding a network in a loopy system allowing the user to interact. Indeed, the network inputs must include the user feedback, which depends on the network outputs. This creates a dependency between the inputs and outputs of the network, which is poorly resolved by a regular training process from static data. Creating such interactive systems exploiting deep learning is nonetheless fundamental to simplify, speed up and secure the performance of segmentation in the clinical environment.

We propose a general multi-class deep learning interactive segmentation framework and training methods. Our system consists of an embedded network, a user interaction loop and an interaction memory. First, the user reviews the current segmentation result and, if satisfied, accepts. Otherwise, the user may quickly make simple corrections by placing points and strokes to refine the segmentation, which is achieved by a special input configuration of the embedded network. Indeed, this network inputs the image, user correction masks, and possibly other memorised parameters, and outputs the segmentation probability maps. The system then loops back to the user review step, whilst updating the interaction memory to keep track of the user corrections through the interactions. Our contributions are two-fold. First, a general deep learning-based inter-

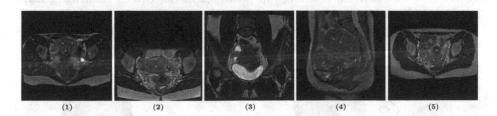

Fig. 1. MRI female pelvis dataset samples, main difficulties indicated with green arrows, series 1 to 5: (1) presence of an IUD, not seen in the training set; (2,5) unclear contours, blurriness of the uterine cavity; (3) similarity of the uterine (left) and cervix cavities (right); (4) strong uterus deformation due to tumours, with here five tumours. (Color figure online)

active multi-class image segmentation framework, with a user interaction loop, dynamic data training process and an interaction memory. Second, a sequential interaction memory, which keeps track of the segmentation results and user corrections, maintaining sequentiality within the system. We demonstrate our framework in semantic multi-class MRI segmentation of the female pelvis for which we introduce a new dataset. For this task, we instantiate our system with an existing encoder-decoder architecture optionally featuring RNN [38] modules. We validate the results against automatic and existing interactive systems with the standard metrics and perform an ablation study of our system's components. We report results of a preliminary user study conducted with medical users, using a specifically developed graphical user interface connected to our system.

2   Related Work

We review classical and deep learning approaches to medical image segmentation, distinguishing automatic and interactive approaches for each.

Classical automatic segmentation encompasses a wide variety of methods [30]. Their performance are usually insufficient to achieve clinically-acceptable accuracy and they have been largely taken over by deep learning. In contrast, classical interactive methods are still widely used. The most well known ones are probably the Graph Cuts [2], Random Walker [9] and Geodesic Image Segmentation (GeoS) [4]. They achieve acceptable performance for simple cases. However, medical data often features structures with complex shapes and poorly defined contours, noise and artefacts. This results in a substantial increase of user time required to perform segmentation and limited achievable accuracy. Deep learning-based automatic segmentation includes a multitude of methods. A review and evaluation of over 100 methods [19] was conducted with ResNet [12] extensively used as a backbone, represented by EMANet [16] with top scores on the PASCAL VOC dataset. Most of the models use an encoder-decoder architecture [19]. This includes the U-Net [20], with a wide spectrum of applications [23], and recent variants [7,24] reaching top positions in the BraTS challenge 2021. Automatic MRI segmentation was attempted for various targets, including the kidney [14], the prostate [10] and brain tumours [11]. These methods demonstrate state-of-the-art performance in their respective tasks. However, they are

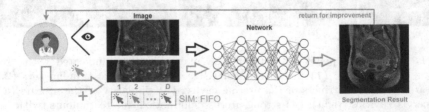

Fig. 2. Proposed interactive system.

automatic and do not allow the user to interact. Automatic segmentation is highly appropriate in applications which can not involve user interactions, such as real-time organ tracking. In contrast, many applications require validation and corrections from a certified user. For such applications, the direct use of automatic deep learning methods is inappropriate.

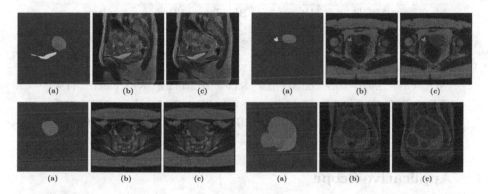

Fig. 3. Segmentation results, where uterus - green, bladder - yellow, tumour - red, cavity - pink and user clicks - cyan: **(a)** ground truth; **(b)** auto; **(c)** human user-controlled DDG-SIM. (Color figure online)

The integration of deep learning within interactive segmentation systems is a major challenge. A simple approach is to use a classical interactive method to post-process the result from an automatic deep learning method [26] or correct it manually [22]. Such systems inherit the intrinsic limitations of the chosen classical method. A more advanced approach is to use a neural network to process user feedback in a loopy structure [1,17,21,27–29]. These methods use a network which takes the image and user interaction masks as inputs. Training is challenging owing to the loop. Existing approaches generate user interaction masks from labelled data, either statically before training or dynamically during training. Static data training methods [27–29] limit the system's generalisation and interaction effectiveness. Dynamic data training methods [1,17] improve performance. They simulate user interaction by randomly sampling mis-segmented regions. This is done once from a single prediction [1] or from the latest segmentation result [17]. These methods diversify the training data, but do not reproduce the typical sequentiality of real user interactions. The lack of sequentiality is also a consequence of the interaction memory used in these systems, which simply accumulates the user corrections, discarding ordering. A sequential memory was used in [29] to 'transfer' the user interaction recorded on one slice to the other slices, but was not used to exploit sequentiality during slice segmentation. An open-source interactive segmentation platform [6] was recently made available, which offers both deep learning-based [21,26] and classical methods [2], inheriting their limitations.

In contrast to existing work, our framework uses a sequential interaction memory which captures the sequentiality of user interactions at training and inference times. It is also the first framework to cope with multiple classes.

Table 1. Experimental evaluation results where bold means best.

Method	BGD		Uterus		Bladder		Tumours		Cavity	
	IoU	Dice	IoU	Dice	IoU	Dice	IoU	Dice	IoU	Dice
Auto	99.2	99.6	64.7	78.6	71.9	83.6	60.4	75.3	40.4	57.6
SDG-base	99.1	99.6	61.7	76.3	70.1	82.4	62.5	76.9	21.1	34.9
SDG-CIM	99.3	99.7	66.5	79.9	83.9	91.2	72.8	84.3	29.0	44.9
DDG-CIM	**99.6**	**99.8**	77.4	87.3	**87.4**	**93.3**	77.7	87.4	39.6	56.7
DDG-SIM	**99.6**	**99.8**	**79.8**	**88.7**	87.0	93.0	**79.0**	**88.3**	**57.8**	**73.3**

3 Applicative Scope

While our framework may be applied to numerous segmentation problems, we focus on the interactive female pelvis MRI segmentation, involving five classes: uterus, bladder, uterine cavity, tumours and background. The intended use is surgical planning and surgical augmented reality [3]. We create public female pelvis MRI dataset, consisting of 97 MRI series with 3066 slices in total, manually annotated in 3D Slicer [13] and in MITK [8] by expert radiologists. This took from 10' to 50' per series with 25' on average, which is clearly infeasible in the clinical setting. The segmentation of anatomical structures of the female pelvis is particularly challenging due to a large variance in their representation, including shape, size, position, orientation and texture among the patients, with and without pathologies. Difficult samples can be seen in Fig. 1. Moreover, the target anatomical structures form a naturally imbalanced dataset, where background takes 96.15%, uterus 2.11%, bladder 1.02%, tumours 0.67% and uterine cavity 0.05%. The strongest imbalance is observed for the uterine cavity and the background, whose average ratio of volumes is 0.057%. Our objective is to develop a segmentation system which minimises the time required to complete the segmentation with acceptable accuracy, while allowing an expert reviewer to have control and guide the segmentation, as and when necessary.

4 Methodology

4.1 System

Structure. We build the proposed system shown in Fig. 2 starting with a basic interactive segmentation system named base, featuring an interaction loop. This system does not have a memory of user corrections or previous segmentation results and processes each set of user corrections in isolation. The interaction loop allows iterative refinement by forming new inputs through a combination of network outputs and user corrections. The system is generic as it does not depend on a specific network architecture, as long as the network takes both the image and the user corrections as inputs. The user corrections are represented by N binary masks, where N is the number of classes. The network inputs are concatenated to a single tensor of size $H \times W \times C$, where $H \times W$ is the image size and C is the number of channels, varying depending on the system. For the base system $C_{\text{base}} = 1 + N$. Indeed, as there is no memory, the network takes the image as the first channel and the binary masks of the user corrections for the N classes for next N channels. This strongly harms user experience as the past user corrections would be forgotten by the system at the next interaction [26,27].

Sequential Interaction Memory. Existing works use the type of interaction memory, which aggregates the raw system states by merging the successive interaction masks [1,17,28]. We call this a cumulative interaction memory (CIM). The network takes the image and the merged user correction masks, and its input tensor thus has $C_{\text{cim}} = C_{\text{base}} = 1 + N$ channels. This type of memory discards the ordering of interactions - the sequentiality, typical of user corrections. We introduce a second type of interaction memory which, in contrast to CIM, preserves the past D system states, hence the user's sequential behaviour. We call this a sequential interaction memory (SIM). We call the number of states D the SIM's size or depth. For the task of multi-class segmentation, a single state consists of a probability map for the network outputs and a binary mask for the user corrections, for each of the N classes. The network takes an image and the SIM, which are automatically combined to form the input tensor with $C_{\text{sim}} = 1 + 2DN$. It is important to make a distinction between the proposed SIM and internal RNN memory. SIM tracks and stores system states, represented by inputs and outputs of the network. Indeed, SIM is external to the network and does not depend on a specific network architecture. The RNN memory, however, is specific to the network architecture, enabled by passing hidden state from step to step and represented by weights. In our ablation study we show that RNN's suitability for sequential data may further reinforce the proposed framework.

4.2   Training with Dynamic Data Generation

A regular training process from static data will poorly reproduce the real system usage at test time and hence limit the achievable accuracy and user interaction efficiency. To resolve this, we propose a dynamic training approach, where the training data is generated from the labelled dataset during training by a virtual user. The basic idea of the virtual user is to generate corrections similarly to a real user, whose involvement in training is not feasible. These corrections are represented by one binary mask per class, populated by foreground clicks for each class. The click is handled by an interaction-control process, which exploits the difference image between the previous network output and the ground truth.

Training with the proposed SIM means filling its D states with realistic values produced by the virtual user. We thus run the system for D iterations with fixed weights to populate the SIM with simulated user input data prior to backpropagation. We choose D experimentally with the goal of maximizing the performance with the minimum number of interactions.

Table 2. User evaluation results given as Time, IoU and number of interactions per class as 'Int.' ;'A' - gynecologic surgeon; 'B', 'C' - certified radiologists. Tumour presence is in proportion to that of the whole dataset.

Series	Time	BGD		Uterus		Bladder		Tumours		Cavity		mIoU	Total Int.
		IoU	Int.	IoU	Int.	IoU	Int.	IoU	Int.	IoU	Int.		
1-A	1'44"	99.7	–	69.5	23	92.0	5	–	–	44.0	–	76.3	28
1-B	3'00"	99.6	–	64.1	12	93.6	6	–	–	41.4	2	74.7	20
1-C	3'19"	99.6	8	67.6	30	93.5	6	–	–	37.7	9	74.6	53
2-A	3'10"	99.3	–	67.0	21	79.4	9	71.7	–	35.0	10	70.5	40
2-B	2'42"	99.3	–	69.9	20	78.4	7	71.7	–	42.6	1	72.4	28
2-C	5'04"	98.2	11	51.9	29	52.3	12	71.8	–	46.6	13	64.1	65
3-A	3'10"	99.6	–	70.3	7	76.1	15	–	–	38.5	6	71.1	28
3-B	2'50"	99.6	1	72.2	5	76.8	14	–	–	42.6	5	72.8	25
3-C	4'13"	99.6	6	70.7	12	77.8	11	–	–	21.8	9	67.4	38
4-A	7'08"	98.1	–	63.0	3	71.9	6	81.0	137	44.0	27	71.6	173
4-B	8'30"	98.2	8	66.8	21	76.6	9	58.6	27	41.9	–	68.4	65
4-C	8'47"	98.0	13	53.0	–	80.0	11	72.7	96	34.7	–	67.6	120
5-A	2'38"	99.8	–	61.0	17	93.2	14	–	–	24.9	1	69.7	32
5-B	4'17"	99.9	11	68.0	5	93.5	11	–	–	30.6	6	73.0	33
5-C	3'51"	99.8	13	66.9	29	93.2	12	–	–	29.3	13	72.3	67

5   Experimental Results

5.1   Setup

We instantiate our system with an existing encoder-decoder architecture featuring RNN modules. Namely, we use a ResNet34 [12] encoder pre-trained on ImageNet [5] and a decoder equipped with a pair of standard convolutional layer and a matching convolutional LSTM layer at every step of the upsampling path. To counter the dataset imbalance, we use the focal loss [18] and dataset-wide precalculated per-class weights. The dataset split is as follows: training set - 77 series/2449 slices, validation set - 10 series/308 slices and test set - 10 series/309 slices. We preprocessed all data via normalisation, standardisation and N4BFC [25] and performed random data augmentation: vertical and horizontal flipping, intensity shifting, gamma correction, blurring and unsharp masking.

5.2   Automated Evaluation

We compare one automatic method and four interactive methods, where SDG is Static Data Generation and DDG is Dynamic Data Generation: 1) Auto: U-Net with ResNet34 encoder [15]; 2) SDG-base: memory-less system trained with SDG, as described in [1]; 3) SDG-CIM: network from SDG-base used with a CIM overlay; 4) DDG-CIM: system with CIM trained with DDG; 5) DDG-SIM: complete proposed system with SIM trained with DDG. The evaluation setup is a ResNet34 encoder with (1–4) a generic decoder or (5) an LSTM-decoder as in Sect. 5.1. At test time, clicks are generated via the virtual user. The metrics are reported in Table 1. We observe that DDG-SIM outperforms the other methods with a minor disadvantage for bladder, for which DDG-CIM is slightly better with 87.4% against 87.0% IoU. The ablation study shows a steady increase in performance, starting with SDG-base and adding the proposed components towards DDG-SIM. Auto outperforms both SDG-base on uterus, bladder and cavity, and SDG-CIM on cavity. This can be attributed to static data generation, which does not perform well for smaller numbers of interactions. In our experience, the higher the number of interactions at training, the lower the effectiveness of individual interactions at test time. While the opposite is also true, it can be observed from the results that certain systems may not be able to learn efficiently from a small number of interactions at training. We observe a comparatively lower accuracy for cavity, whose IoU lies between 21.1% and 57.8%. We explain this with its low volume, which accounts for only 0.054% of the dataset.

5.3   User Evaluation

We performed a preliminary user study with DDG-SIM involving three senior medical experts, using a specifically developed graphical user interface. We randomly selected 6 test series containing 144 slices in total, where 1 series is used to familiarise the users with the graphical user interface and 5 series are used in a random order for user evaluation. MRI image samples from each of the series can be seen in Fig. 1. We evaluate the user performance in Table 2 using elapsed time, IoU and the number of interactions employed per class. The segmentation result is compared with Auto method in Fig. 3.

We note that the time is low enough to be clinically feasible, even if the users are barely acquainted with the system. Indeed, the average elapsed time for all series is 4'18", which is largely below the reported average of 25' for existing systems. Series 4 was a complex case with 11 tumours and a heavy deformation of the uterus shape, taking 8'08" on average for our system and 40' for existing systems.

6   Conclusion

We have proposed a general deep learning-based interactive multi-class image segmentation framework, with a user interaction loop and a sequential inter-action memory. We have demonstrated our framework in female pelvis MRI segmentation, using a new dataset. We have evaluated our framework against existing work with the standard metrics and conducted a user evaluation. This shows that our framework largely outperforms existing systems in accuracy and drastically reduces the average user segmentation time from 25' to 4'18".

Prospect of Application: We plan to further improve the proposed solution towards its clinical usage. First, through application to other segmentation tasks and expansion of the user study. Second, by using it to aid annotation, reducing interaction demand through SIM initialization with automatic segmentation. Third, by directly applying it to 3D images, to further shorten the segmentation time.

References

1. Amrehn, M., et al.: UI-Net: interactive artificial neural networks for iterative image segmentation based on a user model. In: Eurographics Workshop on Visual Computing for Biology and Medicine. The Eurographics Association (2017)
2. Boykov, Y., Jolly, M.P.: Interactive graph cuts for optimal boundary & region segmentation of objects in N-D images. In: Proceedings Eighth IEEE International Conference on Computer Vision. ICCV 2001, vol. 1, pp. 105–112 (2001)
3. Collins, T., et al.: Augmented reality guided laparoscopic surgery of the uterus. IEEE Trans. Med. Imaging **40**(1), 371–380 (2021)
4. Criminisi, A., Sharp, T., Blake, A.: GeoS: geodesic image segmentation. In: Forsyth, D., Torr, P., Zisserman, A. (eds.) ECCV 2008. LNCS, vol. 5302, pp. 99–112. Springer, Heidelberg (2008). https://doi.org/10.1007/978-3-540-88682-2_9
5. Deng, J., et al.: Imagenet: a large-scale hierarchical image database. In: 2009 IEEE Conference on Computer Vision and Pattern Recognition, pp. 248–255 (2009)
6. Diaz-Pinto, A., et al.: Monai label: a framework for AI-assisted interactive labeling of 3D medical images. ArXiv abs/2203.12362 (2022)
7. Futrega, M., Milesi, A., Marcinkiewicz, M., Ribalta, P.: Optimized U-Net for brain tumor segmentation. ArXiv abs/2110.03352 (2021)
8. Goch, C.J., Metzger, J., Nolden, M.: Abstract: medical research data management using MITK and XNAT. In: Bildverarbeitung für die Medizin 2017. I, pp. 305–305. Springer, Heidelberg (2017). https://doi.org/10.1007/978-3-662-54345-0_68
9. Grady, L.: Random walks for image segmentation. IEEE Trans. Pattern Anal. Mach. Intell. **28**(11), 1768–1783 (2006)
10. Guo, Y., Gao, Y., Shen, D.: Deformable MR prostate segmentation via deep feature learning and sparse patch matching. IEEE Trans. Med. Imaging **35**(4), 1077–1089 (2016)
11. Havaei, M., et al.: Brain tumor segmentation with deep neural networks. Med. Image Anal. **35**, 18–31 (2017)
12. He, K., Zhang, X., Ren, S., Sun, J.: Deep residual learning for image recognition. In: 2016 IEEE Conference on Computer Vision and Pattern Recognition (CVPR), pp. 770–778 (2016)
13. Kikinis, R., Pieper, S.D., Vosburgh, K.G.: 3D slicer: a platform for subject-specific image analysis, visualization, and clinical support. In: Jolesz, F.A. (ed.) Intraoperative Imaging and Image-Guided Therapy, pp. 277–289. Springer, New York (2014). https://doi.org/10.1007/978-1-4614-7657-3_19

14. Kline, T.L., et al.: Performance of an artificial multi-observer deep neural network for fully automated segmentation of polycystic kidneys. J. Digit. Imaging **30**(4), 442–448 (2017)
15. Le'Clerc Arrastia, J., et al.: Deeply supervised UNet for semantic segmentation to assist dermatopathological assessment of basal cell carcinoma. J. Imaging **7**(4), 71 (2021)
16. Li, X., Zhong, Z., Wu, J., Yang, Y., Lin, Z., Liu, H.: Expectation-maximization attention networks for semantic segmentation. In: 2019 IEEE/CVF International Conference on Computer Vision (ICCV), pp. 9166–9175 (2019)
17. Liao, X., et al.: Iteratively-refined interactive 3d medical image segmentation with multi-agent reinforcement learning. In: 2020 IEEE/CVF Conference on Computer Vision and Pattern Recognition (CVPR), pp. 9391–9399 (2020)
18. Lin, T.Y., Goyal, P., Girshick, R.B., He, K., Dollár, P.: Focal loss for dense object detection. In: 2017 IEEE International Conference on Computer Vision (ICCV), pp. 2999–3007 (2017)
19. Minaee, S., Boykov, Y.Y., Porikli, F., Plaza, A.J., Kehtarnavaz, N., Terzopoulos, D.: Image segmentation using deep learning: a survey. IEEE Trans. Pattern Anal. Mach. Intell. 1 (2021)
20. Ronneberger, O., Fischer, P., Brox, T.: U-Net: convolutional networks for biomedical image segmentation. In: Navab, N., Hornegger, J., Wells, W.M., Frangi, A.F. (eds.) MICCAI 2015. LNCS, vol. 9351, pp. 234–241. Springer, Cham (2015). https://doi.org/10.1007/978-3-319-24574-4_28
21. Sakinis, T., et al.: Interactive segmentation of medical images through fully convolutional neural networks. ArXiv abs/1903.08205 (2019)
22. Shan, F., et al.: Lung infection quantification of COVID-19 in CT images with deep learning. ArXiv (2020)
23. Siddique, N., Paheding, S., Elkin, C.P., Devabhaktuni, V.: U-net and its variants for medical image segmentation: a review of theory and applications. IEEE Access **9**, 82031–82057 (2021)
24. Siddiquee, M.M.R., Myronenko, A.: Redundancy reduction in semantic segmentation of 3D brain tumor MRIS. ArXiv abs/2111.00742 (2021)
25. Tustison, N.J., et al.: N4ITK: improved N3 bias correction. IEEE Trans. Med. Imaging **29**(6), 1310–1320 (2010)
26. Wang, G., et al.: Interactive medical image segmentation using deep learning with image-specific fine tuning. IEEE Trans. Med. Imaging **37**, 1562–1573 (2018)
27. Wang, G., et al.: Deepigeos: a deep interactive geodesic framework for medical image segmentation. IEEE Trans. Pattern Anal. Mach. Intell. **41**, 1559–1572 (2019)
28. Zhou, B., Chen, L., Wang, Z.: Interactive deep editing framework for medical image segmentation. In: Shen, D., et al. (eds.) MICCAI 2019. LNCS, vol. 11766, pp. 329–337. Springer, Cham (2019). https://doi.org/10.1007/978-3-030-32248-9_37
29. Zhou, T., Li, L., Bredell, G., Li, J., Konukoglu, E.: Quality-aware memory network for interactive volumetric image segmentation. In: de Bruijne, M., et al. (eds.) MICCAI 2021. LNCS, vol. 12902, pp. 560–570. Springer, Cham (2021). https://doi.org/10.1007/978-3-030-87196-3_52
30. Zhu, H., Meng, F., Cai, J., Lu, S.: Beyond pixels: a comprehensive survey from bottom-up to semantic image segmentation and cosegmentation. J. Vis. Commun. Image Represent. **34**, 12–27 (2016)

Deep Neural Network Pruning for Nuclei Instance Segmentation in Hematoxylin and Eosin-Stained Histological Images

Amirreza Mahbod[1]([⊠]), Rahim Entezari[2,3], Isabella Ellinger[1],
and Olga Saukh[2,3]

[1] Institute for Pathophysiology and Allergy Research, Medical University of Vienna,
Vienna, Austria
amirreza.mahbod@meduniwien.ac.at
[2] Institute of Technical Informatics, Technical University Graz, Graz, Austria
[3] Complexity Science Hub, Vienna, Austria

Abstract. Recently, pruning deep neural networks (DNNs) has received a lot of attention for improving accuracy and generalization power, reducing network size, and increasing inference speed on specialized hardwares. Although pruning was mainly tested on computer vision tasks, its application in the context of medical image analysis has hardly been explored. This work investigates the impact of well-known pruning techniques, namely layer-wise and network-wide magnitude pruning, on the nuclei instance segmentation performance in histological images. Our utilised instance segmentation model consists of two main branches: (1) a semantic segmentation branch, and (2) a deep regression branch. We investigate the impact of weight pruning on the performance of both branches separately, and on the final nuclei instance segmentation result. Evaluated on two publicly available datasets, our results show that layer-wise pruning delivers slightly better performance than network-wide pruning for small compression ratios (CRs) while for large CRs, network-wide pruning yields superior performance. For semantic segmentation, deep regression and final instance segmentation, 93.75%, 95%, and 80% of the model weights can be pruned by layer-wise pruning with less than 2% reduction in the performance of respective models.

Keywords: Neural networks · Pruning · Nuclei segmentation · Machine learning · Deep learning · Medical imaging

1 Introduction

Deep learning-based approaches have shown excellent performances for various computer vision tasks such as classification, detection, and segmentation problems [11]. They have also been extensively used in various medical image analysis settings [1]. While deep neural network (DNN) algorithms perform better than other image processing or classical machine learning approaches, they comprise

---

A. Mahbod—The first two authors contributed equally to this work.

S. Wu et al. (Eds.): AMAI 2022, LNCS 13540, pp. 108–117, 2022.
https://doi.org/10.1007/978-3-031-17721-7_12

millions of trainable parameters that slow down training and inference, and need powerful computational and storage resources [4].

In recent years, various pruning techniques have been proposed, and their impact on DNN performance was explored. As shown in former studies, pruning can increase generalization capability, DNN performance, and at times decrease inference time [7]. Especially in the medical context where resource-constrained hardware might be used, exploiting pruning methods can be highly beneficial [9].

Pruning methods can be generally classified into two main categories: structured and unstructured pruning. In structured pruning only specific weight patterns can be pruned, e.g. a whole row or column can be removed from the weight matrix, resulting in higher speedup. Unstructured pruning does not have such limitation and is thus more fine-grained, resulting in better accuracy, higher compression rates and better size reduction [7].

While pruning techniques have widely been used for natural image analysis [7], they have rarely been exploited in the context of medical image processing. In contrast to former studies that used DNN pruning for image classification [3,16] or image semantic segmentation [9], in this work, we exploited pruning for nuclei instance segmentation in hematoxylin and eosin (H & E)-stained histological images. Nuclei instance segmentation plays an essential role in the analysis of histological whole slide images and can be considered as a fundamental step for further analysis [19]. Parameters such as nuclei density or count can be extracted from instance segmentation masks. In the next step this information is used for disease detection, diagnosis and treatment planning [10]. The most promising approaches for automatic nuclei instance segmentation are based on supervised learning [12,14]. Localization-based methods, ternary segmentation approaches and regression-based algorithms are among the most promising models for nuclei instance segmentation [2,5,12,15].

In this study, we utilised a recently developed model for nuclei instance segmentation [15]. The model has two main branches, namely a semantic segmentation branch and a deep regression branch. We also modified the model by incorporating pre-trained ResNet-34 models [6] in the encoder section of both segmentation and regression branches. We investigated the impact of DNN magnitude pruning for two strategies, i.e. networks-wide and layer-wise (see Sect. 2.3) on both branches, and final instance segmentation results. By doing so, we explore the pruning impact on three distinct image analysis tasks, namely semantics segmentation, regression and instance segmentation. To the best of our knowledge, the effect of DNN pruning on the nuclei instance segmentation and deep regression performance has not yet been investigated in the related literature. Evaluated on two publicly available nuclei instance segmentation datasets, namely MoNuSeg [12] and TNBC [17], our results show that 80% of the model's weights can be pruned with only up to 2% drop in the nuclei instance segmentation performance.

2   Method

The workflow of a DNN pruning approach for nuclei instance segmentation is depicted in Fig. 1. The left branch does semantic segmentation while the right branch performs deep regression. To compress the model, each branch is trained and pruned iteratively. Then, the final compressed networks for both branches are merged together for the final post-processing of the resulting instance segmentation model. In the following subsections, we first describe the datasets used, and detailed model in each branch. We then explain the pruning step and the final merging step, which complete the processing pipeline.

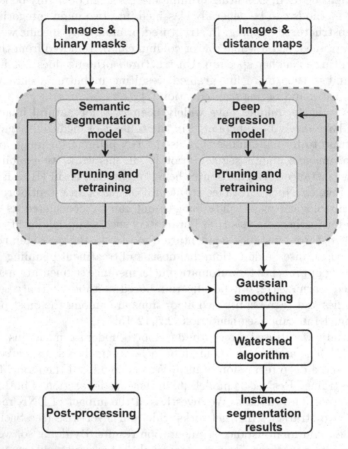

Fig. 1. The generic workflow of the proposed method. Iterative pruning and training for semantic segmentation and regression models are shown in blue boxes. (Color figure online)

2.1 Datasets

We investigate the performance of our pruning strategies on two publicly available datasets, MoNuSeg [12] and TNBC [17]. MoNuSeg dataset consists of 44 H & E-stained histological images with a fixed image size of 1000 × 1000 pixels. The image patches were extracted from the TCGA database and nine human organs (breast, kidney, liver, prostate, lung, bladder, colon, stomach, and brain).

All images were acquired at 40× magnification, and the entire dataset has more than 28,000 manually segmented nuclei. As described in [12], the dataset was divided into a training (30 images) and a test set (14 images). Further details about the MoNuSeg dataset can be found in [12]. TNBC dataset consists of 50 H & E-stained histological images with a fixed image size of 512 × 512 pixels. The whole slide images were acquired and scanned at 40× magnification by Curie Institute, Paris, France. The dataset consists of images from one organ (breast). More than 4,000 nuclei were manually segmented in this dataset. Further details are provided in [17].

2.2   Segmentation and Regression Models

Our instance segmentation model for nuclei segmentation is inspired by [15]. As shown in Fig. 1, the proposed pruning pipeline processes two models separately, namely a semantic segmentation model and a deep regression model. The main task of the semantic segmentation model to separate the background from the foreground, while the main task of the deep regression model is to predict the nuclei distance maps. The architectures of the utilised models are the same. Both are encoder-decoder-based models with skip connections between encoder and decoder parts. In contrast to the original architecture presented in [15], which uses four convolutional and max-pooling layers in the encoder part, we integrate the ResNet-34 architecture [6] as the encoder for both semantic segmentation and deep regression models as using pre-trained models in the encoder part of the U-Net-alike architectures has shown to improve the performance [12]. Both models have the same number of trainable parameters, which makes around 24.4 million parameters in total. As the semantic segmentation model dealt with a binary segmentation task, we used the sigmoid activation function in the last layer with the Dice loss function. For the deep regression model, however, we use a linear activation function in the last layer with a mean square error loss function to handle the regression task. Aside from these two differences, the model architectures, the training and the inference procedures are identical in both branches. We use Adam optimizer with a batch size of 2 for model training. The initial learning rate was set to 0.001 with a cosine annealing learning rate scheduler [13]. We trained each model for 1000 epochs. As the DNN models were trained with limited training samples, we made use of a number of augmentation techniques suggested in prior studies [14,15]. We applied resizing (only for the MoNuSeg dataset to match them to 1024 × 1024 pixels), random horizontal flipping, random scaling and shifting, random Gaussian filtering, and random perspective transformation as the main augmentation techniques.

2.3   Pruning

Existing literature suggests multiple ways to make use of sparsity during and after model training. [7] provides a comprehensive survey on model sparsification strategies. Among all these methods, magnitude pruning has gained a lot of attention mainly for two reasons: it features superior performance than

---

Algorithm 1. Network-wide/layer-wise magnitude pruning

1: **procedure** ITER-MAG-PRUNE(p_type, CR)
2:     Train neural network until convergence
3:     $i = \log_2 CR$ ▷ number of iterations
4:     **while** $i \geq 1$ **do**
5:         **if** p_type = network-wide **then**
6:             Sort all weights in ascending order
7:             Prune the smallest 50% of weights
8:         **else if** p_type = layer-wise **then**
9:             Sort parameters in each layer
10:            Prune the smallest 50% of weights per layer
11:        Retrain the network until convergence
12:        $i = i - 1$

---

many other pruning strategies, and it is computationally inexpensive, i.e. there is no need to compute Hessians, etc. In this work, we employ two versions of magnitude pruning, namely network-wide (also known as global) and layer-wise magnitude pruning. Algorithm 1 illustrates the pseudo-code for these two pruning techniques. Related work [18] shows that iterative pruning achieves better performance than one-shot pruning.

2.4   Merging and Post-processing

To form the final instance segmentation masks, we merged the results from the semantic segmentation and deep regression branches as shown in Fig. 1. The merging scheme is similar to [15]. First, we apply a Gaussian smoothing filter on the predicted nuclei distance maps from the deep regression model to prevent false-positive local maxima detection. The estimated average nuclei size from the segmentation model determines the kernel size of the Gaussian filter [15]. From the smoothed distance maps, we then extract local maxima and use them as seed points for the marker-controlled Watershed algorithm. We use the predicted binary segmentation masks from the semantic segmentation model to determine the background in the instance segmentation masks. Finally, we apply two straightforward post-processing steps as suggested in former studies [12]. Using morphological operations, we remove tiny objects from the segmentation masks (area <30 pixels) and fill the holes in the predicted instances.

2.5   Evaluation Metrics

To evaluate the final instance segmentation performance, we use Aggregate Jaccard Index (AJI) [12] and Panoptic Quality (PQ) score [5] as the primary evaluation scores. Moreover, to evaluate the performance of each DNN model (i.e. the semantic segmentation model and the deep regression model), we utilise Dice similarity score and Mean Square Error (MSE) as evaluation indexes. Further details about these scores can be found in [5].

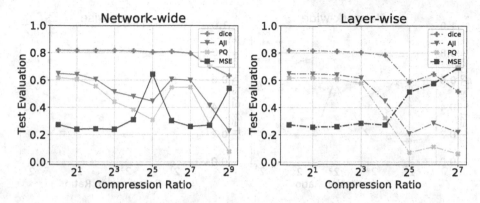

Fig. 2. Impact of two pruning methods on the semantic segmentation (Dice), regression (MSE), and instance segmentation (AJI, PQ) performances on the MoNuSeg test set. Nuclei semantic segmentation is extremely robust against both pruning methods. Layer-wise pruning shows better performance for smaller compression ratios, while enforcing larger pruning ratios to each layer harms the total performance.

3   Results and Discussion

In our experiments, we use the training set of the MoNuSeg dataset to train and iteratively prune the model. Figure 2 and Fig. 3 present performance results of the pruned models on the test set of the MoNuSeg dataset and the entire TNBC dataset, respectively.

Table 1. Theoretical speedup. Layer-wise pruning yields higher speed-ups, as it prunes more weights in the early layers that have small kernels applied to a large input, requiring more FLOPS. $CR > 2^7$ is impossible to achieve with layer-wise pruning due to loss of connectivity inside the model.

Pruning method	Compression ratio (CR)								
	2	4	8	16	32	64	128	256	512
Network-wide	1.49	2.13	3.07	4.46	6.59	9.90	15.01	23.80	45.02
Layer-wise	1.99	3.99	7.97	15.89	31.57	62.27	121.18	–	–

Figure 2 shows that nuclei semantic segmentation network is extremely robust against pruning, where removing 0.992% of the parameters in network-wide ($CR = 2^7$) and 0.937% ($CR = 2^4$) in layer-wise fashion is possible with only 2% reduction in Dice. It also shows that layer-wise pruning is a better choice (for all measures and tasks) for smaller compression ratios, while enforcing extreme pruning ratios ($CR > 2^5$) to each layer harms the total performance. That is due to losing small yet important kernels in the early layers. Extreme pruning ratios ($CR > 2^8$) are also not possible to achieve with layer-wise pruning because this leads to removing the whole layer.

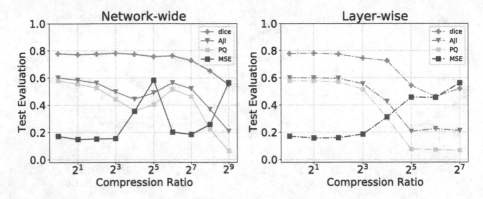

Fig. 3. Impact of pruning on model performance under distribution shift, i.e. training and pruning on MoNuSeg and test on TNBC dataset. All evaluation metrics are identical to Fig. 2. Layer-wise pruning shows less robustness to the distribution shift.

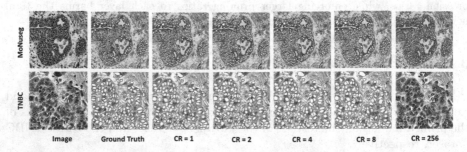

Fig. 4. Visualizing the layer-wise pruning impact on the final instance segmentation performance for two example images from MoNuSeg (top) and TNBC dataset (bottom). The first column shows the raw input images, the second column shows the ground truth instance segmentation masks, and the rest shows the predicted masks by the model with different compression ratios (CRs).

Another interesting observation in Fig. 2 (network-wide) is that pruning deep regression model first increase MSE and then decrease MSE (and ultimately results in high MSE values due to extreme compression ratios). This observation is aligned to previous works [18], where the authors observe the performance improvement when pruning. We conjecture that iterative pruning and training helps to find better global optima in the loss landscape. Such a performance improvement results in extreme compression ratios ($CR = 2^7$) for network-wide instance segmentation pruning while only losing 2 % in AJI and PQ.

Figure 3 evaluates model performance under distribution shift, i.e. training and pruning on MoNuSeg and test on the TNBC dataset. All evaluation metrics are close to Fig. 2, showing that our pruning schemes are robust to potential natural distribution shifts presented by a different dataset. Comparing network-wide and layer-wise pruning shows that the latter presents less robustness to the distribution shift. Similar evaluation patterns also can be seen in the TNBC dataset, i.e. for smaller CRs, layer-wise is a better choice for instance segmentation. We also observe the performance decrease and then increase for network-wide pruning, as better solutions are found using iterative pruning and training.

Table 1 shows the theoretical speedup that can potentially be achieved by proper hardware supporting model sparsity for both pruning techniques along different CRs. As expected, layer-wise pruning gains much higher speed-ups, as it stronger prunes early layers.

Figure 4 provides qualitative evaluation of the impact of pruning on the final instance segmentation for different CRs. DNN pruning with small CRs (CR $\approx$ 2^3 and smaller) has not drastically changed the predicted instance segmentation masks. However, the instance segmentation performance has been significantly degraded for very large CR ($CR = 2^8$).

This work can be extended in a number of ways that we are planning to address in future studies. We plan to investigate the effect of architecture on instance segmentation by using different pre-trained models. Another interesting direction is to investigate the observed distribution shift for different target datasets. It is also interesting to see whether fine-tuning on the target distribution helps the out-of-distribution generalization. Another potential research question, inspired by [8] is to investigate which instances (classes) are more prone to neural network compression. Finally, it would be interesting to explore structured pruning techniques, especially those which allow practical speedups when using special hardware such as NVIDIA Ampere [20].

4 Conclusion

In this work, we apply two magnitude-based pruning techniques, namely network-wide and layer-wise pruning for nuclei instance segmentation in H&E-stained histological images. Our results suggest that with layer-wise pruning and a certain CR level, the weights from the semantic segmentation and deep regression models can be pruned with less than 2% drop in the evaluation indexes. We observe that nuclei semantic segmentation is highly robust against pruning i.e. Dice score is barely reduced even in extreme compression ratios. Our results also shows that both pruning methods show high robustness again distribution shift with high importance on critical real world applications.

Prospect of Application: Further research is needed to explore other pruning techniques and investigate their impact on the nuclei instance segmentation performance for in-distribution and out-of-distribution regimes. We also plan to extend this work to to investigate instances affected by different pruning strategies and focus on avoiding accuracy reduction across all classes.

Acknowledgements. This project was supported by the Austrian Research Promotion Agency (FFG), No. 872636. This study was conducted retrospectively using human subject data made available through open access. Ethical approval was not required as confirmed by the license attached with the open access data.

References

1. Anwar, S.M., Majid, M., Qayyum, A., Awais, M., Alnowami, M., Khan, M.K.: Medical image analysis using convolutional neural networks: a review. J. Med. Syst. **42**(11), 1–13 (2018). https://doi.org/10.1007/s10916-018-1088-1
2. Bancher, B., Mahbod, A., Ellinger, I., Ecker, R., Dorffner, G.: Improving mask r-cnn for nuclei instance segmentation in hematoxylin & eosin-stained histological images. In: MICCAI Workshop on Computational Pathology, pp. 20–35. PMLR (2021)
3. Entezari, R., Saukh, O.: Class-dependent compression of deep neural networks. In: Proceedings of the International Workshop on Machine Learning on Edge in Sensor Systems (2020)
4. Entezari, R., Saukh, O.: Class-dependent pruning of deep neural networks. In: IEEE Second Workshop on Machine Learning on Edge in Sensor Systems, pp. 13–18 (2020). https://doi.org/10.1109/SenSysML50931.2020.00010
5. Graham, S., et al.: Hover-Net: simultaneous segmentation and classification of nuclei in multi-tissue histology images. Med. Image Anal. **58**, 101563 (2019). https://doi.org/10.1016/j.media.2019.101563
6. He, K., Zhang, X., Ren, S., Sun, J.: Deep residual learning for image recognition. In: Conference on Computer Vision and Pattern Recognition, pp. 770–778. IEEE (2016)
7. Hoefler, T., Alistarh, D., Ben-Nun, T., Dryden, N., Peste, A.: Sparsity in deep learning: pruning and growth for efficient inference and training in neural networks. J. Mach. Learn. Res. **22**(241), 1–124 (2021)
8. Hooker, S., Courville, A., Clark, G., Dauphin, Y., Frome, A.: What do compressed deep neural networks forget? arXiv preprint arXiv:1911.05248 (2019)
9. Jeong, T., Bollavaram, M., Delaye, E., Sirasao, A.: Neural network pruning for biomedical image segmentation. In: Medical Imaging 2021: Image-Guided Procedures, Robotic Interventions, and Modeling, vol. 11598, pp. 415–425. SPIE (2021). https://doi.org/10.1117/12.2579256
10. Jørgensen, A.S., et al.: Using cell nuclei features to detect colon cancer tissue in hematoxylin and eosin stained slides. Cytometry Part A, **91**(8), 785–793 (2017). https://doi.org/10.1002/cyto.a.23175, https://onlinelibrary.wiley.com/doi/abs/10.1002/cyto.a.23175
11. Khan, S., Rahmani, H., Shah, S.A.A., Bennamoun, M.: A guide to convolutional neural networks for computer vision. Synth. Lect. Comput. Vis. **8**(1), 1–207 (2018). https://doi.org/10.2200/S00822ED1V01Y201712COV015
12. Kumar, N., et al.: A multi-organ nucleus segmentation challenge. IEEE Trans. Med. Imaging **39**(5), 1380–1391 (2020). https://doi.org/10.1109/TMI.2019.2947628
13. Loshchilov, I., Hutter, F.: Sgdr: stochastic gradient descent with warm restarts. arXiv preprint arXiv:1608.03983 (2016)
14. Mahbod, A., Schaefer, G., Bancher, B., Löw, C., Dorffner, G., Ecker, R., Ellinger, I.: CryoNuSeg: a dataset for nuclei instance segmentation of cryosectioned H & E-stained histological images. Comput. Biol. Med. **132**, 104349 (2021). https://doi.org/10.1016/j.compbiomed.2021.104349
15. Mahbod, A., Schaefer, G., Ellinger, I., Ecker, R., Smedby, Ö., Wang, C.: A two-stage U-Net algorithm for segmentation of nuclei in H & E-stained tissues. In: Reyes-Aldasoro, C.C., Janowczyk, A., Veta, M., Bankhead, P., Sirinukunwattana, K. (eds.) ECDP 2019. LNCS, vol. 11435, pp. 75–82. Springer, Cham (2019). https://doi.org/10.1007/978-3-030-23937-4_9

16. Muckatira, S.: Properties of winning tickets on skin lesion classification. arXiv preprint arXiv:2008.12141 (2020)
17. Naylor, P., Laé, M., Reyal, F., Walter, T.: Segmentation of nuclei in histopathology images by deep regression of the distance map. IEEE Trans. Med. Imaging **38**(2), 448–459 (2019). https://doi.org/10.1109/TMI.2018.2865709
18. Renda, A., Frankle, J., Carbin, M.: Comparing rewinding and fine-tuning in neural network pruning. arXiv preprint arXiv:2003.02389 (2020)
19. Skinner, B.M., Johnson, E.E.P.: Nuclear morphologies: their diversity and functional relevance. Chromosoma **126**(2), 195–212 (2016). https://doi.org/10.1007/s00412-016-0614-5
20. Zhou, A., et al.: Learning n: M fine-grained structured sparse neural networks from scratch. arXiv preprint arXiv:2102.04010 (2021)

Spatial Feature Conservation Networks (SFCNs) for Dilated Convolutions to Improve Breast Cancer Segmentation from DCE-MRI

Hyunseok Seo[1]($\boxtimes$) (iD), Seohee So[1], Sojin Yun[1], Seokjun Lee[1], and Jiseong Barg[2]

[1] Korea Institute of Science and Technology (KIST), Seoul 02792, Korea
seo@kist.kr
[2] Korea Advanced Institute of Science and Technology (KAIST), Daejeon 34141, Korea

Abstract. Target delineation in the medical images can be utilized in lots of clinical applications, such as computer-aided diagnosis, prognosis, or radiation treatment planning. Deep learning has tremendously improved the performances of automated segmentation in a data-driven manner as compared with conventional machine learning models. In this work, we propose a spatial feature conservative design for feature extraction in deep neural networks. To avoid signal loss from sub-sampling of the max pooling operations, multi-scale dilated convolutions are applied to reach the large receptive field. Then, we propose a novel compensation module that prevents intrinsic signal loss from dilated convolution kernels. Furthermore, an adaptive combination method of the dilated convolution results is devised to enhance learning efficiency. The proposed model is validated on the delineation of breast cancer in DCE-MR images obtained from public dataset. The segmentation results clearly show that the proposed network model provides the most accurate delineation results of the breast cancers in the DCE-MR images. The proposed model can be applied to other clinical practice sensitive to spatial information loss.

Keywords: Deep learning · MRI · Segmentation · Signal loss · Spatial information

1 Introduction

Medical image delineation in a manual way for various clinical applications is often a labor-intensive and time-consuming task. The delineation results are affected by inter- or even intra-operator variations [1]. In addition, specialized expertise is required and a high-level consistency in the results has to be addressed [2]. So automated delineation algorithms for medical images have been vigorously studied to overcome the limitation of the manual segmentations [3–8].

The emergence of deep learning has shifted a paradigm in medical image analysis, which results in increase of the reliability of computer vision in clinical practices [9, 10]. Especially, deep learning models have an intrinsic ability to effectively learn high-dimensional relationships in the prior information [11], and medical image segmentation

© The Author(s), under exclusive license to Springer Nature Switzerland AG 2022
S. Wu et al. (Eds.): AMAI 2022, LNCS 13540, pp. 118–127, 2022.
https://doi.org/10.1007/978-3-031-17721-7_13

is one of the major applications of them. For example, U-Net [12] is the basic network model to provide high quality segmentation results of the biomedical images, which has been utilized as a backbone structure of the various deep learning models. Many algorithms for improving the delineation performance with deep learning have been studied [13]. Efficient decision-making in medical image segmentation was studied by devising an adaptive loss function [14]. It guides the optimization process to better direction via avoiding class imbalance in training process. Other studies that can use more information have been introduced. Most of that way is to incorporate slice information into in-plane images. 2.5D or 3D-based models are the results for better extraction of visual features via additional information in slice direction [15, 16].

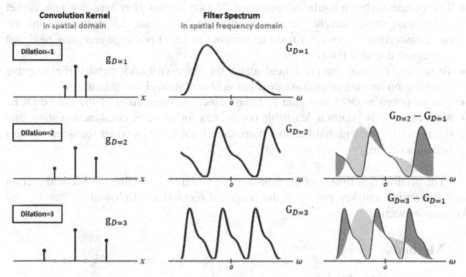

Fig. 1. Problem in the dilated convolutions. One-dimensional convolutional kernels (g) with different dilation factors (D) and corresponding filter spectrum (G) in the spatial frequency domain. The rightmost column represents the difference between the filter spectrum and that with a dilation factor of one.

In spite of previous improvements, there is an intrinsic limitation in deep neural networks because the networks usually rely on the small size of kernels (3 × 3) for feature extraction that has narrow receptive fields. Max pooling operation is a popular solution to increase receptive fields. There are some merits of max pooling operation, which can provide a form of translation invariance and a form of noise smoothing [17]. However, it is a kind of sub-sampling causing spatial signal loss that is severe to the small or unclear targets. mU-Net [18] was introduced to cope with loss of spatial information from pooling operations. Dilated convolution is another way to expand receptive fields without pooling operations [19–21]. So, it can capture the visual details that are likely to be removed with the max pooling operation. But, in terms of the digital signal processing theory [22], convolution kernels are broadened by a dilation factor and it causes shrinkage of filter width, as shown in Fig. 1, which is the smoothing effects.

In this paper, we design a network model to extremely minimize the loss of spatial information for delineation of the small and unclear target in the medical images. To this end, we do not utilize pooling layers. Instead, multi-scale dilated convolutions are applied to increase the receptive field. Furthermore, the compensation module is proposed to hinder the loss of spatial information due to broadened kernels in dilated convolutions. Then, we define learnable parameters for combining the results of each dilated convolution to make flexible feature extraction along depth or stage of the network. The key contributions of this study are summarized as follows.

- Our network model prevents loss of spatial information during feature extraction for robust segmentation under the scenarios of small or unclear targets.
- The compensation module is composed of two convolution layers where kernel weights are same (weight sharing) but dilation factors are different. We combine two convolutions in a way of residual learning to grab both large receptive field and conservative spatial information.
- To achieve optimal receptive field along the stage (network depth), the adaptive combination method of multi-scale dilation convolutions is proposed.
- The proposed model has a gain in breast cancer segmentation of the public DCE-MRI datasets. In addition, learnable parameters for adaptive combination show that the network learns global features more than local features when the depth (stage) becomes deeper.

The detailed description of the proposed algorithms is explained in Method section and the results and key points of the proposed method are followed in Results and Discussion section.

2   Methods

2.1   Compensation Module

Dilated convolution does not lose spatial information from sub-samplings because there are no pooling operations. However, broaden kernel due to dilation generates narrow filters in the frequency domain, and some spectral components relevant to spatial information are filtered out (gray shadow in Fig. 1). Simply, there is a trade-off between the dilated factor and spatial information. Thus, the visual features in image details might be ignored if dilated factor becomes large to increase the receptive field. To regenerate lost spatial information due to dilated convolution, we can come up with two convolutions. Both have the same convolution kernel weights (weight sharing), but dilation factors are not the same. One of them has a dilated factor of one ($D = 1$) and the other has a dilated factor of d ($D = d$). Then, $F_{s,d}$ is defined for the features extracted by dilated convolution with a dilated factor of d at stage s. The lost spatial information, $LSI_{s,d}$, from broaden kernels by dilated convolutions can be inferred as follows.

$$LSI_{s,d} \equiv F_{s,1}^d - F_{s,d} \qquad (1)$$

where $F_{s,1}^d$ stands for the features extracted by dilated convolution with a dilated factor of one and whose kernel weights are copied from $F_{s,d}$. By doing this, we can recover

$LSI_{s,d}$ gone by dilated convolution (with a dilated factor of d) which has a narrower filter width than that of a dilated factor of one in the frequency domain, as shown in Fig. 1. In other words, $LSI_{s,d}$ enables to include the features of the visual details that cannot be extracted by a large dilated factor of d. Finally, to achieve both large receptive field and detailed features, the compensated features for dilated convolution (dilated factor: d), $CF_{s,d}$, can be defined with $LSI_{s,d}$ as follows,

$$CF_{s,d} \equiv k \cdot F_{s,d} + LSI_{s,d}$$

$$= k \cdot F_{s,d} + \left(F^d_{s,1} - F_{s,d} \right) = (k-1)F_{s,d} + F^d_{s,1} \qquad (2)$$

Here, we use a scale factor of $k = 2$ for $F_{s,d}$ instead of other numbers as $CF_{s,d}$ can be easily re-expressed to a form of the residual learning. Besides, we can avoid a logical issue that final $CF_{s,d}$ excludes $F_{s,d}$ when a scale factor is one. Therefore, from Eq. 2, we can design a compensation module, as shown in Fig. 2(a).

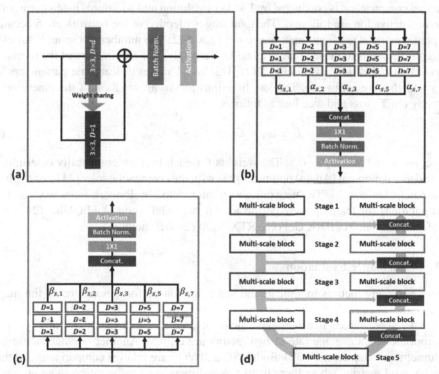

Fig. 2. (a) The compensation module for a dilated factor of d. (b) The multi-scale block composed of the compensation modules in (a) for encoding part of U-Net at stage s. (c) The multi-scale block for decoding part of U-Net. (d) The final model of the proposed network.

Then, there are multiple compensation modules that have different dilation factors at each stage as we do not know which dilation factor is optimal for each stage. Moreover, the results from respective compensation modules are weighted by learnable parameters and combined adaptively. The weights of the small dilation factor become increased if local features are significant for inference. In contrast, high weights of the large dilation factor imply that extraction of global features is important. These learnable weights can make more flexible learning. Furthermore, they can provide a clue where the network learns global or local features.

2.2 Network Architecture

The backbone network is a vanilla U-Net. However, all convolution layers in the U-Net composed of convolution operations, batch normalization, and activations are replaced with our compensation modules. All pooling and up-pooling layers in the U-Net are removed to avoid signal loss by the sub-sampling. There are five dilated convolutions where dilated factors are 1, 2, 3, 5, and 7 so that receptive fields are corresponded to 3×3, 5×5, 7×7, 11×11, and 15×15, respectively. Next to the compensation module, the compensated features are weighted by learnable parameters and concatenated. Then, channel compression is conducted by 1×1 convolution and additional batch normalization and activation are followed. The total stages (depths) of the network are 5 because in-plane matrix size of our input image is 512×512. The number of channels for each stage corresponds to those of the original U-Net study. The architecture of the proposed network model is described in Fig. 2(d). The initial values of learnable parameters for $\alpha_{s,d}$ and $\beta_{s,d}$ are set to one. The loss functions are an aggregation of the binary cross entropy (BCE) loss and dice loss as follows.

$$\mathcal{L} \equiv \omega_1 \times \mathcal{L}_{BCE} + \omega_2 \times \mathcal{L}_{dice} \tag{3}$$

Here, $\omega_1 = 0.2$ and $\omega_2 = 0.8$. The weights for each loss are empirically determined. The adaptive moment (Adam) optimizer [23] with the cosine scheduler [24] was applied. The batch size was 24. The network was implemented by Pytorch framework and all computations for learning were performed on two Intel Xeon Gold 6248R (24 cores, 3.0 GHz) and one NVIDIA GeForce RTX 3090 (24 GB memory).

2.3 Performance Evaluation

There are many metrics to validate the segmentation performance. One of the major evaluation methods is the dice similarity coefficient (DSC). DSC score is equivalent to the F_1 score which is a harmonic mean of precision and recall (sensitivity). It is appropriate when average rate of two factors are critical. Another popular metric is a volumetric overlap error (VOE). Both DSC and VOE are relative comparisons and they can be good metrics where there is no voxel dimensional information in anonymized dataset. The definitions of DSC and VOE are well described in the relevant studies [18, 25]. All processing for data analysis and evaluation were implemented using MATLAB software (9.8.0.1721703, R2020a, The MathWorks Inc., CA).

2.4 Image Dataset and Data Preparation

In our study, the public dataset for breast MRI was applied. This dataset is composed of 922 biopsy-confirmed invasive breast cancer patients over a decade and they were retrospectively collected at a single institute [26]. All images were obtained by dynamic contrast enhanced (DCE)-MRI. The original dataset provides bounding box annotations generated by radiologists. So, we requested additional segmentation annotations based on these bounding boxes from two other clinical experts.

Table 1. Quantitative scores of the breast-cancer segmentation results.

Methods	DSC	VOE
U-Net [12]	0.56 ± 0.07	0.52 ± 0.13
H-DenseUNet [15]	0.63 ± 0.04	0.43 ± 0.08
mU-Net [18]	0.64 ± 0.04	0.43 ± 0.07
DIU-Net [21]	0.63 ± 0.05	0.44 ± 0.07
Proposed network	$\mathbf{0.65 \pm 0.03}$	$\mathbf{0.41 \pm 0.07}$
mU-Net-based output-consistency regularization [27]	0.67 ± 0.02	0.39 ± 0.06
DIU-Net-based output-consistency regularization	0.66 ± 0.03	0.41 ± 0.06
Proposed network-based output-consistency regularization	$\mathbf{0.69 \pm 0.02}$	$\mathbf{0.38 \pm 0.04}$

In the original dataset, in-plane matrix size is not all same so we resized the image to 512×512. Another key point is to apply multi-phase images. In our network model, input data has four channels to include four different phase images. To this end, 15 patient data was discarded because of data consistency. Consequently, total 752 patient data for training and 155 patient data for validation were used. In other words, there were 20,095 slice images of each phase for training and 4,019 slice images of each phase for validation. We conducted five-fold cross validations to validate our model more strictly. All subsets for the cross validation were prepared by patient-level splits so that any slice images of the same patient belong to only one of training or validation set. Then, this dataset was applied to deep learning-based state-of-the-art (SOTA) segmentation algorithms under the same conditions.

3 Results

The DSC and VOE scores are calculated in Table 1. Among U-Net [12], H-DenseUNet [15], mU-Net [18], DIU-Net [21], and the proposed method, the U-Net provides the lowest score in DSC and the highest score in VOE. H-DenseUNet, mU-Net, and DIU-Net have similar scores. The proposed network model has the highest score in DSC and the lowest score in VOE. The t-test for the proposed method was performed under null hypothesis that the score from the proposed method is equal to that from the compared method. We can reject this null hypothesis at the significance level of 0.05 since all *p*-values are calculated less than 0.05. Likewise, we measured the DSC and VOE scores when our method is combined with output-consistency regularization scheme [27]. The original output-consistency regularization scheme was implemented on mU-Net. Here, we did not apply this scheme to H-DenseUNet due to memory limitation in our workstation. The proposed network with output-consistency regularization achieves the highest score in terms of DSC and the lowest score in terms of VOE. We did *t*-test for the proposed network-based output-consistency regularization as well. In our study, all *p*-values were clearly calculated under 0.001.

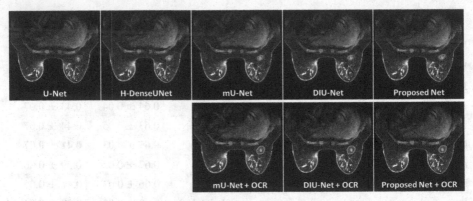

Fig. 3. The visual results of the segmentation (Red: Ground truth and Green: Prediction). OCR denotes the output-consistency regularization. (Color figure online)

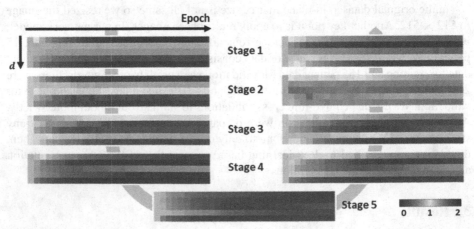

Fig. 4. Evolution of $\alpha_{s,d}$ and $\beta_{s,d}$ of the multi-scale blocks in encoding and decoding parts, respectively.

Figure 3 shows the segmentation results from each method in Table 1. The visual results also aligned to those of DSC and VOE scores. In Fig. 4, for the adaptive combinations, evolutions of the weights defined as $\alpha_{s,d}$ and $\beta_{s,d}$ are displayed. The weights for the small dilated factor are large at the shallow stage, however, those for the large dilated factors become larger when the deeper the stage goes. It is more noticeable in encoding part.

4 Discussion and Conclusion

Currently, deep learning-based segmentation algorithms have been improved [28]. However, there is intrinsic loss of spatial information during feature extractions. It is more critical in the small or unclear target delineations. Because those targets are easily vulnerable to spatial information loss. mU-Net was introduced to alleviate this issue caused by the pooling operations and dilated convolution was devised to replace direct subsamplings. In this study, we bring up a new network architecture where there are no pooling operations and loss of spatial information.

In the proposed network model, multi-scale dilated convolutions are applied instead of the pooling operations. Then, the compensation module recovers lost spatial information due to dilation effect of the kernels. Moreover, the learnable weights for the feature combinations enable more efficient training. Specifically, we can infer that the network extracts the low-level features with the local features as the local features are obtained with small dilation factors and are highly weighted in the early stage of the network. In contrast, the high-level features are extracted with the global features because the weights for large dilated factors are increased when the network depth goes to the bottleneck stage. This insight is consistent with the conventional analysis with the VGG model that the low-level features are relevant to the local features and high-level features are related to the global features. To make sure more generality of the proposed method, we repeated the same learning process five times with different subsets of training and validation data. Here, careful patient-level splits were applied to guarantee that the network never sees the validation images during training process. Furthermore, to fully use dynamic information, the network has multi-phase input data. Because, it is not easy to recognize breast cancers in conventional MR images such as normal T_1- or T_2-weighted images. We input the four phase images sequentially along the channel directions. The quantitative scores, statistical t-test, and visual results (Table 1 and Fig. 3) clearly show that the proposed method is better than other compared methods. We can see that the proposed method has power even when it is combined with multi-output-consistency regularization.

There is more room to improve the proposed model. In our study, all stages have the fixed dilated factors that were determined empirically. The receptive field highly depends on these dilated factors so we can find smarter ways to search the optimal factors. Additionally, the public dataset applied to our study provides other metadata about imaging features such as size, shape, and texture. Then, we can come up with a method incorporating those meta data into our learning process.

This study proposes a spatial feature conservative design in deep neural networks to improve breast cancer segmentation. To avoid spatial information loss from pooling operations, dilated convolutions are applied. Dilated convolutions also have intrinsic loss of spatial information so a compensation module is designed. Moreover, adaptive combination of the results from multiple dilated convolutions is proposed.

Prospect of Application: The proposed method can be extended to pooling operations in other deep learning models or to other practical applications sensitive to spatial information loss.

Acknowledgements. This work was partially supported by KIST Institutional Programs (Grant 2E31602, Grant 2E31613, Grant 2E31571, and Grant 2E31511).

References

1. Dou, Q., et al.: 3D deeply supervised network for automated segmentation of volumetric medical images. Med. Image Anal. **41**, 40–54 (2017)
2. Moradmand, H., Aghamiri, S.M.R., Ghaderi, R.: Impact of image preprocessing methods on reproducibility of radiomic features in multimodal magnetic resonance imaging in glioblastoma. J. Appl. Clin. Med. Phys. **21**(1), 179–190 (2020)
3. Li, D., et al.: Augmenting atlas-based liver segmentation for radiotherapy treatment planning by incorporating image features proximal to the atlas contours. Phys. Med. Biol. **62**(1), 272 (2016)
4. Luo, Q., et al.: Segmentation of abdomen MR images using kernel graph cuts with shape priors. Biomed. Eng. Online **12**(1), 124 (2013)
5. Wu, W., et al.: Automatic liver segmentation on volumetric CT images using supervoxel-based graph cuts. Comput. Math. Methods Med. **2016** (2016)
6. Li, G., et al.: Automatic liver segmentation based on shape constraints and deformable graph cut in CT images. IEEE Trans. Image Process. **24**(12), 5315–5329 (2015)
7. Chartrand, G., et al.: Liver segmentation on CT and MR using Laplacian mesh optimization. IEEE Trans. Biomed. Eng. **64**(9), 2110–2121 (2016)
8. Zheng, Y., et al.: Feature learning based random walk for liver segmentation. PLoS One **11**(11), e0164098 (2016)
9. Shen, L., Zhao, W., Xing, L.: Patient-specific reconstruction of volumetric computed tomography images from a single projection view via deep learning. Nat. Biomed. Eng. **3**(11), 880–888 (2019)
10. Seo, H., Shin, K.M., Kyung, Y.: A dual domain network for MRI reconstruction using gabor loss. In: 2021 IEEE International Conference on Image Processing (ICIP). IEEE (2021)
11. Jin, K.H., et al.: Deep convolutional neural network for inverse problems in imaging. IEEE Trans. Image Process. **26**(9), 4509–4522 (2017)
12. Ronneberger, O., Fischer, P., Brox, T.: U-net: convolutional networks for biomedical image segmentation. In: Navab, N., Hornegger, J., Wells, W., Frangi, A. (eds.) MICCAI 2015. LNCS, vol. 9351, pp. 234–241. Springer, Cham (2015). https://doi.org/10.1007/978-3-319-24574-4_28
13. Wang, R., et al.: Medical image segmentation using deep learning: a survey. IET Image Proc. **16**(5), 1243–1267 (2022)
14. Seo, H., Bassenne, M., Xing, L.: Closing the gap between deep neural network modeling and biomedical decision-making metrics in segmentation via adaptive loss functions. IEEE Trans. Med. Imaging **40**(2), 585–593 (2020)
15. Li, X., et al.: H-DenseUNet: hybrid densely connected UNet for liver and tumor segmentation from CT volumes. IEEE Trans. Med. Imaging **37**(12), 2663–2674 (2018)

16. Çiçek, Ö., et al.: 3D U-Net: learning dense volumetric segmentation from sparse annotation. In: Ourselin, S., Joskowicz, L., Sabuncu, M., Unal, G., Wells, W. (eds.) MICCAI 2016. LNCS, vol. 9901, pp. 424–432. Springer, Cham (2016). https://doi.org/10.1007/978-3-319-46723-8_49

17. Zhang, R.: Making convolutional networks shift-invariant again. In: International Conference on Machine Learning. PMLR (2019)

18. Seo, H., et al.: Modified U-Net (mU-Net) with incorporation of object-dependent high level features for improved liver and liver-tumor segmentation in CT images. IEEE Trans. Med. Imaging **39**(5), 1316–1325 (2019)

19. Li, Y., Zhang, X., Chen, D.: CSRNet: dilated convolutional neural networks for understanding the highly congested scenes. In: Proceedings of the IEEE Conference on Computer Vision and Pattern Recognition (2018)

20. Seo, H., et al.: Machine learning techniques for biomedical image segmentation: an overview of technical aspects and introduction to state-of-art applications. Med. Phys. **47**(5), e148–e167 (2020)

21. Cahall, D.E., et al.: Dilated inception U-net (DIU-net) for brain tumor segmentation. arXiv preprint arXiv:2108.06772 (2021)

22. Candy, J.C., Temes, G.C.: Interpolation and decimation of digital SignalsA tutorial review (1992)

23. Kingma, D.P., Ba, J.: Adam: a method for stochastic optimization. arXiv preprint arXiv:1412. 6980 (2014)

24. Loshchilov, I., Hutter, F.: SGDR: stochastic gradient descent with warm restarts. arXiv preprint arXiv:1608.03983 (2016)

25. Park, S., et al.: Deep learning-based automatic segmentation of mandible and maxilla in multi-center CT images. Appl. Sci. **12**(3), 1358 (2022)

26. Saha, A., et al.: A machine learning approach to radiogenomics of breast cancer: a study of 922 subjects and 529 DCE-MRI features. Br. J. Cancer **119**(4), 508–516 (2018)

27. Seo, H., et al.: Deep neural network with consistency regularization of multi-output channels for improved tumor detection and delineation. IEEE Trans. Med. Imaging **40**(12), 3369–3378 (2021)

28. Isensee, F., et al.: nnU-Net: a self-configuring method for deep learning-based biomedical image segmentation. Nat. Methods **18**(2), 203–211 (2021)

The Impact of Using Voxel-Level Segmentation Metrics on Evaluating Multifocal Prostate Cancer Localisation

Wen Yan[1,2,3]($\boxtimes$), Qianye Yang[2,3], Tom Syer[4], Zhe Min[2,3], Shonit Punwani[4], Mark Emberton[5], Dean Barratt[2,3], Bernard Chiu[1], and Yipeng Hu[2,3]

[1] Department of Electrical Engineering, City University of Hong Kong, 83 Tat Chee Avenue, Hong Kong, China
wenyan6-c@my.cityu.edu.hk
[2] Department of Medical Physics and Biomedical Engineering, University College London, Gower St, London WC1E 6BT, UK
[3] Wellcome/EPSRC Centre for Interventional and Surgical Sciences, University College London, Gower St, London WC1E 6BT, UK
[4] Centre for Medical Imaging, Division of Medicine, University College London, Foley Street, London W1W 7TS, UK
[5] Division of Surgery and Interventional Science, University College London, Gower St, London WC1E 6BT, UK

Abstract. Dice similarity coefficient (DSC) and Hausdorff distance (HD) are widely used for evaluating medical image segmentation. They have also been criticised, when reported alone, for their unclear or even misleading clinical interpretation. DSCs may also differ substantially from HDs, due to boundary smoothness or multiple regions of interest (ROIs) within a subject. More importantly, either metric can also have a nonlinear, non-monotonic relationship with outcomes based on Type 1 and 2 errors, designed for specific clinical decisions that use the resulting segmentation. Whilst cases causing disagreement between these metrics are not difficult to postulate, one might argue that they may not necessarily be substantiated in real-world segmentation applications, as a majority of ROIs and their predictions often do not manifest themselves in extremely irregular shapes or locations that are prone to such inconsistency. This work first proposes a new asymmetric detection metric, adapting those used in object detection, for planning prostate cancer procedures. The lesion-level metrics is then compared with the voxel-level DSC and HD, whereas a 3D UNet is used for segmenting lesions from multiparametric MR (mpMR) images. Based on experimental results using 877 sets of mpMR images, we report pairwise agreement and correlation 1) between DSC and HD, and 2) between voxel-level DSC and recall-controlled precision at lesion-level, with Cohen's $\kappa \in [0.49, 0.61]$ and Pearson's $r \in [0.66, 0.76]$ (*p-values*<0.001) at varying cut-offs. However, the differences in false-positives and false-negatives, between the actual errors and the perceived counterparts if DSC is used, can be as high as 152 and 154, respectively, out of the 357 test set lesions. We therefore carefully conclude that, despite of the significant correlations,

© The Author(s), under exclusive license to Springer Nature Switzerland AG 2022
S. Wu et al. (Eds.): AMAI 2022, LNCS 13540, pp. 128–138, 2022.
https://doi.org/10.1007/978-3-031-17721-7_14

voxel-level metrics such as DSC can misrepresent lesion-level detection accuracy for evaluating localisation of multifocal prostate cancer and should be interpreted with caution.

Keywords: Prostate cancer · Multi-parametric MR · Lesion-level localisation metrics · Voxel-level segmentation metrics

1   Introduction

Prostate cancer is one of the most frequently occurring malignancies in adult men [24]. Transrectal ultrasound-guided (TRUS) biopsy is the gold standard for detecting and grading prostate cancer; however, it has side effects such as bleeding, pain, and infection. Multiparametric MR (mpMR) scan has been suggested as a non-invasive assessment tool before a biopsy [1]. In addition, mpMR scans can be performed after a biopsy or a treatment to investigate if any cancer found in the prostate has progressed. Radiologists read mpMR images and give lesions a score of 1–5 by using a Likert scoring system [12] or the Prostate Imaging Reporting and Data System (PI-RADS) [7, 25]. Both scoring systems are used to describe the level of evidence for detecting lesions and to standardize radiological assessment.

Recently, deep learning approaches have been proposed for diagnosing patients with suspicion of clinically significant prostate cancer and segment prostate lesions directly from mpMR images [4, 6, 10, 22, 26]. In addition to evaluating patient-level cancer detection - an image classification problem, results from image segmentation using UNet and its variant [20] have also been reported, as the mpMR-detected lesions may need histo-pathological examination or treatment, for example, through targeted biopsy [16] and focal ablation [2]. Further examples of mpMR-based procedure planning are discussed in Sect. 2.1.

Voxel-level segmentation metrics including Dice similarity coefficient (DSC) and Hausdorff distance (HD), defined in Sect. 2.2, have long been established to evaluate segmentation accuracy and reported for this application [4, 6, 10, 15, 22, 26]. However, they have also been debated for their consistency and clinical relevance. These limitations are particularly evident with multiple regions-of-interest (ROIs). As illustrated in a1 and a2, Fig. 1, when the number of predicted (green) and ground-truth (red) ROIs differ, the HDs become dependent on the distance from the missed ground-truth to the others, but the DSCs do not. Other factors include boundary smoothness that are more sensitive to HDs than DSCs.

Perhaps more relevant to clinical practice, either DSC or HD can disagree with other metrics that are related to clinical decision making. Examples include lesion-level detection accuracy that is of interest in this study. Shown in Fig. 1, one ground-truth ROI is entirely missed in b1 while both ground-truth ROIs are, albeit partially, detected in b2. These two cases measure to similar DSCs (here, ≈ 0.5). The lesion-level accuracy is important in many biomedical imaging applications. In our applications, described in Sect. 2.1, the heterogeneity within

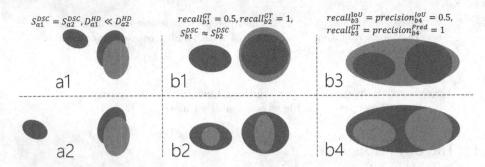

Fig. 1. Illustration of the prediction (green) overlaid with the ground-truth lesion (red), details are described in Sect. 2 (Color figure online).

individual foci has motivated diagnostic sampling and treating these lesions individually, rather than a uniform coverage of all cancerous regions, partly due to the natural history of the pathology [2].

Lesion-level metrics used in object detection literature are arguably appropriate for quantifying lesion detection, even when segmentation algorithms are used, which have produced promising results in this application, perhaps due to well-tuned algorithms such as UNet [21]. The object detection metrics are discussed in Sect. 2.2, together with their limitations in evaluating segmentation output. We propose a new asymmetric lesion-level measure in Sect. 2.4.

We investigate the following specific questions in this application. **(1) Do cases, such as those in Fig.1 that cause disagreement between these metrics, exist in clinical data with a competent segmentation network? and (2) To what extent, the presence of these cases affects the ability of voxel-level segmentation metrics in evaluating lesion-level detection?** The correlation between these metrics can be dependent on the radiological/histopathological ground-truth, the adopted segmentation networks and the clinical tasks that utilise these detected lesions, while this study is intended to answer these questions in specific clinical applications described in Sect. 2.1. In Sect. 3, we report both voxel- and lesion-level results from prostate lesion segmentation on clinical mpMR and summarise the overall disagreement levels and correlations at a range of cut-off values. These metric results are presented together with the quantified impact, due to adopting the segmentation metrics, on false-positive and false-negative numbers in this application.

2   Materials and Methods

2.1   Prostate Lesion Segmentation for Procedure Planning

The mpMR images were acquired from 850 prostate cancer patients, with a total of 877 studies from part of several clinical trials conducted at University College London Hospital, including biopsy and treatment patient cohorts, including SmartTarget [11], PICTURE [23], ProRAFT [17], Index [8], PROMIS

[3] and PROGENY [13]. All trial patients gave written consents and the ethics was approved as part of the respective trial protocols. Radiologist contours were obtained for all lesions with Likert-scores$\geq$3 and served as ground-truth labels in this study. 192, 325, 232 and 106 studies have 1, 2, 3 and $\geq$4 lesions, respectively. Image volumes were resampled to $0.5 \times 0.5 \times 1.0\,\mathrm{mm}^3$ with normalised intensities [0,1], before being centre-cropped to a size of $192 \times 192 \times 96$ voxels using gland segmentation masks, primarily for computational consideration. No other pre-processing was applied.

Three MR volumes, T2-weighted, ADC and diffusion with high-b values ($b = 1000$ or $b = 2000$), were channel-wise concatenated as the input to a 3D UNet. 877$\times$3 mpMR images were divided into 503, 190 and 184, as training-, validation- and test sets without same patients in different sets. The network was trained with equally-weighted cross-entropy and Dice losses [14] for 100 epochs, using an Adam optimiser with a weight decay of 0.0001. The networks and training strategies were otherwise non-optimised for this application to provide a reference performance. While clustering ROIs from voxel-level segmentation algorithms remain an open research question, individual lesions were separated, for the purpose of this study, by testing the neighbouring 26-connected voxels, before filtering out any isolated ROIs with fewer than 8 voxels.

For targeted biopsy planning, 3–6 biopsy needle positions are planned for individual detected lesions [16]. Missing clinically-significant lesions could mean missed opportunity for early detection of tumours that are still amenable for less radical treatment. In a number of treatments such as focal therapy [2] and nerve-sparing surgery [5,19], accurately identifying individual lesions does not only ensure adequate coverage of cancers, but also supports different function-preserving surgical options, as false-positive lesions could invalidate less-invasive treatment options with less-complications and quicker recovery. In this work, we focus on lesion-level accuracy as an example type of clinically-relevant metrics to examine voxel-level DSC and HD.

2.2 Voxel-Level Segmentation Metrics

DSC measures the overlap between the predicted segmentation Y_p and the ground-truth Y_g, $\mathcal{S}^{DSC} = 2 \times |Y_p \cap Y_g|/(|Y_p| + |Y_g|)$. HD measures the greatest surface distance between the boundaries of the predicted segmentation and the ground-truth. In Sect. 3, we report the 95th percentile of surface distances, denoted as $\mathcal{D}^{HD}$, as a robust alternative.

2.3 Lesion-Level Object Detection Metrics

In object detection literature, the accuracy metrics are computed typically for comparing overall performance from different algorithms, by first defining the individual *true-positives* that represent correctly detected ROIs (i.e. instances or, here, lesions), based on an overlap measure intersection over union (IoU), $\mathcal{S}^{IoU} = (Y_p \cap Y_g)/Y_p \cup Y_g$, between the predicted Y_p and the ground-truth Y_g

ROIs. The predicted ROIs with greater and less than a given overlap *thresh-old* s^{IoU} are considered true-positives and false-positives, respectively. Ground-truth lesions that are not detected by any predicted ROIs are false-negatives. Individual predicted or ground-truth ROIs are counted once with their highest-overlapping counterparts [18]. True-negative ROIs are not defined. These metrics are customarily defined between bounding-boxes representing instances in object detection algorithms, whilst these are reported at voxel-level in Sect. 3 with respect to the evaluated segmentation algorithms.

The lesion-level accuracy can, in turn, be summarised by counting the numbers of true-positive, false-positive and false-negative ROIs, denoted as TP, FP and FN, respectively, $precision^{IoU} = TP^{IoU}/(TP^{IoU} + FP^{IoU})$ and $recall^{IoU} = TP^{IoU}/(TP^{IoU} + FN^{IoU})$ where the superscripts IoU indicate the IoU-based definitions.

Marginalising over varying prediction probability *cut-off* values obtains summary metrics such as average precision, area under the precision-versus-recall curve. However these metrics are not discussed further in this work, as they may be appropriate for comparing different methods but lacks direct clinical interpretation in specific applications [9]. We instead compare precision with controlled recall at individual cut-off values, whereas this cut-off applies on voxel class probabilities in the segmentation task, rather than on ROI (instance) probabilities in a typical object detection algorithm.

Limitations in Evaluating Multifocal Cancer Localisation. Direct applying the object detection metrics was found challenging to interpret in our multifocal cancer application, which considers multiple ROIs of the same type[1] described in Sect. 2.1. Object detection algorithms allow flexible and many more ROI candidate proposals before thresholding on overlaps. This is in contrast to typical segmentation results, in which no overlapping ROIs are predicted. To balance the flexibility in region proposals and avoiding over-predicting, TP^{IoU}, FP^{IoU} and FN^{IoU} are designed with an arguably more stringent criterion. As described above, a) a symmetric overlap measure IoU is used, and b) individual predicted and ground-truth ROIs are not allowed to be counted more than once. For example, one of the two ground-truth ROIs is considered as false-negative in Fig. 1.b3, while the left green ROI is likely to be a false-positive in Fig. 1.b4. We observed that disregarding ROIs with substantial overlap in these two cases, by using object detection metrics on segmentation output, makes it difficult to account for varying detection and coverage levels. In other words, changing cut-off does not differentiate cases, in which both ground-truth ROIs were "detected" or both predicted ROIs collectively "covered" the disease area, from others.

In general, it is its symmetric nature of the overlap measure $\mathcal{S}^{IoU}$ (and $\mathcal{S}^{DSC}$) that lead to $precision^{IoU}$ and $recall^{IoU}$ being insensitive to the different combinations of false-negative- and false-positive *voxels*, where the cut-off applies for segmentation output. As we show in Table 1 in Sect. 3, different values in $precision^{IoU}$ indeed lead to similar or even the same $recall^{IoU}$ values, vice versa.

---

[1] This work uses binary segmentation as an example, though the discussion may generalise to multiclass segmentation by considering lesions of different grades separately.

This indifference to the "costs" associated with respective false-negatives and false-positives could have direct clinical consequences. However, adapting the definition of individual ROIs, such that they are amenable to these metrics, is not trivial.

Furthermore, for the purpose of assessing other metrics, voxel-level segmentation metrics in this work, such insensitive lesion-level metrics may over-estimate their correlation due to limited numerical and statistical precision determined by practical factors such as noise in the data and size of the subjects.

2.4 Lesion Detection Metrics for Multifocal Segmentation Output

To address some of the above-discussed limitations with $precision^{IoU}$ and $recall^{IoU}$ for assessing the segmentation output in this clinical applications, we propose an asymmetric measure, such that the voxel-level cut-off becomes sensitive to, thus practically useful for, balancing the two error types.

For each of N ground-truth lesions $\{Y_g^n\}_{n=1,...,N}$, it is considered as a true-positive lesion if it has overlap with any of the M predictions $\{Y_p^m\}_{m=1,...,M}$, single or multiple, that is greater than a pre-defined overlap threshold s^{GT}, otherwise false-negative. Thus, $\mathcal{S}^{GT} = \sum_{m=1}^{M}(Y_p^m \cap Y_g^n)/Y_g^n$ where the superscripts GT indicating the ground-truth-based definitions, with which false-positive lesions is not defined. The recall thus can be computed, $recall^{GT} = TP^{GT}/(TP^{GT} + FN^{GT})$ where TP^{GT} and FN^{GT} are the numbers of true-positive and false-negative lesions using the ground-truth-based definitions, respectively.

For individual predicted lesions Y_p^m, a true-positive lesion requires the overlap with ground-truth regions Y_g^n to be greater than s^{Pred}, otherwise false-positive. Thus, $\mathcal{S}^{Pred} = \sum_{n=1}^{N}(Y_g^n \cap Y_p^m)/Y_p^m$ where the superscripts $Pred$ for the prediction-based definitions and undefined FN^{Pred}. Therefore, $precision^{Pred} = TP^{Pred}/(TP^{Pred} + FP^{Pred})$.

2.5 Correlation, Pairwise Agreement and Impact on Evaluation

Pearson's r is reported to measure the linear correlation between $\mathcal{S}^{DSC}$ and $\mathcal{D}^{HD}$ and that between voxel-level $\mathcal{S}^{DSC}$ and lesion-level $precision^{Pred}/precision^{IoU}$, on 100 bootstrapping samples with a sample size of 20, from the holdout set. Cohen's Kappa coefficient κ is computed, between two metrics, to measure the level of pairwise agreement on judging the better one from two randomly sampled holdout cases. For example, a higher $\mathcal{S}^{DSC}$ agrees (true) with a higher $precision^{Pred}$ but disagrees (false) with a higher $\mathcal{D}^{HD}$, if measured from the same case of the two. For comparison purposes, an overlap threshold of 0.3 was used for S^{IOU}, S^{Pred} and S^{GT}, approximating the mean $\mathcal{S}^{DSC}$ on holdout set, with varying cut-off values. Other non-extreme threshold values did not alter the conclusions summarised in Sect. 3.

Table 1. Summary of the voxel- and lesion-level results, with varying cut-off (c/o) values. Estimated $\hat{FP}$ and $\hat{FN}$ are derived from linear relationship between DSC and lesion-level metrics. Results are based on 357 lesions in holdout patients.

c/o	Lesion-level				Voxel-level		Dice-est./Actual	
	$prec.^{Pred}$	$rec.^{GT}$	$prec.^{IoU}$	$rec.^{IoU}$	$\mathcal{S}^{DSC}$	$\mathcal{D}^{HD}$	$\hat{FP}/FP$	$\hat{FN}/FN$
0.1	0.26	0.69	0.12	0.17	0.33(0.18)	20.40(10.41)	257/409	86/106
0.2	0.36	0.61	0.21	0.27	0.34(0.19)	18.20(10.20)	214/306	101/136
0.3	0.42	0.54	0.23	0.27	0.34(0.20)	18.50(9.75)	232/273	103/154
0.4	0.44	0.52	0.25	0.29	0.33(0.20)	18.25(10.13)	256/253	111/169
0.5	0.47	0.49	0.25	0.28	0.33(0.21)	19.02(10.70)	216/237	104/178
0.6	0.49	0.45	0.25	0.28	0.32(0.21)	18.97(10.63)	219/213	101/194
0.7	0.52	0.42	0.27	0.27	0.31(0.21)	19.71(11.57)	179/190	101/208
0.8	0.58	0.37	0.26	0.26	0.29(0.21)	20.00(12.54)	132/158	98/227
0.9	0.64	0.31	0.27	0.23	0.26(0.21)	22.63(13.37)	114/115	101/255

The DSC results are used as an example to estimate the false-positive and false-negative cases, using the linearly fitted correlation models (see Fig. 2 for examples). The differences, between these Dice-estimated and the actual errors, provide quantitative evidence of the clinical impact on evaluating lesion localisation using segmentation metrics.

3   Results

The segmentation results are reported in Table 1, showing that the $precision^{Pred}$ and $recall^{GT}$ are more sensitive to the cut-off than $precision^{IoU}$ and $recall^{IoU}$ are. This was indeed due to the difference between the symmetric overlap measure $\mathcal{S}^{IoU}/\mathcal{S}^{DSC}$ and the asymmetric $\mathcal{S}^{GT}/\mathcal{S}^{Pred}$, discussed in Sects. 2.2 and 2.4. Figure 2 provides examples of the lesion segmentation with their quantitative results.

3.1   Comparison Between DSC and HD

Figure 2 a) observe a monotonic relationship between $\mathcal{S}^{DSC}$ and $\mathcal{D}^{HD}$, with a correlation of $r=-0.6462$ ($p-value=0.000$) and a "moderate" pairwise agreement of $\kappa=0.57$. However, examples were found that the two metrics disagree on which case of a given pair is a "better" segmentation. For example, the case in Fig. 3 c) yielded a lower $\mathcal{S}^{DSC}$ and a lower $\mathcal{D}^{HD}$, compared with those measured from the cases in a) and b). This indeed indicates that variable number of ROIs may be a factor of such disagreement, due to their sizes and locations.

3.2   Comparison Between Voxel- and Lesion-Level Metrics

Figure 2 b-d) illustrate that both lesion-level metrics are increasingly correlated with $\mathcal{S}^{DSC}$ with higher cut-offs, ranging from 0.35 to 0.85 and from 0.66 to 0.76, for $recall^{GT}$ and $precision^{Pred}$, respectively.

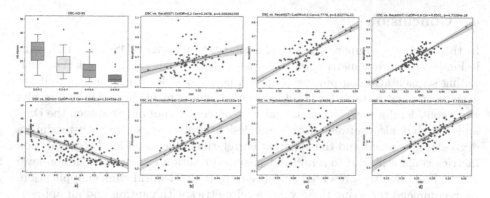

Fig. 2. Quantitative comparison on holdout set, a) shows the correlation between $\mathcal{S}^{DSC}$ and $\mathcal{D}^{HD}$ in box plot and scatter plot, respectively. b-d) show the correlation between DSC and Precision/Recall under different cut-offs.

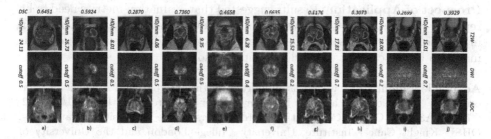

Fig. 3. Holdout set segmentation results, with ground-truth (predicted) lesions in red (green), showing examples of a-c) inconsistency between DSC and HD, d) good prediction in all evaluation metrics, e) single lesion with multiple predictions, f) two lesions with one prediction, g-h) poorer performance with higher cut off, and i-j) better performance with higher cut-off. (Color figure online)

In Fig. 3, Cases d-f) show examples of levels of correlation and agreement between the voxel- and lesion-level metrics, Cases g-j) show the effect of different cut-off values on two cases. It is noteworthy that these cases were cherry-picked to show various scenarios that motivated $recall^{GT}/precision^{Pred}$ and the overall comparison reported in Fig. 2. Visual examples are generally consistent with the reported quantitative correlation and agreement results and showed an interestingly strong correlation between the voxel- and lesion-level evaluation metrics.

As summarised in the last two columns of Table 1, the ratio of Dice-estimated false-positives to true false-positives rises, partly due to the reduced number of false-negative lesions as the cut-off increases. The DSC may therefore be considered a good evaluation metric at a cutoff close to 0.9. The opposite trend can be observed for the false-negatives. However, the differences in general cannot be overlooked, with the maximum being 37% (152) and 60% (154) of the respective true errors.

4   Conclusion

In this work, we compare voxel-level segmentation metrics DSC and HD, with lesion-level accuracy metrics, on the prostate lesion segmentation task. For evaluating segmentation output, we proposed new lesion detection metrics that are asymmetric and suitable for voxel-level cut-off adjustment. Experimental results show considerable correlation and pairwise agreement not only between the DSC and HD, but also between voxel- and lesion-level metrics. Notwithstanding a degree of agreement and the apparent correlations, the voxel-level segmentation metrics could still lead to significant misinterpretation in lieu of the lesion-level errors. Following the presented evidence from the real-world clinical application, we recommend reporting these voxel-level metrics with caution and an appreciation of their limitations. Future work includes studies with wider clinical downstream tasks that use automated segmentation and a comparison between these metrics as loss functions for network training.

Prospect of Application: Results suggested that evaluation metrics need to be reported with respect to the downstream tasks of prostate cancer segmentation, in addition to widely used voxel-level overlap or boundary distances, and this may also be the case for wider clinical applications.

Acknowledgment. This work was supported by the International Alliance for Cancer Early Detection, an alliance between Cancer Research UK [C28070/A30912; C73666/A31378], Canary Center at Stanford University, the University of Cambridge, OHSU Knight Cancer Institute, University College London and the University of Manchester. This work was also supported by the Wellcome/EPSRC Centre for Interventional and Surgical Sciences [203145Z/16/Z].

References

1. Ahmed, H.U., et al.: Diagnostic accuracy of multi-parametric MRI and TRUS biopsy in prostate cancer (PROMIS): a paired validating confirmatory study. Lancet **389**(10071), 815–822 (2017)
2. Ahmed, H.U., Hindley, R.G., Dickinson, L., Freeman, A., et al.: Focal therapy for localised unifocal and multifocal prostate cancer: a prospective development study. Lancet Oncol. **13**(6), 622–632 (2012)
3. Bosaily, A.E.S., et al.: PROMIS-prostate MR imaging study: a paired validating cohort study evaluating the role of multi-parametric MRI in men with clinical suspicion of prostate cancer. Contemp. Clin. Trials **42**, 26–40 (2015)
4. Cao, R., Zhong, X., Shakeri, S., Bajgiran, A.M., et al.: Prostate cancer detection and segmentation in multi-parametric MRI via CNN and conditional random field. In: 2019 IEEE 16th International Symposium on Biomedical Imaging (ISBI 2019), pp. 1900–1904. IEEE (2019)
5. Catalona, W.J., Bigg, S.W.: Nerve-sparing radical prostatectomy: evaluation of results after 250 patients. J. Urol. **143**(3), 538–543 (1990)
6. Chiou, E., Giganti, F., Punwani, S., Kokkinos, I., Panagiotaki, E.: Harnessing uncertainty in domain adaptation for MRI prostate lesion segmentation. In: Martel, A.L., et al. (eds.) MICCAI 2020. LNCS, vol. 12261, pp. 510–520. Springer, Cham (2020). https://doi.org/10.1007/978-3-030-59710-8_50

7. Dickinson, L., Ahmed, H.U., Allen, C., Barentsz, J.O., et al.: Scoring systems used for the interpretation and reporting of multiparametric MRI for prostate cancer detection, localization, and characterization: could standardization lead to improved utilization of imaging within the diagnostic pathway? J. Magn. Reson. Imaging **37**(1), 48–58 (2013)
8. Dickinson, L., et al.: A multi-centre prospective development study evaluating focal therapy using high intensity focused ultrasound for localised prostate cancer: the INDEX study. Contemp. Clin. Trials **36**(1), 68–80 (2013)
9. Halligan, S., Altman, D.G., Mallett, S.: Disadvantages of using the area under the receiver operating characteristic curve to assess imaging tests: a discussion and proposal for an alternative approach. Eur. Radiol. **25**(4), 932–939 (2015). https://doi.org/10.1007/s00330-014-3487-0
10. Hambarde, P., Talbar, S., Mahajan, A., Chavan, S., et al.: Prostate lesion segmentation in MR images using radiomics based deeply supervised U-Net. Biocybernetics Biomed. Eng. **40**(4), 1421–1435 (2020)
11. Hamid, S., et al.: The smartTarget biopsy trial: a prospective, within-person randomised, blinded trial comparing the accuracy of visual-registration and magnetic resonance imaging/ultrasound image-fusion targeted biopsies for prostate cancer risk stratification. Eur. Urol. **75**(5), 733–740 (2019)
12. Jung, J.A., Coakley, F.V., Vigneron, D.B., et al.: Prostate depiction at endorectal MR spectroscopic imaging: investigation of a standardized evaluation system. Radiology **233**(3), 701–708 (2004)
13. Linch, M., et al.: Intratumoural evolutionary landscape of high-risk prostate cancer: the PROGENY study of genomic and immune parameters. Ann. Oncol. **28**(10), 2472–2480 (2017)
14. Ma, J., Chen, J., Ng, M., Huang, R., et al.: Loss odyssey in medical image segmentation. Med. Image Anal. **71**, 102035 (2021)
15. Menze, B.H., Jakab, A., Bauer, S., Kalpathy-Cramer, J., et al.: The multimodal brain tumor image segmentation benchmark (BRATS). IEEE Trans. Med. Imaging **34**(10), 1993–2024 (2014)
16. Moore, C.M., Kasivisvanathan, V., Eggener, S., Emberton, M., et al.: Standards of reporting for MRI-targeted biopsy studies (START) of the prostate: recommendations from an international working group. Eur. Urol. **64**(4), 544–552 (2013)
17. Orczyk, C., et al.: Prostate radiofrequency focal ablation (ProRAFT) trial: a prospective development study evaluating a bipolar radiofrequency device to treat prostate cancer. J. Urol. **205**(4), 1090–1099 (2021)
18. Padilla, R., Passos, W.L., Dias, T.L.B., Netto, S.L., da Silva, E.A.B.: A comparative analysis of object detection metrics with a companion open-source toolkit. Electronics **10**(3) (2021). https://doi.org/10.3390/electronics10030279, https://www.mdpi.com/2079-9292/10/3/279
19. Rob, L., Halaska, M., Robova, H.: Nerve-sparing and individually tailored surgery for cervical cancer. Lancet Oncol. **11**(3), 292–301 (2010)
20. Ronneberger, O., Fischer, P., Brox, T.: U-Net: convolutional networks for biomedical image segmentation. In: Navab, N., Hornegger, J., Wells, W.M., Frangi, A.F. (eds.) MICCAI 2015. LNCS, vol. 9351, pp. 234–241. Springer, Cham (2015). https://doi.org/10.1007/978-3-319-24574-4_28
21. Schelb, P., Kohl, S., Radtke, J.P., Wiesenfarth, M., et al.: Classification of cancer at prostate MRI: deep learning versus clinical PI-RADS assessment. Radiology **293**(3), 607–617 (2019)

22. Schelb, P., Tavakoli, A.A., Tubtawee, T., Hielscher, T., et al.: Comparison of prostate MRI lesion segmentation agreement between multiple radiologists and a fully automatic deep learning system. In: RöFo-Fortschritte auf dem Gebiet der Röntgenstrahlen und der bildgebenden Verfahren, vol. 193, pp. 559–573. Georg Thieme Verlag KG (2021)

23. Simmons, L.A., et al.: Accuracy of transperineal targeted prostate biopsies, visual estimation and image fusion in men needing repeat biopsy in the PICTURE trial. J. Urol. **200**(6), 1227–1234 (2018)

24. Sung, H., Ferlay, J., Siegel, R.L., Laversanne, M., et al.: Global cancer statistics 2020: GLOBOCAN estimates of incidence and mortality worldwide for 36 cancers in 185 countries. CA: Cancer J Clin. **71**(3), 209–249 (2021)

25. Weinreb, J.C., Barentsz, J.O., Choyke, P.L., Cornud, F., et al.: PI-RADS prostate imaging-reporting and data system: 2015, version 2. Eur. Urol. **69**(1), 16–40 (2016)

26. Winkel, D.J., Wetterauer, C., Matthias, M.O., Lou, B., et al.: Autonomous detection and classification of PI-RADS lesions in an MRI screening population incorporating multicenter-labeled deep learning and biparametric imaging: proof of concept. Diagnostics **10**(11), 951 (2020)

OOOE: Only-One-Object-Exists Assumption to Find Very Small Objects in Chest Radiographs

Gunhee Nam[⊠], Taesoo Kim, Sanghyup Lee, and Thijs Kooi

Lunit Inc., Seoul, South Korea
{ghnam,taesoo.kim,eesanghyup,tkooi}@lunit.io

Abstract. The accurate localization of inserted medical tubes and parts of human anatomy is a common problem when analyzing chest radiographs and something deep neural networks could potentially automate. However, many foreign objects like tubes and various anatomical structures are small in comparison to the entire chest X-ray, which leads to severely unbalanced data and makes training deep neural networks difficult. In this paper, we present a simple yet effective 'Only-One-Object-Exists' (OOOE) assumption to improve the deep network's ability to localize small landmarks in chest radiographs. The OOOE enables us to recast the localization problem as a classification problem and we can replace commonly used continuous regression techniques with a multi-class discrete objective. We validate our approach using a large scale proprietary dataset of over 100K radiographs as well as publicly available RANZCR-CLiP Kaggle Challenge dataset and show that our method consistently outperforms commonly used regression-based detection models as well as commonly used pixel-wise classification methods. Additionally, we find that the method using the OOOE assumption generalizes to multiple detection problems in chest X-rays and the resulting model shows state-of-the-art performance on detecting various tube tips inserted to the patient as well as patient anatomy.

Keywords: Point detection · Localization · Object segmentation

1 Introduction

A common and effective application of deep neural networks in the domain of automated Chest X-ray (CXR) analysis is the localization of foreign objects and human anatomy [32]. For example, the ability to segment and locate foreign objects, such as catheters, tubes, and lines has tremendous potential to optimize clinical workflow and ultimately improve patient care [6–8]. The innovations in object detection and segmentation methods for natural images [5,21,25,26] have sparked progress in detecting foreign objects and anatomy in CXR images [4,18, 28]. However, despite unique challenges associated with finding objects in CXR images, many of the methods designed for equivalent tasks in natural images are applied to CXR images without significant architectural modifications.

© The Author(s), under exclusive license to Springer Nature Switzerland AG 2022
S. Wu et al. (Eds.): AMAI 2022, LNCS 13540, pp. 139–149, 2022.
https://doi.org/10.1007/978-3-031-17721-7_15

Compared to most objects in natural images, foreign objects and human anatomy viewed in CXR images are much smaller in scale. Training deep neural network to detect small scale objects is challenging, because the number of background pixels far outweighs the foreground pixel count [3,22,29]. Frid-Adar *et al.* [4] proposed to generate training data by synthesizing images with augmented endotracheal tubes (ETT). Their method addresses data imbalance and improves performance of an image level classification, but does not provide a solution for the small object detection problem. Kara *et al.*[15] proposed a regression based cascade method to localize the tip of ETT and the carina. In comparison, we provide a classification based solution to the detection problem which is often reported to outperform regression based methods for various detection tasks in natural images [12,19,20,24,27].

In this work, we present a solution to the problem of detecting small foreign objects or anatomical structures in chest radiographs. We introduce the '*Only-One-Object-Exists*' (OOOE) assumption, a simple yet effective assumption, that limits the number of observable instances of a particular object we want to detect to one per image and reduces the detection problem to a point localization problem. Using these assumptions, the localization problem can be cast as a classification problem that can be solved with a spatial-softmax operation.

We validate our approach for (1) detecting ETT tip and (2) detecting the carina, on the publicly available RANZCR-CliP Kaggle Challenge dataset. Additionally, we also provide results on a large scale proprietary dataset of over 100K chest X-ray images. Our method inspired by the OOOE assumption outperforms two commonly used baselines: (1) a simple segmentation model [23,26] and (2) a regression based detection approach [15]. We additionally demonstrate that our approach leads to a model that generalizes better across datasets and makes better use of global context information.

2   Methods

We address the problem of detecting small objects in an image, using the assumption that they occur once and only once. We also observe that small objects, such as the tip of a tube or a certain landmark of an anatomy, can essentially be represented as a single point in an image.

Our solution to the point detection problem consists of two parts: a feature extractor F and a detection head g, which will be described in detail in the following sections.

2.1   Feature Extractor

A feature extractor is a function that satisfies the following:

$$X = F(\mathbf{I}), \tag{1}$$

where $\mathbf{I} \in \mathbb{R}^{H \times W \times C}$ is an input image with spatial dimensions H, W and with C channels. The feature extractor F is a transformation such that the output

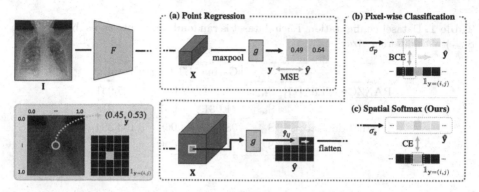

Fig. 1. Comparison to regression and pixel-wise classification methods. Given a CXR image **I**, our objective is to find the ground-truth **y** point location. (a) The regression method predicts $\hat{\mathbf{y}} = [\hat{\mathbf{y}}_1, \hat{\mathbf{y}}_2]$ directly. (b) The pixel-wise classification method predicts absence/presence of an object for all pixels. (c) Our method assumes only one instance of an object exists in an image.

feature $X \in \mathbb{R}^{h \times w \times c}$ is a tensor with spatial dimensions h, w such that $h < H, w < W$ and with c channels. In this work, we implement F with a widely used convolutional neural network with residual connections (ResNet34) [9].

2.2 Point Detection Head

In a point detection problem, we assume that the ground truth location of an object of interest is represented as a single 2D location on a image $\mathbf{y} \in \mathbb{R}^2$. The objective of the point detection head g is to predict $\hat{\mathbf{y}}$ given X. Depending on how $\hat{\mathbf{y}}$ is computed and how g is trained, a detection algorithm is considered to be either a regression or a classification method.

Regression based approaches such as [15] are trained by directly minimizing the mean-square-error (MSE) between the predicted location $g(X) = \hat{\mathbf{y}}_{reg} \in \mathbb{R}^2$ and the ground truth location $\mathbf{y}$ as depicted in (a) of Fig. 1.

Despite the simplicity of regression based detection methods, classification based methods have outperformed them in practice across multiple detection problems [12,13,19,20,24,27]. In a classification setup, the model instead outputs an activation map $g(X) = \hat{\mathbf{y}} \in \mathbb{R}^{H \times W}$ where the value located at (i, j) is $\mathbf{y}_{ij} = g(\mathbf{x}_{ij})$ and $F(\mathbf{I}) = \mathbf{X} = [\mathbf{x}_{11}, \mathbf{x}_{12}, ..., \mathbf{x}_{WH}]$. As shown in (b) of Fig. 1, the presence of an object at $\hat{\mathbf{y}}_{ij}$ is learned by computing a *pixel-wise binary cross-entropy* (BCE) loss with $\mathbf{y}_{ij}$ where $\mathbf{y}_{ij} = 1$ when the ground truth location of the object is at i, j and $\mathbf{y}_{ij} = 0$ otherwise.

One of the main intuition of this paper is that we can often and naturally bound the number of positive detections in $\hat{\mathbf{y}}$ by using application driven prior knowledge. It is often true for practical applications that the expected number of object/anatomy is known a priori and is equal to one (e.g. humans only have one carina, only one endo-tracheal tube is inserted at any given time). Our idea is to encode this strong prior using the *spatial softmax* operator (as opposed

Table 1. Dataset configuration. Each dataset is randomly split into two subsets (S_{train}, S_{test}) with different sizes.

		Carina	ETT tip	Total
RANZCR-CLiP [17]	S_{train}	4,244	2,057	5,931
	S_{test}	1,031	937	1,818
Internal dataset	S_{train}	98,382	43,066	103,394
	S_{test}	1,544	609	1,633

to pixel-wise BCE) which leads to our OOOE point detection head formulation which we describe below.

Spatial Softmax. The spatial softmax allows the detection head to produce a relative probability for each pixel, by applying the softmax function along the spatial axis. This leads to the OOOE assumption we make in this paper which states one and only one instance of the object is present in the image.

The spatial softmax σ_s operation over the activation map $\hat{\mathbf{y}}$ and the resulting value at spatial location i, j is defined as follows:

$$\sigma_s(\hat{\mathbf{y}}_{ij}) = \frac{e^{\hat{\mathbf{y}}_{ij}}}{\sum_{j=1}^{H} \sum_{i=1}^{W} e^{\hat{\mathbf{y}}_{ij}}}. \tag{2}$$

Then, the point detection model is optimized to minimize the following negative log-likelihood objective:

$$\mathcal{L}(\mathbf{y}, \hat{\mathbf{y}}) = \frac{1}{HW} \sum_{j=1}^{H} \sum_{i=1}^{W} -\mathbf{y}_{i,j} \log(\sigma_s(\hat{\mathbf{y}}_{ij})), \tag{3}$$

where $\mathbf{y}_{i,j} = 1$ when the object is located at point (i, j). The final point detection prediction $\hat{\mathbf{y}}_{cls}$ using classification based the spatial softmax approach is defined as the location (i, j) with the highest activation value $\hat{\mathbf{y}}_{ij}$:

$$\hat{\mathbf{y}}_{cls} = \underset{i,j}{\operatorname{argmax}} \, \hat{\mathbf{y}}_{ij} \tag{4}$$

Visual comparison to the regression and pixel-wise classification approaches is depicted in (c) of Fig. 1.

3   Experiments

3.1   Datasets

We evaluate the point detection performance on a relatively small public RANZCR-CLiP [17] dataset and a large internal dataset. The differences are noted in Table 1. For both datasets, we define two subsets (S_{train}, S_{test}) and cases in each split are randomly selected without patient id overlap between the splits.

RANZCR-CLiP [17] is a dataset used in a recent Kaggle challenge for mal-positioning classification of endotracheal and nasogastric tubes, and catheters. This dataset consists of 30K cases with case-level labels. Additionally, tube line annotations for a subset of (~3K cases for ETT) are provided. Using these line annotations, we create a ETT tip point annotation by taking the bottom most point in the ETT line annotation as the tip point. For the same dataset, we use the trachea bifurcation (*i.e.* carina) point annotations provided by Konya *et al.* [16].

Internal Dataset refers to a large proprietary dataset. The cases are collected from public data [2,11,14,30] as well as private sources consisting of various sites in multiple countries. Most of the cases are antero-posterior (AP) images since the cases with tube objects are mostly from ill patients in a bedridden state. For the dataset, 100K cases are annotated by 20 board-certified radiologists with previous CXR annotation experience.[1]

3.2   Evaluation Metrics

Previous studies for carina and ETT tip detection adopt an *absolute error* to measure the model performance [15]. Various statistics such as the mean, median and standard deviation are reported. However, some of these statistics are sensitive to outliers.

In this paper, we additionally use precision plots which is a general metric to evaluate point detection performance. These plots are commonly used in object tracking literature [1,10,31]. The precision plot shows the percentage of cases where the location error between the prediction and ground-truth is within a distance threshold δ on the y-axis against multiple prediction thresholds on the x-axis. This method reduces the effect of outliers, so that overall performance can be seen without severe bias.

Since the RANZCR-CLiP data does not provide information about the pixel spacing of the radiograph, we measure the distance relative to the size of the image and choose the maximum distance threshold $\delta = 0.15$. To summarize the performance, we report area-under-curve (AUC) of the precision plots. We made use of bootstrapping to generate confidence bounds around the AUC values.

In S_{test} of the internal data, however, the DICOMs of some cases (1,413 cases for carina, 524 cases for ETT tip) have pixel spacing information so that the absolute distance can be retrieved. To compare our method to related work, we report the same statistics used in [15] (*e.g.* mean, median, etc.) of absolute errors for these cases including AUC of the precision plots. For the precision plots by the absolute distance, we choose the maximum distance threshold $\delta = 50\,mm$.

---

[1] Unfortunately, we are not in the position to disclose this data at this time.

Table 2. Experiment configurations. Each experiment (E) uses different set for its training and test set. Diamond ($\Diamond$) represents training set, and star($\star$) represents test set for the experiment.

Split	RANZCR-CLiP [17]		Internal dataset	
	S_{train}	S_{test}	S_{train}	S_{test}
$E_{I \to I}$			$\Diamond$	$\star$
$E_{R \to R}$	$\Diamond$	$\star$		
$E_{I \to R}$		$\star$	$\Diamond$	
$E_{R \to I}$	$\Diamond$			$\star$

$\Diamond$: Training set, $\star$: Test set

Table 3. Model performance for various experimental settings (see Table 2). We report the area under the curve of precision plots (Prec.) and its 95% confidence interval (95% CI). Our spatial softmax (SS) method outperforms other methods in all experimental settings.

(%)		$E_{I \to I}$		$E_{R \to I}$		$E_{R \to R}$		$E_{I \to R}$	
		Prec.	95% CI	Prec.	95% CI	Prec.	95% CI	Prec.	95% CI
Carina	Reg	74.5	73.7–75.3	46.5	45.2–47.7	59.2	57.8–60.6	69.1	68.2–70.2
	PC	85.7	85.0–86.4	71.4	70.6–72.3	87.0	86.4–87.5	79.2	78.4–79.8
	Ours	**86.8**	86.1–87.5	**72.1**	71.1–72.9	**89.3**	88.7–89.9	**81.1**	80.7–81.6
ETT Tip	Reg	69.1	67.1–70.9	35.1	32.8–37.9	42.4	41.0–44.0	67.2	65.5–68.8
	PC	82.9	81.1–84.3	60.8	58.7–63.6	67.5	65.8–69.1	75.1	73.1–76.9
	Ours	**87.4**	86.3–88.8	**73.6**	71.7–75.3	**70.4**	68.8–71.8	**76.8**	74.9–78.7

Reg: Regression, **PC**: Pixel-wise Classification, **Ours**: Spatial Softmax

3.3   Implementation Details

For the *pixel-wise classification* method, we balance weights between positive and negative samples with the same ratio. Otherwise, the model too easily overfits to negative samples given the severe data imbalance; only one pixel in an image is positive for the point detection. For the *regression* method, we choose a learning rate of 0.001 by grid hyper-parameter search.

Experimental Settings: We trained and validated the model on different permutations of the data, described in Table 2. For $E_{I \to I}$ and $E_{R \to R}$ settings, we train and validate on the cases from the same source. Furthermore, we defined $E_{I \to R}$ and $E_{R \to I}$ experiments to test our model's ability to generalize across different data sources. Given this setup, we can also observe the effect of training set size on model's performance.

3.4   Comparison to Other Methods

First, we compare our model to the regression based approach [15] in Table 3. Our spatial softmax method outperforms all other methods across all settings.

Table 4. Absolute distance error between predictions and ground-truths.

Error (mm)		Mean	Median	Max	Min	Std	Q1	Q3	Prec.(%)	count
Carina	Reg	14.46	12.51	107.00	0.04	9.75	7.70	18.34	71.29	1,413
	PC	7.81	5.64	**86.59**	0.01	**7.64**	3.19	9.64	84.40	
	Ours	**7.46**	**4.75**	229.51	**0.00**	10.58	**2.66**	**8.71**	**85.56**	
ETT Tip	Reg	18.38	13.72	141.38	**0.00**	15.97	8.34	23.54	65.00	524
	PC	9.73	5.46	128.32	**0.00**	13.33	3.00	9.53	81.41	
	Ours	**7.28**	**3.95**	**98.75**	**0.00**	**11.80**	**2.40**	**6.64**	**86.28**	

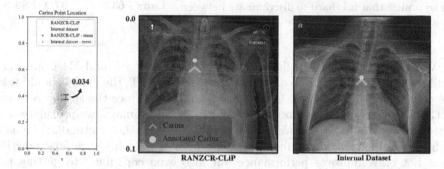

Fig. 2. Between the annotations from RANZCR-CLiP and the internal dataset, the intrinsic annotation inconsistency exists. *(Left)* The carina point location plot of S_{test} in each dataset and its mean value. The mean location difference in relative distance is 0.034 between the two dataset. *(Right)* The visualization of the annotated carina and the actual carina point for each dataset. The carina is annotated slightly upper than the actual point in RANZCR-CLiP.

The performance of carina detection is actually relatively worse when trained on a larger dataset (i.e. $E_{R\rightarrow R} > E_{I\rightarrow R}$). We suspect this is an effect of domain gap; there exists annotation style difference between the two datasets as shown in Fig. 2.

Table 4 summarizes various statistical measures including the AUC of the precision plots of the absolute distance errors on $E_{I\rightarrow I}$. Overall, our method shows the best performance compared to the other methods when measuring performance with respect to absolute distance error.

3.5   A Closer Look at ET-tube vs. T-tube Detection Performance

Upon qualitative analysis of our model's performance on the RANZCR-CLiP dataset, some cases classified as ETT actually turned out to be tracheostomy tubes (TT). TT is a short, curved airway tube that is inserted through a surgically generated stoma at the anterior neck, for prolonged respiratory support. TT is visually similar to ETT but TT can be discriminated from ETT by its typical course and short length.

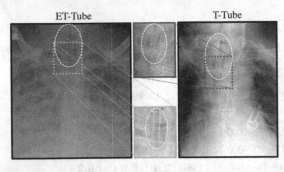

ET-Tube   T-Tube

Fig. 3. ETT and TT in CXR. The local appearances are so similar that it is hard to discriminate between the two without the global view.

Table 5. AUC of precision plots (Prec.) and AUCROC (AUC) for ETT tip vs. TT. I^- denotes the internal dataset excluding TT from ETT annoations.

(%)	$E_{I^-\to R}$	$E_{I^-\to I^-}$	
	Prec.	Prec.	AUC
Reg	55.3	61.4	-
PC	**67.8**	83.5	80.6
Ours	63.2	**87.1**	**88.3**

When looked at with a limited field of view, the TT and ETT are very similar as shown in Fig. 3. To discriminate ETT from TT, the model should take the context into account and look at the whole scan. Since the spatial softmax method compares relative scores from all pixels in the image, we postulate it is better at discriminating between ETT and TT than other methods. This is a highly desirable trait for a tube detection model as reducing such false positive cases not only improves performance but also even contribute to getting the trust of users of automated detector in practice.

To test this hypothesis, we excluded cases with TT annotations from our internal dataset (I^-). The resulting performance of the different models is shown in Table 5. Our spatial softmax method indeed outperforms the pixel-wise classification method for $E_{I^-\to I^-}$. On the other hand, our method shows much lower performance for its ETT tip detection performance than $E_{I\to R}$ in Table 3 while the pixel-wise classification method achieves relatively consistent performance. This indicates that the spatial softmax method is able to discriminate ETT from TT while the pixel-wise classification method does not.

In addition to precision, we also report the AUC of the receiver operating characteristic curve (AUCROC) on $E_{I^-\to I^-}$ in Table 5 for detecting ETT tips. Here, positives are cases with an ETT and negatives are cases with an TT tube, respectively. We used the maximum score from the prediction map as the prediction score. The spatial softmax method outperforms the pixel-wise classification method by a large performance gap, which was found to be significant using a DeLong test ($p = 0.0007$).

4   Conclusion

In this paper, we presented a method for the detection of small single objects in medical images, inspired by work from landmark detection in natural images. The method is simple to implement and outperforms other commonly used techniques such as methods based on regression or pixel-wise segmentation by a large margin on two different detection tasks in chest X-ray, using two different datasets. Although we prove the effectiveness of our method in CXR images, the detection of small single objects for other modality remains undiscovered. This may have potential to expand into other medical imaging areas, such as detecting a clip markers in mammograms. As part of future work, the method could be extended to assume a variable number of instances (*e.g.* 2 or more) and would increase the range of possible applications. We hope an expert knowledge driven automated system as presented in this paper contributes to increased application of automated methods in real world practice.

Prospect of Application: The ability to detect the position of inserted endotracheal tube tip with respect to the patient's carina from chest X-rays has the potential to enable malpositioning detection of the tube.

References

1. Babenko, B., Yang, M.H., Belongie, S.: Robust object tracking with online multiple instance learning. IEEE Trans. Pattern Anal. Mach. Intell. **33**, 1619–1632 (2010)
2. Bustos, A., Pertusa, A., Salinas, J.M., de la Iglesia-Vayá, M.: Padchest: a large chest x-ray image dataset with multi-label annotated reports. Med. Image Anal. **66**, 101797 (2020)
3. Chen, C., Liu, M.-Y., Tuzel, O., Xiao, J.: R-CNN for small object detection. In: Lai, S.-H., Lepetit, V., Nishino, K., Sato, Y. (eds.) ACCV 2016. LNCS, vol. 10115, pp. 214–230. Springer, Cham (2017). https://doi.org/10.1007/978-3-319-54193-8_14
4. Frid-Adar, M., Amer, R., Greenspan, H.: Endotracheal tube detection and segmentation in chest radiographs using synthetic data. In: Shen, D., et al. (eds.) MICCAI 2019. LNCS, vol. 11769, pp. 784–792. Springer, Cham (2019). https://doi.org/10.1007/978-3-030-32226-7_87
5. Girshick, R.: Fast R-CNN. In: Proceedings of the IEEE International Conference on Computer Vision (2015)
6. Godoy, M.C., Leitman, B.S., De Groot, P.M., Vlahos, I., Naidich, D.P.: Chest radiography in the ICU: Part 1, evaluation of airway, enteric, and pleural tubes. Am. J. Roentgenolo. **198**, 536–571 (2012)
7. Godoy, M.C., Leitman, B.S., De Groot, P.M., Vlahos, I., Naidich, D.P.: Chest radiography in the ICU: Part 2, evaluation of cardiovascular lines and other devices. Am. J. Roentgenol. **198**, 572–581 (2012)
8. Gupta, P.K., Gupta, K., Jain, M., Garg, T.: Postprocedural chest radiograph: impact on the management in critical care unit. Anesth. Essays Res. **8**, 139 (2014)
9. He, K., Zhang, X., Ren, S., Sun, J.: Deep residual learning for image recognition. In: Proceedings of the IEEE Conference on Computer Vision and Pattern Recognition (2016)
10. Henriques, J.F., Caseiro, R., Martins, P., Batista, J.: Exploiting the circulant structure of tracking-by-detection with kernels. In: Fitzgibbon, A., Lazebnik, S., Perona, P., Sato, Y., Schmid, C. (eds.) ECCV 2012. LNCS, vol. 7575, pp. 702–715. Springer, Heidelberg (2012). https://doi.org/10.1007/978-3-642-33765-9_50
11. Irvin, J., et al.: Chexpert: a large chest radiograph dataset with uncertainty labels and expert comparison. In: Proceedings of the AAAI Conference on Artificial Intelligence (2019)
12. Jakab, T., Gupta, A., Bilen, H., Vedaldi, A.: Unsupervised learning of object landmarks through conditional image generation. Adv. Neural Inf. Process. Syst. **31** (2018)

13. Jeon, S., Nam, S., Oh, S.W., Kim, S.J.: Cross-identity motion transfer for arbitrary objects through pose-attentive video reassembling. In: Vedaldi, A., Bischof, H., Brox, T., Frahm, J.-M. (eds.) ECCV 2020. LNCS, vol. 12369, pp. 292–308. Springer, Cham (2020). https://doi.org/10.1007/978-3-030-58586-0_18

14. Johnson, A.E., et al.: MIMIC-CXR, a de-identified publicly available database of chest radiographs with free-text reports. Sci. Data **6**, 1–8 (2019)

15. Kara, S., Akers, J.Y., Chang, P.D.: Identification and localization of endotracheal tube on chest radiographs using a cascaded convolutional neural network approach. J. Digit. Imaging **34**, 898–904 (2021). https://doi.org/10.1007/s10278-021-00463-0

16. Kónya, S.: 5k trachea bifurcation on chest xray. https://www.kaggle.com/sandorkonya/5k-trachea-bifurcation-on-chest-xray (2021)

17. Law, M., et al.: Ranzcr-clip - catheter and line position challenge. https://www.kaggle.com/c/ranzcr-clip-catheter-line-classification (2021)

18. Lee, H., Mansouri, M., Tajmir, S.H., Lev, M.H., Do, S.: A deep-learning system for fully-automated peripherally inserted central catheter (PICC) tip detection. J. Digit. Imaging **31**, 393–402 (2017). https://doi.org/10.1007/s10278-017-0025-z

19. Li, C., Bai, J., Hager, G.D.: A unified framework for multi-view multi-class object pose estimation. In: Proceedings of the European Conference on Computer Vision (ECCV) (2018)

20. Li, C., Zeeshan Zia, M., Tran, Q.H., Yu, X., Hager, G.D., Chandraker, M.: Deep supervision with shape concepts for occlusion-aware 3D object parsing. In: Proceedings of the IEEE Conference on Computer Vision and Pattern Recognition (2017)

21. Lin, T.Y., Dollár, P., Girshick, R., He, K., Hariharan, B., Belongie, S.: Feature pyramid networks for object detection. In: Proceedings of the IEEE Conference on Computer Vision and Pattern Recognition (2017)

22. Lin, T.Y., Goyal, P., Girshick, R., He, K., Dollár, P.: Focal loss for dense object detection. In: Proceedings of the IEEE International Conference on Computer Vision (2017)

23. Long, J., Shelhamer, E., Darrell, T.: Fully convolutional networks for semantic segmentation. In: Proceedings of the IEEE Conference on Computer Vision and Pattern Recognition (2015)

24. Oh, S.W., Kim, S.J.: Approaching the computational color constancy as a classification problem through deep learning. Pattern Recognit. **61**, 405–416 (2017)

25. Ren, S., He, K., Girshick, R., Sun, J.: Faster R-CNN: towards real-time object detection with region proposal networks. Adv. Neural Inf. Process. Syst. **28** (2015)

26. Ronneberger, O., Fischer, P., Brox, T.: U-Net: convolutional networks for biomedical image segmentation. In: Navab, N., Hornegger, J., Wells, W.M., Frangi, A.F. (eds.) MICCAI 2015. LNCS, vol. 9351, pp. 234–241. Springer, Cham (2015). https://doi.org/10.1007/978-3-319-24574-4_28

27. Su, H., Qi, C.R., Li, Y., Guibas, L.J.: Render for CNN: viewpoint estimation in images using CNNs trained with rendered 3D model views. In: Proceedings of the IEEE Conference on Computer Vision and Pattern Recognition (2015)

28. Sullivan, R., Holste, G., Burkow, J., Alessio, A.: Deep learning methods for segmentation of lines in pediatric chest radiographs. In: Medical Imaging 2020: Computer-Aided Diagnosis (2020)

29. Tong, K., Wu, Y., Zhou, F.: Recent advances in small object detection based on deep learning: a review. Image Visi. Comput. **97**, 103910 (2020)

30. Wang, X., Peng, Y., Lu, L., Lu, Z., Bagheri, M., Summers, R.: Hospital-scale chest x-ray database and benchmarks on weakly-supervised classification and localization of common thorax diseases. In: Proceedings of the IEEE Conference on Computer Vision and Pattern Recognition (2017)
31. Wu, Y., Lim, J., Yang, M.H.: Online object tracking: a benchmark. In: Proceedings of the IEEE Conference on Computer Vision and Pattern Recognition (2013)
32. Çallı, E., Sogancioglu, E., van Ginneken, B., van Leeuwen, K.G., Murphy, K.: Deep learning for chest x-ray analysis: a survey. Med. Image Anal. **72**, 102125 (2021)

Wavelet Guided 3D Deep Model to Improve Dental Microfracture Detection

Pranjal Sahu[1]([⊠]), Jared Vicory[1], Matt McCormick[1], Asma Khan[2], Hassem Geha[2], and Beatriz Paniagua[1]

[1] Kitware Inc., Carrboro, NC, USA
{pranjal.sahu,jared.vicory,matt.mccormick,
beatriz.paniagua}@kitware.com
[2] University of Texas in San Antonio, San Antonio, USA
{khana2,geha}@uthscsa.edu

Abstract. Epidemiological studies indicate that microfractures (cracks) are the third most common cause of tooth loss in industrialized countries. An undetected crack will continue to progress, often with significant pain, until the tooth is lost. Previous attempts to utilize cone beam computed tomography (CBCT) for detecting cracks in teeth had very limited success. We propose a model that detects cracked teeth in high resolution (hr) CBCT scans by combining signal enhancement with a deep CNN-based crack detection model. We perform experiments on a dataset of 45 ex-vivo human teeth with 31 cracked and 14 controls. We demonstrate that a model that combines classical wavelet-based features with a deep 3D CNN model can improve fractured tooth detection accuracy in both micro-Computed Tomography (ground truth) and hr-CBCT scans. The CNN model is trained to predict a probability map showing the most likely fractured regions. Based on this fracture probability map we detect the presence of fracture and are able to differentiate a fractured tooth from a control tooth. We compare these results to a 2D CNN-based approach and we show that our approach provides superior detection results. We also show that the proposed solution is able to outperform oral and maxillofacial radiologists in detecting fractures from the hr-CBCT scans. Early detection of cracks will lead to the design of more appropriate treatments and longer tooth retention.

Keywords: Isotropic wavelets · Cracked teeth · Deep learning

1 Introduction

Epidemiological studies report that cracked (incomplete fractures) teeth are the third most common cause of tooth loss in industrialized countries after caries and periodontal disease [1]. Cracks are defined as thin surface disruptions of enamel and dentin that initiate from the crown of the tooth and extend subgingivally in a

S. Wu et al. (Eds.): AMAI 2022, LNCS 13540, pp. 150–160, 2022.
https://doi.org/10.1007/978-3-031-17721-7_16

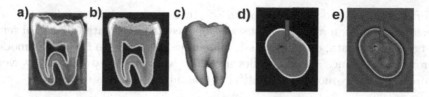

Fig. 1. Sample of a) hr-CBCT; b) registered micro-CT ; c) registered micro-CT geometry; d) micro-CT image e) corresponding phase image. Red arrows indicate the cracks. (Color figure online)

mesio-distal direction. Cracks are invariably colonized by bacteria [2,3] which can infect the dental pulp and periapical tissues resulting in pain, swelling, and bone resorption [4,5]. If left untreated, cracks progress and result in tooth loss. Non-invasive methods to detect cracks and interventions to prevent crack propagation are effective strategies to prevent the adverse sequalae of pulpal and periapical infections, and to avert tooth loss [6–11].

There is an important gap in dental diagnostics as the detection of incipient cracks in teeth is clinically challenging for two main reasons. First, the signs and symptoms are variable and often discontinuous with periods of remission [12–14]. Some patients present with sharp pain on biting, cold sensitivity, or deep probing depths [6,15,16], while others have no signs and symptoms until the pulp and periapical tissues are irreversibly infected. Second, available clinical diagnostic tools often cannot determine the presence of cracks. Imaging approaches used to detect cracks include 2D intraoral radiographs and 3D Cone Beam Computed Tomography (CBCT) scans, but they have challenges such as those arising from qualitative and subjective human evaluation [17,18]. Intraoral radiographs often fall short in their ability to detect non-displaced cracks because cracks which are not aligned with the x-ray beam do not result in subject contrast and will not be recorded; superimposition of overlying structures and the three-dimensional nature of the cracks limits subject contrast and hampers interpretation. CBCT addresses these limitations but introduces new ones. Challenges of CBCT are more limited spatial resolution, potential presence of artifacts from adjacent high-density structures (i.e., beam hardening caused by restorations or root canal obturation materials), and difficulty for clinicians to effectively and quantitatively analyze the 3D information to visualize the crack [18,19]. Early detection and localization of cracks in a non-invasive, data-driven, quantitative way is of utmost importance in ensuring appropriate treatment and in preventing tooth loss [20].

These motivations drive the development of the work presented here, where we propose an algorithm to enhance detection and visualization of incipient tooth cracks by coupling hr-CBCT with advanced image analysis methods and machine learning. We use micro-computed tomography (micro-CT) as our ground truth. Micro-CT is a very high-resolution imaging modality that is capable of capturing bony structures with high fidelity, but due to the high radiation needed it cannot be applied in living patients. Both hr-CBCT and micro-CT will be used to test our algorithms, our hypothesis is that hr-CBCT will have a comparable performance to micro-CT, but due to the increased resolution, micro-CT will have larger detection rates. Previously, it has been demonstrated that in absence of large training data, coupling classical imaging features with deep CNN models improve performance [21,22]. Following this, we propose to combine wavelet features with CNN models in identifying fine micro fractures in teeth.

2   Materials

We conduct our experiments on a dataset comprised of 45 teeth. We induced cracks in a subsample of that data (n = 31), while the other sound teeth were used as controls (n = 14). To create the cracks, a continuous force ($\geq$400 N) was exerted on the grooves using an Instron E3000 Electropuls machine. All the teeth were then examined with and without transillumination by two investigators. The presence/absence of superficial micro cracks, their location, extent, and orientation were recorded. We confirmed that our standardized method induces cracks in extracted teeth in a reliable manner (p = 0.017) via Chi square. The induced cracks were mesio-distally oriented and propagated from the crown towards the root of the tooth, which mimics the common clinical presentations of stress induced dental cracks [23].

After crack simulation, the same teeth are then scanned using both micro-CT and hr-CBCT. For micro-CT scanning, the teeth are placed individually into the scanner and acquired as a single structure in the image. For hr-CBCT and in order to increase the similarities with its clinical presentation, the teeth were placed in an ex-vivo human jaw and stabilized with wax. The same jaw is used in this study for placing the teeth, and it is scanned repeatedly for each set of teeth. The teeth were randomly arranged so that the jaw contained 2 molars and 1 premolar, and each set of teeth had 2 fractures and 1 control. The jaw was placed in water to mimic soft tissue. We compare our crack imaging biomarkers computed in hr-CBCT to those computed in micro-CT as our gold standard.

Micro-CT: All teeth were scanned using a desktop micro-CT imaging system (Bruker Skyscan 1172, Belgium) at a pixel size of 11.97 μm, with an exposure set at 1500 ms and voltage at 60 kV, 167 μA, equipped with a 0.5 mm Al filter. Scan settings were set at a 0.30 rotation step with a frame averaging value of 8. Reconstruction was performed with a minimum compressed-sensing (CS) value of 0.00000 and maximum CS value of 0.142390.

High-Resolution CBCT (hr-CBCT): All hr-CBCT volumes were acquired with the Planmeca ProMax 3D Mid ProFace, located at the Oral and Maxillofacial Radiology Clinic at the University of Texas Health San Antonio with acquisition parameters FOV 40 × 50 mm, 90 kV, 12.5 mA, 15 s, endodontic resolution mode, 75 μm voxels. All of the Phase I samples were collected with the Planmeca AINO[TM] noise filter. This is a patented denoising technology owned by Planmeca, that is used by default in the endodontic mode.

Tooth Segmentation: Since micro-CT teeth are scanned by themselves in a single sample tube, the tooth structure in this image modality can be segmented using Otsu thresholding [24] (see Fig. 1(b)) followed by an opening operation and a fill holes filter to segment the whole tooth (pulp, dentin and enamel). A rough segmentation from the tooth and mandibular geometries in the hr-CBCT was obtained from a fixed threshold. Since the dry skull was always scanned in the same location, it was possible to perform a rough alignment of the micro-CT to the hr-CBCT by applying a known deformation custom to pre, first or second molars and then refined via the Closest Point algorithm [25]. A sample of registered micro-CT and hr-CBCT tooth is shown in Fig. 1.

Crack Annotation: Micro-CT data captures finer details better and therefore is used to perform crack annotation. In this study, only fractures in 11 out of the 31 cracked teeth are annotated. After annotating the cracks in micro-CT, we transfer the annotations to hr-CBCT by performing registration of the micro-CT to the hr-CBCT scan of the same tooth and propagating the segmentation. Finally the annotated dataset of 11 cracked teeth is randomly divided into train (8 cases) and validation (3 cases) sets. The remaining 34 cases are used for testing the trained model. The cases remain the same in micro-CT and hr-CBCT splits.

3   Methods

Due to the limited number of training samples we propose to guide the CNN network using classical wavelet based features. Wavelets provide a signal decomposition framework that allows for good localization in both the spatial and frequency domains. The model is trained using the manual annotations to segment the cracks in the tooth. The segmentation model is then used to obtain crack probability maps which is next utilized to classify the cracked and control tooth. Classical wavelet based feature extraction, training of proposed deep segmentation CNN and finally the cracked tooth detection is described next.

Classical Wavelets Based Feature Extraction: The entire crack tooth detection pipeline is shown in Fig. 2. As shown, we first compute classical wavelet based features. This involves image pre-processing, computation of a wavelet pyramid based on the signal present in the input image, monogenic signal generation, phase analysis, and inverse wavelet pyramid construction (spatial reconstruction). In the image pre-processing step, each tooth is cropped from the scan by computing the smallest bounding box that includes the whole tooth geometry. This volume is then padded until all dimensions are multiples of 256 in order to avoid overlap of spatial bands while performing wavelet decomposition.

Wavelet Pyramid: The implementation of the wavelet transform is generally called wavelet pyramid construction [26,27] in image processing. This involves passing an image through successive filters where at each level the image is

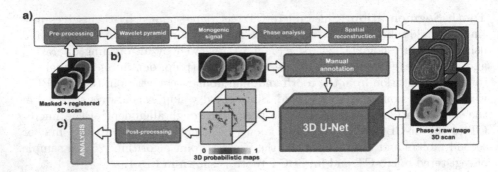

Fig. 2. Algorithm workflow. (a) Wavelet Feature computation, in blue (b) Fracture segmentation, in green (c) Analytical assessment, in red. (Color figure online)

down-sampled and non-overlapping band-pass filters are applied to capture different frequency ranges of the input image. By changing the number of high-pass bands, we can capture a wide range of frequencies, including those responsible for sharp edges such as those created by a crack. By changing the number of levels, we can generate multi-scale versions of an image, where certain scales capture specific features better than others. The ultimate result of this wavelet pyramid construction is a set of wavelet coefficients. The forward wavelet pyramid outputs a series of wavelet coefficients containing information about each scale. A steerable filter [26,28] can be applied to select the orientation where the feature of interest is maximum. In our experiments, we use the Simoncelli steerable filter with 3 scales and 3 high-pass filters.

Monogenic Signal and Phase Analysis: The monogenic wavelet [29] is a generalization of the 1D analytical wavelet signal [30]. Instead of using the Hilbert transform to convolve the wavelet coefficients, it uses the Riesz transform to generalize the computation to higher dimensions, making it suitable for image analysis applications. The monogenic signal allows for the decomposition of multidimensional signals $f \in L_2(\mathbb{R}^d)$ into phase and amplitude. The monogenic signal is defined as the $d+1$ dimensional vector, $f_m(\boldsymbol{x}) = (f(x), \mathscr{R}_1 f(x), \ldots, \mathscr{R}_d f(x))$, where $\mathscr{R}_i$ denotes the Riesz transform to the dimension i. The phase of the monogenic signal is defined as,

$$\alpha_f = arctan \frac{\sqrt{(\mathscr{R}_1 f^2) + \ldots (\mathscr{R}_d f^2)}}{f} \tag{1}$$

This phase component contains information about the structure of the signal in the image and is resistant to local changes in brightness caused by artifacts.

Spatial Reconstruction: The last step is to compute the inverse wavelet pyramid to reconstruct the phase images in the spatial domain. This reconstruction produces an image that enhances thin microfractures and filaments. The features obtained after phase analysis is shown in Fig. 2.

Table 1. Cracked tooth detection results on test split for different network architectures in micro-CT, as well as in hr-CBCT for final architecture.

Dataset	Model	AUC	Accuracy	Precision	Recall
Micro-CT	2D U-Net (without phase)	0.55	0.56	0.62	0.65
Micro-CT	3D U-Net (without phase)	0.63	0.68	0.76	0.65
Micro-CT	2D U-Net (with phase)	0.77	0.71	0.81	0.65
Micro-CT	3D U-Net (with phase)	**0.88**	0.82	0.82	0.90
hr-CBCT	3D U-Net (with phase)	0.56	0.56	0.63	0.60

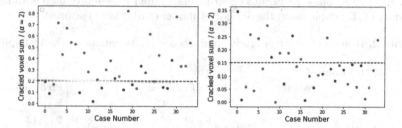

Fig. 3. Predicted probability for crack presence for each case in test split for micro-CT (with phase 3D U-Net)(left) and CBCT (with phase 3D U-Net)(right) images. With cracks in (orange) and Without cracks in (blue). (Color figure online)

Wavelet Guided Deep 3D Model for Fracture Segmentation: We use a 3D U-Net [31] model that takes as input a tooth volume and the corresponding phase image as the two channels. We use the implementation present in the open source library called MONAI. Since the number of training samples is less, we reduce the count of filters in each layer by a factor of 4. We find that increasing the number of filters beyond this has no additional benefits on the validation set. The dimension of the input image is $256 \times 256 \times 256$. To increase the number of training samples we randomly extract crops of dimension $256 \times 256 \times 8$ from the tooth. The thin nature of cracks increases the network training difficulty and therefore we must dilate the annotations. The output of the CNN is a two channel volume denoting the probability of crack/no-crack at each voxel location. The network is trained using a cross entropy loss function. We use the Adam optimizer [32] with a learning rate of 0.001. The network is trained for a maximum of 500 epochs and the weights with best validation set performance in terms of Dice score is selected for inference on the test split. Our model is implemented in PyTorch. Training is done on a Nvidia 3090 GPU and each model takes approximately 3 h to train.

We also performed experiments using a 2D U-Net [33] model. For this experiment the crops taken were of dimension $256 \times 256 \times 1$ i.e. only one slice from the volume. The hyperparameters and training settings remain the same as we find no improvement from changing the learning rate or number of epochs. To study the benefit of wavelet features we also conduct an experiment with only the orig-

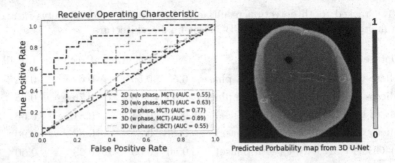

Fig. 4. (left) ROC plots for various experiments; (right) Probability map obtained on a test micro-CT sample using the 3D U-Net model (with phase features).

Table 2. Results of observer study conducted with 3 dentists on the test split.

(a) **micro-CT**		Predicted		(b)		Predicted		(c)		Predicted	
		F	C			F	C			F	C
Actual	F	16	4	Actual	F	13	7	Actual	F	7	13
	C	6	8		C	4	10		C	2	12

(d) **hr-CBCT**		Predicted		(e)		Predicted		(f)		Predicted	
		F	C			F	C			F	C
Actual	F	7	13	Actual	F	1	19	Actual	F	0	20
	C	7	7		C	1	13		C	0	14

*(F = Fractured, C = Control)

inal images as input. Due to having stronger signal present, we first perform this study on the micro-CT dataset. Based on the findings on micro-CT, we select the best model to train on the hr-CBCT dataset separately.

Tooth Fracture Detection Based on Crack Segmentation: While performing inference on a given tooth volume using 3D U-Net model, we extract non-overlapping crops of dimension $256 \times 256 \times 8$ from top through bottom and obtain the crack voxel probability by performing a softmax operation on the two channel output of the 3D U-Net. The binary labels for each voxel are obtained by taking the maximum probability class index. In each crop, we perform connected component analysis to remove components having size less than 50 voxels (using 26 connectivity). The ratio of cracked voxels to tooth volume in each crop is obtained and this ratio is then summed for all the crops in that tooth. The obtained value is then divided by a constant ($\alpha = 2$) for normalization to obtain final tooth crack probability ($\in [0, 1]$).

4   Results and Discussion

Using the technique described in Sect. 3, we obtain the probability for crack presence in a tooth. In Fig. 3, we plot this probability for each tooth in the test split. The black line denotes the optimal threshold for maximizing classification accuracy. This threshold could be used as an operating point to separate cracked teeth from non-cracked teeth. In addition, based on the probability values we perform ROC analysis to quantify the separation of cracked vs non-cracked teeth as seen in Fig. 4 (left). The results of this analysis are also shown in Table 1. The accuracy, precision, and recall are calculated by taking the threshold that maximizes accuracy for each experiment. In Fig. 3, the black line denotes the best threshold for that model. We see a good separation between cracked and control teeth in case of the micro-CT dataset, see Fig. 3 (left). We also observe that crack detection is much harder in hr-CBCT compared to micro-CT as significant overlap between the groups can be seen in Fig. 3 (right).

This measure gives us the ability to flag such images as having a high likelihood of having a crack. In addition, visually inspecting the images and probability maps below this threshold allow the physician to quickly inspect and determine if the highlighted area is a crack or not.

Observer Study: We compared the efficacy of our proposed model by conducting an observer study to obtain baseline diagnostic fracture detection accuracy from radiologists. Three Oral and Maxillofacial Radiologists at the clinic in the University of Texas Health San Antonio separately evaluated the anonymized scans. Results of this study are shown in Table 2. As can be seen, the trained dentists find it hard to detect the fractures even for the micro-CT dataset and their performance is inferior compared to the best model which is 3D U-Net with phase features, refer Table 1. The proposed model's performance in the micro-CT dataset is encouraging as the model was trained with only 8 samples and further improvement may be seen with the increase in training data. The performance on the hr-CBCT dataset, however, is not optimal both for observers and the proposed model. One encouraging outcome of this study is that the wavelet enhanced CNN model is able to outperform human observers in terms of accuracy for hr-CBCT. The human observers have an accuracy in the range of 0.38–0.41, see Table 2, while the CNN model is able to achieve accuracy of 0.56.

Discussion: The superior performance of the proposed model has been made possible due to the combination of a highly customizable isotropic wavelet backbone that can be configured to be sensitive to features in any orientation and scale. Since the clinical treatment of fractured teeth would be the same independently of the nature of the fracture, the goal of this project is fracture detection, not segmentation. Because of this, we restricted our study to binary classification of cracked and non-cracked tooth. In future study, we will collect more crack annotations and will perform analysis on the degree of accuracy by quantifying the severity of the crack.

We are aware that the current performance on hr-CBCT is inferior and not suitable for clinical practice. On further investigation, we found that one cause for inferior performance is that the endodontic mode in hr-CBCT often uses smoothing filters that are intended to provide visually appealing images without the presence of artifacts. These filters are useful to better perceive the gross tooth structure, however, such excessive smoothing can destroy features like microfractures. Our future work will perform this study on hr-CBCT tooth reconstructed without the smoothing filters.

Prospect of Application: The proposed algorithm addresses the need for quantitative, reproducible, and evidence-based ways to detect cracks in teeth that can potentially lead to improved tooth loss prevention. Our method has the potential to improve the diagnostic accuracy of dental professionals by using the phase images resulting from wavelet analysis to train a deep learning classifier that creates probabilistic maps for microfractures.

Acknowledgement. This work has been supported by The National Institutes of Health, under Project Number 2R44DE027574-02A1.

References

1. Lynch, C.D., McConnell, R.J.: The cracked tooth syndrome. J.-Can. Dent. Assoc. **68**(8), 470–475 (2002)
2. Ricucci, D., Siqueira, J.F., Jr., Loghin, S., Berman, L.H.: The cracked tooth: histopathologic and histobacteriologic aspects. J. Endodontics **41**(3), 343–352 (2015)
3. Kahler, B., Moule, A., Stenzel, D.: Bacterial contamination of cracks in symptomatic vital teeth. Aust. Endod. J. **26**(3), 115–118 (2000)
4. Iqbal, M., Kim, S., Yoon, F.: An investigation into differential diagnosis of pulp and periapical pain: a PennEndo database study. J. Endodontics **33**(5), 548–551 (2007)
5. Portman-Lewis, S.: An analysis of the out-of-hours demand and treatment provided by a general dental practice rota over a five-year period. Prim. Dent. Care **3**, 98–104 (2007)
6. Krell, K.V., Rivera, E.M.: A six-year evaluation of cracked teeth diagnosed with reversible pulpitis: treatment and prognosis. Br. Dent. J. **204**(9) (2008)
7. Olivieri, J.G., et al.: Outcome and survival of endodontically treated cracked posterior permanent teeth: a systematic review and meta-analysis. J. Endodontics **46**(4), 455–463 (2020)
8. Wu, S., Lew, H.P., Chen, N.N.: Incidence of pulpal complications after diagnosis of vital cracked teeth. J. Endodontics **45**(5), 521–525 (2019)
9. Abbott, P., Leow, N.: Predictable management of cracked teeth with reversible pulpitis. Aust. Dent. J. **54**(4), 306–315 (2009)
10. Opdam, N.J., Roeters, J.J., Loomans, B.A., Bronkhorst, E.M.: Seven-year clinical evaluation of painful cracked teeth restored with a direct composite restoration. J. Endodontics **34**(7), 808–811 (2008)
11. Kang, S.H., Kim, B.S., Kim, Y.: Cracked teeth: distribution, characteristics, and survival after root canal treatment. J. Endodontics **42**(4), 557–562 (2016)

12. Gibbs, J.W.: Cuspal fracture odontalgia. Dent. Digest **60**, 158–160 (1954)
13. Ritchey, B., Mendenhall, R., Orban, B.: Pulpitis resulting from incomplete tooth fracture. Oral Surg. Oral Med. Oral Pathol. **10**(6), 665–70 (1957)
14. Cameron, C.E.: Cracked-tooth syndrome. J. Am. Dent. Assoc. **68**(3), 405–411 (1964)
15. Rivera, E.M., Williamson, A.: Diagnosis and treatment planning: cracked tooth. Tex. Dent. J. **120**(3), 278–83 (2003)
16. Hilton, T.J., et al.: Associations of types of pain with crack-level, tooth-level and patient-level characteristics in posterior teeth with visible cracks: findings from the national dental practice-based research network. J. Dent. **70**, 67–73 (2018)
17. Setzer, F.C., Hinckley, N., Kohli, M.R., Karabucak, B.: A survey of cone-beam computed tomographic use among endodontic practitioners in the united states. J. Endodontics **43**(5), 699–704 (2017)
18. Brady, E., Mannocci, F., Brown, J., Wilson, R., Patel, S.: A comparison of cone beam computed tomography and periapical radiography for the detection of vertical root fractures in nonendodontically treated teeth. Int. Endod. J. **47**(8), 735–746 (2014)
19. Chavda, R., Mannocci, F., Andiappan, M., Patel, S.: Comparing the in vivo diagnostic accuracy of digital periapical radiography with cone-beam computed tomography for the detection of vertical root fracture. J. Endodontics **40**(10), 1524–1529 (2014)
20. Banerji, S., Mehta, S.B., Millar, B.J.: Cracked tooth syndrome. part 1: aetiology and diagnosis. Br. Dent. J. **208**(10), 459–463 (2010)
21. Buty, M., Xu, Z., Gao, M., Bagci, U., Wu, A., Mollura, D.J.: Characterization of lung nodule malignancy using hybrid shape and appearance features. In: Ourselin, S., Joskowicz, L., Sabuncu, M., Unal, G., Wells, W. (eds.) Medical Image Computing and Computer-Assisted Intervention-MICCAI 2016. Lecture Notes in Computer Science, vol. 9900, pp. 662–670. Springer, Cham (2016)
22. Lin, W., Hasenstab, K., Moura Cunha, G., Schwartzman, A.: Comparison of hand-crafted features and convolutional neural networks for liver MR image adequacy assessment. Sci. Rep. **10**(1), 1–11 (2020)
23. Fox, D., Randall, H., Walter, R., Mol, A., Hernandez-Cerdan, P., Paniagua, B., Khan, A.: Development of a standardized method to induce cracks in extracted human teeth. In: 2019 IADR/AADR/CADR General Session (Vancouver, BC, Canada) (2019)
24. Otsu, N.: A threshold selection method from gray-level histograms. IEEE Trans. Syst. Man Cybern. **9**(1), 62–66 (1979)
25. Zhang, Z.: Iterative point matching for registration of free-form curves and surfaces. Int. J. Comput. Vis. **13**(2), 119 152 (1994)
26. Held, S., Storath, M., Massopust, P., Forster, B.: Steerable wavelet frames based on the Riesz transform. IEEE Trans. Image Process. **19**(3), 653–667 (2009)
27. Chenouard, N., Unser, M.: 3D steerable wavelets in practice. IEEE Trans. Image Process. **21**(11), 4522–4533 (2012)
28. Simoncelli, E.P., Freeman, W.T.: The steerable pyramid: a flexible architecture for multi-scale derivative computation. In: Proceedings., International Conference on Image Processing, vol. 3, pp. 444–447. IEEE (1995)
29. Felsberg, M., Sommer, G.: The monogenic signal. IEEE Trans. Signal Process. **49**(12), 3136–3144 (2001)
30. Selesnick, I.W., Baraniuk, R.G., Kingsbury, N.C.: The dual-tree complex wavelet transform. IEEE Signal Process. Mag. **22**(6), 123–151 (2005)

31. Çiçek, Ö., Abdulkadir, A., Lienkamp, S.S., Brox, T., Ronneberger, O.: 3D U-Net: learning dense volumetric segmentation from sparse annotation. In: Ourselin, S., Joskowicz, L., Sabuncu, M.R., Unal, G., Wells, W. (eds.) MICCAI 2016. LNCS, vol. 9901, pp. 424–432. Springer, Cham (2016). https://doi.org/10.1007/978-3-319-46723-8_49

32. Kingma, D.P., Ba, J.: Adam: a method for stochastic optimization. arXiv preprint arXiv:1412.6980 (2014)

33. Ronneberger, O., Fischer, P., Brox, T.: U-Net: convolutional networks for biomedical image segmentation. In: Navab, N., Hornegger, J., Wells, W.M., Frangi, A.F. (eds.) MICCAI 2015. LNCS, vol. 9351, pp. 234–241. Springer, Cham (2015). https://doi.org/10.1007/978-3-319-24574-4_28

Author Index

Printed in the United States
by Baker & Taylor Publisher Services